1664 312

Co

D1563030

Hard Truths

Hard Truths

Elijah Millgram

WILEY-BLACKWELL

A John Wiley & Sons, Ltd., Publication

Library of Congress Cataloging-in-Publication Data

Millgram, Elijah.
  Hard truths / Elijah Millgram.
    p. cm.
  Includes bibliographical references and index.
  ISBN 978-1-4051-8815-9 (hardcover : alk. paper)
    1. Truth. 2. Reasoning. 3. Metaphysics. I. Title.
    BD171.M49 2009
    121–dc22

                                2008040258

A catalogue record for this book is available from the British Library.

Set in 10.5/13pt Minion by SPi Publisher Services, Pondicherry, India
Printed and bound in Malaysia by Vivar Printing Sdn Bhd

1   2009

Contents

For Hilary Putnam

Acknowledgments

Many people have been kind enough to read and comment on drafts of the manuscript. Ben Crowe, Christoph Fehige, Leslie Francis, James Hawthorne, Erik Johnson, Kathrin Koslicki, John MacFarlane, Cei Maslen, and Paul Teller read through the whole thing. Among those who read one or more chapters—and my apologies if I've lost track of anyone—were Janet Abbate, Chrisoula Andreou, Jody Azzouni, Paul Benacerraf, Sarah Buss, Alice Clapman, Alice Crary, Kate Elgin, Don Garrett, Matt Haber, Eric Hutton, Rachana Kamtekar, Rosanna Keefe, Clifton McIntosh, Ron Mallon, John Martin, Matt Mosdell, Ram Neta, Lex Newman, Shaun Nichols, Bernhard Nickel, Laurie Paul, Anya Plutynski, Hilary Putnam, Diana Raffman, Michael Ranney, Guy Rohrbaugh, Sherri Roush, Laura Schroeter, Bill Talbott, Mariam Thalos, Valerie Tiberius, Johan van Benthem, Candace Vogler, and Gideon Yaffe.

For very helpful conversation, I'm grateful to Irene Appelbaum, Alyssa Bernstein, John Biro, David Chalmers, Charles Chihara, Heather Douglas, John Etchemendy, David Finkelstein, Peter Galison, Michael Glanzberg, Peter Godfrey-Smith, Bob Goodin, Peter Hylton, Jenann Ismael, Gabriel Richardson Lear, Dorothea Lotter, Chris Martin, Emily Rosenzweig, Steve Stich, Jim Tabery, and Jamie Tappenden.

Bits and pieces of this material were presented in various venues, including Kansas State University, the EMST Reasoning Group at UC/Berkeley, the University of Chicago, Vanderbilt University, the Center for Advanced Study in the Behavioral Sciences, Stanford University, the NYU/Columbia Vagueness Reading Group, the IUC Conference on Vagueness, the University of Miami, the University of Oklahoma, the University of Tennessee/Knoxville, Brigham Young University, King's College London, and Reading University. I appreciate the audiences' thoughtful feedback.

For drafting the illustrations, I'm grateful to Joe Ulatowski, and for editing assistance, to Erin Menut.

Work on this book was supported by fellowships from the National Endowment for the Humanities and the Center for Advanced Study in the Behavioral Sciences; I am grateful for the financial support provided through CASBS by the Andrew W. Mellon Foundation. I would also like to thank the Rockefeller Foundation's Bellagio Study and Conference Center, the University of Washington's Helen Riaboff Whiteley Center, and All Souls College for residential fellowships, as well as the University of Utah's Research Council and College of Humanities, for travel and sabbatical support.

1

Introduction

When you call something a hard truth, it's usually an announcement that you're about to say something your audience doesn't want to hear. That's not what the phrase is going to mean here: a hard truth is one that is just flat-out true (and if it weren't, it would be just flat-out false): not sort of true, not true in a way, not true up to a point, not somewhat true, and not any of the indefinitely many other variations on falling short of full truth. But hard truths in the more conversational sense are nonetheless in the offing, because hard truths, I will argue, are a lot fewer and farther between than philosophers have generally supposed, and to get them, you have to do things that philosophers have preferred not to think about or mention in polite company, things that you really can't do too much of the time. It follows that people have to do most of their thinking with the other kind of truth, namely, the truths that are only kind of true. The first part of this book will be given over to motivating the turn to partial truth; the second part will develop the argument for the claim I have just made.

There's a consequence to be drawn, to which the tail end of the book will be devoted: that a great deal of metaphysics is going to have to be substantially revised. That will be unwelcome news to professionals at one end of the philosophy business, but there will be a compensating payoff at the end: a new conception of what metaphysics *is*. By way of persuading you that the apparently not-so-sexy topic of partial truth is worth your attention, I'll start off this Introduction by explaining why that's a payoff to which we should look forward. I'll then quickly sketch some of the main ideas to be expressed by the core argument, and give a chapter-by-chapter overview of the proceedings. I'll wrap up the Introduction with a heads-up regarding the book's stylistic cues and organization.

1.1

Metaphysics (by which I mean not the bookstore shelving category, i.e., a euphemism for superstition, but rather one of the central and perennial concerns of philosophers) has gotten itself a reputation for being the most rarefied, abstruse, and impractical of pursuits. It is thought of not just as a philosophical specialty of merely intellectual interest, but one that does not even serve any intellectual interests other than its own: if you do not *happen* to be curious about such rarefied questions as, oh, what universals are, or what necessity is, or what causation is, or what objects are, and curious about them on their own account, you have no reason to care. Worse, this is the discipline's current self-conception, and not just a prejudice on the part of ignorant outsiders.[1] Metaphysics used to claim that it was the Queen of the Sciences, at a time when that was a proud claim to make, but it now presents itself as the superfluous royal figurehead of a Great Britain, Holland, or Sweden: on display, surrounded by much pomp, decorum, and ritual, and acknowledged to be absolutely useless.

I think that metaphysics is much more interesting and important than that, and if the argument I am going to be developing is correct enough, the conception of metaphysics I've just sketched is a mistake. Metaphysics, or most of it, should be thought of as an *applied* science, one part of which is concerned with determining what approximations or idealizations to use, and the other, an activity with affinities to product design. Metaphysics properly done (or, again, at least most of it: in the Conclusion, I'll return to the question of whether this is *all* of it) is an especially deep form of engineering, one that matters precisely because it is so useful as to be indispensable.

If you survey the history of philosophy, you will find that, throughout, metaphysics has addressed itself to the question: What does the world have to be like, if we are to be able to think about it? The question has come in for many substantively different readings over the course of its history— contrast the very different spins that, for instance, idealists and realists have put on it—but their shared content explains why metaphysics is not the silly enterprise of armchair physics it sometimes seems to be.[2] A philosopher's view of what thought consists in is a picture (or, in especially self-aware and ambitious cases, a theory) of rationality. So, not unreasonably, analytic metaphysics—metaphysics as it is done by analytic philosophers—has been largely a projection onto the world of a widely shared if not very clearly articulated picture of rationality.

In this picture, deductive inference, as first axiomatized by Frege and Russell, and as now taught in standard introductory logic classes, is first-class reasoning, and the prestigious core of rationality.[3] Around it are clustered various second-class forms of reasoning, some still deductive, like modal logics and tense logics, and some that, while no longer extensions of the traditional deductive logic, are still formalized, like Bayesian inference, expected-utility theory, and so on. As we move farther away from the deductive core, we find still less prestigious modes of reasoning, such as inductive and abductive inference, and once we get far enough away, perhaps to arguments by analogy, the honorific title of reasoning is withdrawn. Deductive inference, and specifically the deductive logic taught in all those introductory classes, is *real* inference, and certainly the central, most important variety of it; the closer a form of inference is to such deductive inference, the more real it is.

That picture presupposes two further and related doctrines. First, that reasoning, properly performed, is a matter of eliciting true conclusions from true premises,[4] and second, that truth is all-or-nothing: sentences and beliefs are either flat-out true, or flat-out false. Call the latter idea, that all truth is hard truth, the *bivalence doctrine*;[5] call the former idea *validity as truth preservation*. Philosophers today tend to think of these as different *types* of claim: the one is about inference, and the other about semantics. In Chapter 3, I will explain why they travel together; for now, it is enough that the deductive logic taught in the standard logic class requires both that there be only two truth values, true and false, and that the notion of the validity of an argument is standardly introduced with some such gloss as: necessarily having a true conclusion if it has true premises.[6] To anticipate, in domains of which either or both doctrines were false in the right sort of way, deductive logic would have limited or no applicability, and if most of our thinking were done in such domains, then, as far as practical importance goes, deductive logic would not capture the central or most important forms of inference. If analytic metaphysics really is a projection of this picture of rationality, then coming to see deductive inference as an unusual (though important) special case, rather than rationality's center of gravity, should be expected to have the effect of repositioning traditional views in analytic metaphysics as smallish regions of larger and more varied terrains.

These two doctrines—that valid inference is truth-preserving, and that truth is bivalent—are the philosophically standard view of these matters. But a second glance suggests that they cannot both be right; all too often, the starting points of our inferences are claims that we ourselves take to be only approximately true, or technically true, or officially true, or true for present purposes. I am going to argue that we cannot do without such reasoning, that consequently truth must often be partial, that there must be a way to reason from false premises to conclusions that are, if not true, at any rate satisfactory, and so that we need to have a suitable notion of correctness of inference: that is, a notion of validity that does not amount to truth-preservingness. And I am going to argue further that when the hard (i.e., bivalent) truths of the title are available, special explanation is normally required, specifically, an engineering explanation. The perceived centrality of deductive logic, and the work in metaphysics that is tied to that perception, are the concomitants of a misguided way of thinking about truth. And so I think that revising the way we think about truth is the best way to fix these problems.

Let me now preview the ideas at work in the argument against the bivalence doctrine and validity as truth preservation. In doing so, I will help myself to a bit of philosophical shorthand; if you're not familiar enough with Kant and Nietzsche for the gestures at their views to be helpful, don't worry about it: the moves will be fully spelled out in the sequel.

1.2

Here is a Kantian thought. Suppose the world is a messy, surprising, and irregular place, and things as they are in themselves could be *any* which way. If those things were fully responsible for the inputs that go to make up your experience, then those inputs could also be just any way at all. But inputs that are just any way at all don't make up *experience*; if your cognitive inputs were arbitrarily varied and overwhelmingly multifarious, you would be intellectually overwhelmed by them, and you would, in the end, fail to have anything amounting to a mind. Somehow the raw input must be preprocessed before you see it: it must first be poured into molds. Since experience is the result of pouring raw inputs into molds, the molds have to be there *first*, and so the molds themselves can't be chosen or readjusted on the basis of experience.[7]

Here is a correction to the Kantian thought. Because the world could be just any way at all, pouring your proto-experience into a fixed set of molds will not do. Whatever won't fit into the molds will end up not being part of your mental life; that is, it will become invisible to you. But if the world could be just any way at all, you can't know up front (in philosophers' Latin, a priori) what it's safe to disregard; to ignore you-know-not-what is to invite catastrophic conseqences. And if you try to make everything fit—by *forcing* it in—you will end up breaking the molds. In the Kantian picture, the molds are much of the structure of your mind, so that would mean breaking your mind. Something has to give.

Let's agree that while you will have to pour whatever is going to make up your experience into molds, they don't always have to be the same ones. You can throw out old molds, and install new ones, if experience so warrants; in fact, you will have to, if you are going to maintain a unified mind. Since disposable molds are neither a priori nor necessary, they don't have to be Kant's categories, and we need to keep an open mind about what will replace them; perhaps plain, ordinary names, descriptions, and so on will do most of the time; perhaps special-purpose mathematical descriptions will sometimes be needed to exhibit them.

The corrected Kantian thought needs still further correction. If you could *always* tailor your repertoire of descriptions to what the world serves up—that is, choose molds to fit your experience—you wouldn't have to worry about things getting left out, or about smashing your mind on the world. If the world is as messy as experience suggests, however, too many molds would then be one-use throwaways, which would also leave you short a mind. And if the molds and their contents reflected too much of the messiness of the world, they wouldn't fit together inferentially—that is, in ways that allowed you to reason your way to important and warranted conclusions. Thinking requires thoughts that are repeatable, and which fit together inferentially. The world is such that fitting our thoughts to it trades off against fitting them to one another; the workable compromise is to be generous about what counts as fitting into a mold, and to accept less-than-perfect castings. Our literal vocabulary—or one of them—for saying how our opinions fit the world is our truth vocabulary. Truths that are entirely true—not true up to a point, not just sort of true, not only true in a manner of speaking, and not merely true *enough*—aren't suitable as contents for all, or even most of our thoughts, and we have to get along with soft, partial truth much of the time. This means that you can't always have hard truth.

One more round of revision to the thought we have been morphing. Sometimes you do need hard truth. Allow that Kant was right about this much: if unified intellects are to be possible, the world has to be poured into molds which guarantee that experience (or enough of it, anyway) will be intellectually tractable. If there are fairly close-in limits to how much turnover we can handle in our supply of mental molds, and if we often have to be ungenerous about accepting an imperfect fit, then we will have to give up on the assumption that all the molds are inside or part of your mind. Experience must be shaped into the required configurations *outside* the mind. This idea is perhaps not entirely alien to the development of Kant's own thought. On his way to the central insights of the *Critique of Pure Reason*, Kant wrote that

> if that in us which we call 'representation' were *active* with regard to the *object*, that is, if the object itself were created by the representation (as when divine cognitions are conceived as the archetypes of things), the conformity of these representations to their objects could be understood.[8]

Kant seems to have dismissed this option out of theological modesty; I take it he assumed that getting this solution to work would require omnipotence. And if all objects, all the time, had to be created in the course of representing them, the solution would in fact be unmanageable. But if we need to take this approach only some of the time, then engineering rather than omnipotence will often suffice.

To make thinking that deploys hard truths possible, we have to reengineer the world, by manufacturing objects to conform to our representations. When hard truth is uniformly available with regard to some subject matter, that's normally because we have constructed it. That last claim is easy to take the wrong way these days; but when I say that our truths are constructed, I don't just mean the wishy-washy kind of construction—'social construction'—that you hear so much about from postmodernists. I mean, in the first place, the kind of construction that involves power tools and earth-moving equipment. And so here is how our thrice-revised Kantian thought has come out: having a mind requires both thought that deploys partial truths, and altering some of the objects of thought to make full truth about them possible.

Here is a Nietzschean thought. There are far too many things in the world for us to have dedicated representations of each and every one. So if we are to be able to think about more than a tiny handful of them, we will have to use the same representation for more than one thing. Nietzsche held, at one point, that predication was really just this: the word 'leaf' begins its life as a name for a particular leaf, but is then applied to indefinitely many leaves.[9] But because everything differs from everything else in indefinitely many ways, our predications are falsifications, or, as he moralistically put it, 'lies in the extra-moral sense.' When we call different items 'leaves,' Nietzsche thought, we are forgetting the multitudinous ways in which subsequent leaves differ from that original leaf.

Here is a correction to the Nietzschean thought, one that will strike any sensible contemporary philosopher as simple common sense. When we turn a name into a predicate, we selectively mask most of the detail (and not just the detail) in the original particular: when we call something a 'leaf,' we mean only to say that it resembles the original in precisely one respect, that of being a leaf. We institutionalize this kind of selective masking by introducing a new kind of item, the *property*, to be what it is that a predicate 'names.'[10] Once the restraint in our semantic intentions is appreciated, predication is quite obviously not a falsification or 'extra-moral lie,' after all. What is left of Nietzsche's insistence that we arrive at predication by 'forgetting' is that the choices about which details to mask are very often made thoughtlessly, and consequently unintelligently; as we will see, this is not an unreasonable concern.

Let's run with the Nietzschean thought for a moment. There are too many properties in the world for us to have representations for all of them. If too much of the world is not going to be left invisible to us, we are going to have to recycle our predicative representations. Partial truth is the way (actually, one way) we do this: we apply a predicate when it does not quite apply, that is to say, if you insist on being picky about it, when it really does not apply at all. So-called partial truth is just another lie—to be sure, only in the extra-moral sense. But partial truth allows predication a penumbra in which numerous interstices of the world that would otherwise have remained in darkness are made visible to the intellect.

Here is an analogous correction to the amplified thought. When we advance a predication as a partial truth, we are selectively withdrawing our assent or commitment to the full reach or force of the initial predication. When we say that it's sort of true that it's a leaf, we intend to claim less than that it's a leaf—in just the way that when we claim that it's a leaf, we intend to claim less than that it's token-identical to some *ur*-leaf. Once the restraint in our semantic intentions is appreciated, partial truth becomes quite obviously not a falsification—an 'extra-moral lie'—after all. Partial truth is as innocuous a device as predication, and in a deep sense a very similar device: a means by which a mind whose representational capacities are necessarily quite limited can be cognizant of the plenitude of the world.[11] A philosopher who thinks that predication is fine but partial truth is not occupies an unmotivated and unsustainable position: the pressures that take you from a language (or a 'language') composed of proper names for individuals to a language with terms for properties carry you past that position, to a richer language with expressive devices for partial truth. But we should not forget the analog of Nietzsche's criticism of our choices of predication: that too often we choose our partial truths thoughtlessly and unintelligently.

1.3

Here is how I intend to develop and exploit the ideas I've just described. A substantial amount of additional warm-up is called for, and the first part of the book will be devoted to it. On the one hand, non-philosophers are unlikely to share the conception of truth that I will be contesting; they will wonder why we need an argument for the self-evident fact that many of the things that we think and say are only partially true, and will suspect that a fact as obvious as that is unlikely to have consequences which are both significant and unnoticed. Philosophers, on the other hand, will for the most part divide up into two groups: those who find bivalence self-evident, and specialists who take my concerns to have been already addressed by recent work on vagueness; both groups are likely to think that the claims I have just sketched are still far too impressionistic, and far too thin, to justify launching into an argument against bivalence. So I will begin, in Chapters 2 and 3, by laying out more of the big picture. I will try to make plausible the claim that bivalence is typically the product of engineering, and that because not everything can be engineered, we need to get along without bivalence a good deal of the time. Then I will introduce and criticize what is currently the most popular family of theories of truth (that is, theories that try to answer the question of what truth *is*).

Theories in the family are generically called 'deflationist,' and seem to imply that treatments of truth should not have metaphysical consequences. Since I mean to derive such consequences from my own treatment, I have to say why deflationist accounts of truth do not derail my arguments and my project more broadly conceived. I won't exactly argue against those theories, but I will claim that the best stance to take toward them is diagnostic; once we place deflationist theories of truth in their historical context, their plausibility will diminish, and the associated idea, that there is not much you can *get* by thinking about truth, will be seen to be a mistake. More importantly, by contrasting the function of truth, as deflationists understand it, with the functionality I am going to ascribe to partial truth, I will be explaining what I mean partial truth to be. (However, the reader should be warned that the official definition of partial truth will only be given in Chapter 6.)

Through this point, the focus will have been on motivating the view, rather than on arguing for it. The second part of the book takes up the latter task. I will make two complete passes over the book's core argument, in Chapters 4 and 5. The claim for which I will be arguing, that we reason using partial truths, belongs to logic in the pre-twentieth-century sense: it is a claim about how to think, or about the Laws of Thought. The analytic tradition has historically treated logic as a branch of mathematics, and for the most part let the prescriptive subject matter alone. Not surprisingly, the techniques for thinking about logic so understood have grown rusty with disuse, and one of the topics that has to be on the table is just *how* to conduct such an argument. Accordingly, as I lay out the argument, I will also be explaining what the form of the argument is, and why it is appropriate.

The core argument of the book will be (to appropriate a bit of an older vocabulary, which I will explain in due course) transcendental, and it is a remarkable feature of transcendental arguments that they can normally be put in either of two forms: as a task analysis (that is, the central claim in such an argument has the form: in order to do *this*, you also have to be doing *that*) or as an analysis of what is required for one or another aspect of unity of the self. Chapter 4 will develop the task-analysis version of the argument, to the effect that inference deploying partial truth is legitimate, because you can't make much headway in figuring out the facts without it. And it will also explain how the fact that you can't get along without it shows that an inference form is legitimate. Briefly, I will claim that the elements of thought must repeat themselves if thought is to be possible at all; the world is too messy for elements of thought to repeat themselves often enough, if they merely follow the world; if these two claims are correct, we must abandon both the bivalence doctrine and validity as truth preservation. In the course of the argument, I will also explain why the world has to be messy (and what is involved in my claim that it is).

In Chapter 5 I will throw the argument into the other form taken by transcendental deductions. I will first explain why the preconditions for (aspects of) unity of the self can determine what one's logic—one's guidelines for thinking—must be. I will introduce the notion of a unified intellect, and argue that the beliefs of a disunified intellect are not worth having. I will argue that minds of roughly our cognitive horsepower that do not reason using partial truth fail to manage unified intellects: unified intellects are possible only if the bivalence doctrine and validity as truth preservation are false. Because the world is messy, fitting mental representations to the world does not allow them to be inferentially fitted to each other; partial truth, that is, allowing slack between our representations and the world, is what we need for the bits and pieces of an intellect to be glued together into an intellectually effective mind.

Chapter 6 will complete the core argument by turning to the philosopher's notion of belief. This discussion will allow me to provide, albeit belatedly, a definition of partial truth. It will allow me to address what I have found to be the most frequently pressed objection to the core argument. And it will provide, additionally and incidentally, the first of a series of applications, an illustration of my earlier suggestion that much analytic metaphysics is a projection of a theory of rationality: here, nearly exclusive attention to one kind of inference is responsible for a theory of the contents of people's minds.

Just to provide a sense of what I mean by that, let me pause to sketch how that application will go. Analytic philosophy of mind is focused very largely on beliefs. Belief-desire psychology is the dominant view, roughly, that all you need to talk about, when reconstructing the mental activity that amounts to reasoning, are beliefs and desires;[12] but desires do not have to do with truth at all, and are, on this kind of view, elements of practical rather than theoretical reasoning. So theoretical reasoning—that is, reasoning about what the facts are—is thought to be made up of beliefs, and beliefs alone.[13]

To believe something is to take it to be true, and so the assumption that there are only hard truths explains (much of) the contemporary philosophical commitment to belief psychology. If I am right, and there is a good deal that you only half-take to be true, then there must be steps in your reasoning that are not beliefs. Belief psychology (the theoretical side of belief-desire psychology) *is* appropriate for the special case of reasoning about hard truths. But if, as I am going to argue, hard truths are relatively rare, then beliefs are a good deal less common than is ordinarily believed; they turn out to be best understood as a special case of a broader class of mental items involved in theoretical reasoning. Thus the argument against belief psychology extracts a consequence for the metaphysics of mind from the previous chapters' theses about truth, and so bears out my suggestion that revising one's theory of truth promises important metaphysical payoffs.

With both the account of partial truth and the argument for it in place, I will be in a position to address the most prominent competing approach to the family of phenomena, and I will devote a chapter to recent work on vagueness. The literature is sufficiently specialized so that readers who are not already immersed in it may want to skip this third part of the book. Nonetheless, I will introduce the material I discuss in a way that I hope will make it accessible to those who are encountering it for the first time. And there is work that this chapter does over and above the necessary but unpleasant job of explaining why the apparent alternative is not really live: that of further filling in and supporting the picture of partial truth as coming in indefinitely many qualitatively different varieties.

The fourth and final part of the book pursues the point that there are philosophical consequences to these claims about truth and inference. Because there are many respects in which adopting them can change your substantive metaphysical position, for the first time in the course of the exposition there is a choice to be made as to which further topics to pursue. (Unlike the treatment of belief in Chapter 6, which is forced by the core argument, here I am selecting among many possible applications.) The approach I opt for is historical, and in Chapters 8–11, I will recount the development of one strand of twentieth-century analytic metaphysics, and exhibit how its turning points presupposed the bivalence doctrine. (The central figures in the narrative will be W. V. Quine, Donald Davidson, and David Lewis; that narrative itself, once embarked upon, will not allow much in the way of freedom of choice of topic, except as regards illustrations of its influence on other philosophers.) It will follow that giving up the bivalence doctrine means giving up the positions and methodologies constituting that strand. While the series of positions I will discuss was not by any means all of twentieth-century analytic metaphysics, it was structurally central, framing and motivating subsidiary metaphysical projects, many of which are still alive today, and bivalence figures into it in perhaps as straightforward a manner as we could ask. Abandoning that structurally important strand means abandoning the subsidiary projects as well. In short, I hope to establish that if we reject the bivalence doctrine and validity as truth preservation, then we will have to recognize a great deal of twentieth-century analytic metaphysics to have been a mistake.

If much of the metaphysics in circulation is an error, the natural next question is whether and how it can be replaced. So, finally, Chapter 12 will assess the outcome of the argument. I will return to the claim that metaphysics is a projection of a theory of rationality—a claim I will at that point be in a position to cash out—and I will ask how metaphysics should be reconceived, if I am correct in thinking that hard truths are hard to come by. As already announced, I will argue that we should understand metaphysics as an applied science, one that can and should make our lives (our *day-to-day* lives) better than they now are.

1.4

Those familiar with the conventions of a literary genre allow their reading to be guided by its stylistic cues, but they do not normally pay explicit attention to the cues themselves. Because in this case the cues are likely to be misleading, let me take a moment or two to preempt a handful of misunderstandings.

First, in the business of professional philosophy, publication for the most part divides up into professional journals and books meant to be read solely by specialists, and popular or textbook expositions of material already presented in the professional format. Accessible writing (and especially, rehearsing background that a professional would not need) is accordingly taken to signal that most of argumentation is supposed to have happened elsewhere. Put a bit more bluntly, you're not supposed to take philosophical prose seriously unless nobody who wasn't already a philosopher of the same tribe could read it comfortably.

My own view is that philosophy should always be written to be as broadly accessible as possible, and in this case there is a special reason for making the writing readable to people who are not versed in the current philosophical subspecialties. One intended upshot of the argument of the book is that the approaches taken in a number of philosophical specializations—theory of truth, philosophy of logic, metaphysics, and, incidentally, epistemology—are deeply misguided. If that very ambitious follow-on thesis is taken to heart, philosophers will change the way they work in those areas. (I know, it's a long shot.) If they do, and if the book is written so that only professionals working in those fields, as they are now constituted, can read it, then if the book is successful, it will thereby make itself unreadable. Perhaps it's too ambitious to write for the ages, but I would at least like to be writing for a number of years down the road, even if (especially if) the argument is found convincing. That means writing readably, even to those who do not have the background of contemporary specialists. (There are unavoidable exceptions; I have encapsulated them in notes and an appendix.)

To write for nonspecialists amounts to writing prose that undergraduates can read, and to a professional nowadays, that stylistic choice is likely to convey the impression that the discussion is underargued, and probably that it is loosely organized, as well. Please resist the impression; while the argument proper will not kick in until Chapter 4, it is meant to be as tightly controlled as it gets.

Second, because the argument is ambitious, both as regards its methodology and its conclusions, there are inevitably going to be a lot of pieces on the board. I have found that it pays to disabuse readers of the impression that I am meandering from optional topic to optional topic. Because the argument determines the organization of the material, prior to the turn to applications in Chapter 8, there are almost no open choice points. (A discussion of epistemology in Chapter 6 is an exception, but is there because almost all the work needed to get it going is required by the argument proper.) I will almost always explain what one discussion or another is doing where it is, but I will not always make a big deal out of it. Once again, I am trying to write accessibly, which means departing from the overly verbose conventions of the journal article.

Third and finally, there is an obstacle to following the flow of argumentation that is not merely stylistic. This book argues for a view about what arguments—theoretical arguments, viz., arguments as to what the facts are—have to be like. Professional philosophers are trained to argue from putative flat-out truths to further flat-out truths, and to make their arguments as close to deductively valid as they can. I am claiming that many arguments have to go from 'true enough' to 'true enough,' that those arguments will not be deductive, and that they have to be understood and assessed very differently from deductive arguments.

To the extent that the argumentation in this book is about matters of fact (though bear in mind that there are going to be a number of practical arguments, that is, arguments whose conclusion is about what to do), it will be almost entirely of the very type I am attempting to characterize and defend. That will make it harder for philosophers used to deductively cast argument to see it as argued (and to see it as *tightly* argued). I assure you that the argument is as tight as I can make it, but what it is to make an argument tight, when the argument turns on partial truths, may be different than what you are used to.

Part I
Motivation

2

The Truth in Bivalence

I've suggested that many philosophers have grown up with the bivalence doctrine: the idea that what we assert—internally, in our thoughts, or externally, in our writings and utterances—is either just plain true or just plain false. I think it's fair to say that, with the exception of a few groups of specialists, the bivalence doctrine is very widely held among philosophers, and most of the time, just taken for granted.[1]

However, it's not nearly as widely held among non-philosophers (and philosophers when they're not wearing their philosopher hats). Almost anyone will balk at answering a good many yes-or-no questions with a straight yes or no. Do I want to go hiking tomorrow? *We-ell*, it's hard to give a straight answer to that question. Is the defendant guilty? A lot of jurors would *really* like the option of saying, 'Sort of...' When I am told that Nashville is four hours from Memphis, I take that to be more or less true, but not exactly true. And informed that the dog ate the homework, I may understand that to be false in spirit but not in letter (if, for instance, I know that the student has fed the unfinished homework to the dog); that is, I may take it to be true...in a way. Just going by what ordinary folks say, the bivalence doctrine is false. So who's right, the philosophers or the laity? Is the bivalence doctrine true?

In this chapter, I'm going to suggest that, even though it's not true in the main, the bivalence doctrine has some truth in it. I propose to take a shot at teasing out what it is the bivalence doctrine gets right; on the way, I will try to show how it goes wrong, and to say why it's nonetheless important to appreciate the truth in bivalence.

2.1

First, terminological preliminaries. I'll use the term 'bivalent' in two related ways. Of sentences or statements or thoughts or assertions, taken one by one, I will say that they are bivalent if they are guaranteed to come out flatly true or flatly false when they are held up against some range of backgrounds in which we realistically expect them to be used. (E.g., the background to my use of sentences containing the word 'bald' is a world in which some people have no hair, some have just a little, some have more, and some have very full heads of hair.)[2] Now, although in the course of dealing with our day-to-day affairs, we're usually interested in the truth and falsity of sentences or thoughts, taken one at a time against the actual circumstances in which they present themselves, here we will be concerned primarily with the counterfactual or dispositional behavior of categories of sentences. That is, we'll want to know, not whether the sentence 'John Smith is bald' is true, or even whether it is sure to come out true, but whether, for instance, the class of sentences containing the predicate '... is bald' can be counted on to come out flat true or flat false.[3] So, and here's the second usage, I will say of categories of sentences or thoughts, that they are bivalent, when each of the sentences in the category is bivalent.

   Let me mention four consequences of using our terms this way: First, because bivalence is, here, a dispositional concept, a sentence can fail to be bivalent even if, in a particular case, it comes out flat true or flat false (in just the way that a glass can be fragile even while it is still unbroken). Second, and closely connected to the previous point, a category of sentences that is not bivalent can contain sentences that are bivalent, taken individually: the category of sentences constructed using the predicate '...is bald' is not bivalent, even though 'Somebody or other is bald' is, realistically, inevitably true, and so bivalent. Third, bivalence so understood is sensitive to what is being taken to be the relevant background: in a world somewhat different from our own, in which in-between scalps did not occur, the category of sentences formed using the predicate '...is bald' would be (as far as the predicate went) bivalent after all. And fourth, bivalence, treated this way, can be thought of as a matter of degree, or something like a matter of degree; if *almost* all the occasions for the use of some sentence make it come out fully true or fully false, we may want to ascribe, say, almost complete bivalence.

2.2

We can proceed by treating the layman's view as a working hypothesis. Now, taking seriously the hypothesis that sentences, thoughts, and so on often fail, in one way or another, to be bivalent, means allowing that there is room for explanation when categories of sentences or thoughts *are* bivalent. If bivalence should not be taken for granted, then when one has a thought that is in a position to be either true or false, we can ask how that came about. One way of taking this claim makes it uncontroversial. It is a familiar fact that to have a thought that is true, one must first have a thought that is clear enough to be true or false—a thought capable of engaging the facts that would make it true—and we know from experience that attaining the requisite clarity is hard work. If you're a philosopher by trade, think of the struggle involved in converting your raw and inchoate inspiration into a claim with enough definition to stand a chance at being true or false. And if you're a philosopher with an academic day job, think of the papers your students submit: too often, the problem with student papers is not that they are *wrong*, but that they haven't gotten to the point where they might be so much as wrong. It's no accident that philosophers often think of the alternative to full-truth-or-full-falsity as vagueness.[4]

Sometimes, getting into the position of having a bivalent thought is substantially or entirely a matter of arriving at a clearer formulation of it. And there is a widely held view about beliefs which suggests that this is how bivalence is always managed. On the view in question, beliefs are to be understood in terms of their 'direction of fit': beliefs are supposed to fit the world, and are contrasted with desires, to which the world is to be made to conform. In other words, when there is a mismatch between the world and a desire, as when you want your pantry to be well-stocked, but it is not, the mismatch is addressed by getting provisions to put in the pantry; whereas if you believe your pantry is well-stocked, and it is not, the mismatch is properly addressed by changing your mind as to the pantry's contents.[5]

Consider a case where the mismatch between belief or statement and world amounts to a failure of bivalence. For example, I point out that the cloud up there is shaped like a horse's head. This is not, strictly speaking, true; no horse's head was ever shaped *quite* like that.[6] It is true enough, true in a way, true for present purposes. Now, if for some reason I were to decide that this kind of half-fledged truth was not good enough, an understanding of belief in terms of direction of fit would likely prompt me to address the mismatch between my claim and the cloud by changing my belief so as to make it fully true. I could, for example, replace the predicate 'is shaped like a horse's head' with one precisely fitted to the shape of the cloud. The ensuing sentence would then be fully true.

What I want to drive home is just how deeply impractical a policy of proceeding in this way would be. To begin with, the predicate that perfectly matches the cloud's shape would be very hard to learn, and maybe even just unlearnable. Moreover, it is as likely that I will come across two identical snowflakes as it is that I will run into another cloud with just this shape. So there will be no further occasions to use this predicate. Because no one else will have either reason or opportunity to learn the predicate, I will be unable to use it to communicate informatively. And because it has only one instance, it will not figure in my supply of laws and other generalizations; consequently, the inferences that thoughts containing this predicate enable me to make will be trivial. All in all, acquiring this predicate would be a waste of time, and to make a habit of learning predicates of this sort would be to clutter my mind with perhaps elaborately articulated but completely useless intellectual equipment.

The direction-of-fit view suggests coming to have bivalent thoughts by changing the thoughts, but we have just seen why achieving bivalence this way is often a non-starter. If we want bivalence, and if, as in cases of this kind, the awkwardness of match between belief or statement and world is not to be removed by altering or replacing the belief or statement, it must, we might expect, be removed by altering the world. And this is, I want to claim, how, most of the time, these things actually happen.

Let's take a look at a couple of examples. Sentences to the effect that a particular car is or is not a Honda Civic are pretty much bivalent, and that is not an accident. Your mechanic needs to be able to order parts that will fit; the DMV has to know what registration fee to charge; Honda's commercials will be much more effective if you can go down to the dealer and purchase a car that is not just *sort of* the one advertised. For many, many reasons, it is important for the question, 'Is it a Honda Civic?', to be easily and unequivocally answerable. And so, Honda Civics are *made* that way. Honda tools up its factories to manufacture cars that are easily distinguishable from cars of other makes and models. Cars of the same model resemble each other closely. The vehicles are labeled 'Honda Civic' on easily visible surfaces. They have Vehicle Identification Numbers that can be checked against a list. That is, because it matters, for entirely practical reasons, that sentences like 'This is a Honda Civic' be bivalent, steps are taken so that they are: the class of objects, the concept that matches the objects, and procedures that allow the concept to engage the objects are designed and manufactured jointly. The problem of the bivalence of thoughts about Honda Civics has a very tangible solution: not to change one's beliefs—or not to change one's beliefs *alone*—but to build a factory: to change the world.

Here is a second, rather different, example. There's a conception of property, found in Locke, according to which common resources become your own when you mix your labor with them. We do not employ this conception of property; why not? Quite evidently, because we need to avoid endless wrangling and likely bloodshed, and it would be a bad idea to make the question of who owns what into the issue of how much of whose sweat was mixed with which patch of soil. We have to have—for entirely practical reasons—straightforward yes-or-no answers to questions of ownership. And so there is a different way of doing it: we maintain (more or less) a large book; each page of the book has two columns, the first of which is a list of properties, and the second of which is a list of names of legal persons. We have relatively well-defined procedures for changing the entries in the book, and to deal with cases when those procedures break down and disputes arise, we have empowered certain persons (the ones wearing the black robes and, in England, the wigs) to make it be the case, by so pronouncing, that such-and-such belongs to so-and-so. Here bivalence is produced, not by a factory, but by social institutions designed for the purpose.[7]

We were considering the hypothesis that bivalence is not pervasive, and that hypothesis is starting to seem increasingly plausible, as we have gotten a look or two at how bivalence is brought about. So this is an advantageous juncture to extend the hypothesis a bit further, by adding to it the following claim: that the two cases we have just seen, although in some ways very different from each other, are nevertheless typical. Bivalence does not happen of itself: it is engineered, and when we find ourselves in a position to have thoughts or make assertions that are disposed to be determinately true or false in the ranges of circumstances in which we expect to encounter them, in the background or history of that fact we will normally find changes made, not merely to concepts (or the other items in our mental or linguistic inventories), but to the world—changes whose point is to produce bivalence.[8]

I now want to draw attention to one of the likely consequences of the extended hypothesis. If the bivalence of a category of sentences, or the thoughts those sentences express, is an accomplishment, part of which is a matter of making changes in the world outside the mind, then bivalence costs (at least) whatever those changes cost.[9] Now if the examples we have on the table are any indication, those costs can be sizable: the prices of assembly lines, or of working systems of property ownership, are not to be sneezed at. And with that consequence on the table, we've arrived at a good time to give the hypothesis we're considering a name: I'll call it the *no-free-lunch hypothesis*.

2.3

The hypothesis we are now examining is ambitious, and the payoff is still some distance down the road; to get there, we need first to bypass a number of objections. The no-free-lunch hypothesis has it that bivalence doesn't just happen on its own: it is an achievement, and work has to be done to have sentences or thoughts that are disposed to be either flat true or flat false. But—the first of these objections runs—bivalence can be had so easily as makes no difference, by *loosening up* the thoughts or sentences in question. (Differently put: what we are paying for isn't two-valued truth, but precision.) Language provides a number of handy and generally applicable devices for turning partial into full truth; these devices work, roughly, by anticipating the mismatch between allegation and world in the content of the allegation. If the sentence 'That cloud has the shape of a horse's head' is only approximately true, then the sentence 'That cloud has approximately the shape of a horse's head' is fully true. If 'It's the most charming house you've ever seen' is somewhat true, because true in a way, then the sentence 'In a way, it's the most charming house you've ever seen' is entirely true, no further qualification necessary. Similarity and resemblance are often called upon for this purpose. Alternatively, one can often simply pick a predicate with a larger extension: instead of stating the object's color to be 'burnt crimson,' announce it to be 'reddish.' Full-fledged truth is never more than an additional phrase away, and if it is, it is no more difficult to come by than the phrase, which is to say, not difficult at all.

The fact adduced by the objection is indeed a fact: our language does make it easy enough to manage truth or falsity in just about any particular instance. I will return to the objection in Chapter 6; for now, recall that we are going to be primarily concerned not with actual truth or falsity in particular instances, but with dispositions of sentences or thoughts in given categories to come out either flat true or flat false against the relevant backgrounds. Throwing in an 'approximately' may make this or that sentence (say, the one about the horse-headed cloud) true on this occasion; but it does not generally produce a useful category of sentences that is any more bivalent than before. And likewise, it does not help to point out that *resembling* a horse's head is an elastic predication. There are quite enough clouds of which the claim that they are shaped approximately like horses' heads will be only to a certain extent true, and there are quite enough clouds of which the claim that they resemble horses' heads will be only somewhat true.

Bivalence-by-loosening will usually not solve the practical problems that made bivalence important in the first place. The mechanic who calls his supplier to order parts for the vehicle that is only to a certain extent a Honda Civic will not be able to fix your car, even if he has managed to produce a sentence that, by moving the vagueness into the content, turns out to be flatly true. A legal decision to the effect that each of you is *somewhat* the owner of the property will exacerbate rather than resolve your dispute. Redescribing my upholstery as reddish will be inferentially useless if I am trying to match it to burnt crimson paint. When you get full truth by changing the subject, the mistake is to think that full truth is always available, when what is available is some *other* truth. Loosening looks like a merely verbal maneuver that gets you truth for free; but if the approximate or halfway truth you had before was not what you needed, the full truth the maneuver gives you will not be the truth you need either.[10]

2.4

How far can the no-free-lunch hypothesis be pushed? I'm going to take a look at four especially resistant areas: biological species, the laws of physics, mathematics, and logic. I'll quickly and a bit tentatively sketch ways of getting facts in these domains halfway under the umbrella of the story I'm telling, and while I'm doing that, I'll start to characterize an especially important class of benefits that can, often, make bivalence worth the price.

Think back to the world of our just-barely-human ancestors. In that world, bivalence cannot have been fabricated in the ways I have suggested, because, at that point, human beings had done no fabricating worth mentioning. But presumably even cavemen were able to sort animals into species, and when they did, they were almost always simply right or wrong.[11] So it must be possible to have bivalent truth without paying for it.[12]

One way to think about this kind of case is to say that the work was done before humans came on the scene, but was done nonetheless. It is no accident that there are bivalent truths to be had about membership in a species. Natural selection has produced mechanisms that (with a good many exceptions) prevent the members of different species from interbreeding— and these mechanisms have real adaptive costs.[13] 'What do you get when you cross an elephant and a grape?' is the first line of a joke, and not something farmers need to know, because there are such mechanisms. Here the work was done by evolution; to the extent that we can identify costs paid for benefits received, we can assimilate the process by which bivalent thoughts about species were made possible to the more central cases we already have on the table.[14]

Let me return for a moment to the picture that I used to present the objection. Many of us will remember from our childhoods a stereotype of the proto-human in the pre-artifactual world: the hairy, stooped, and obviously not-all-that-bright Neanderthal. That stereotype probably gets a good deal wrong; we have no reason to think that Neanderthals and other proto-humans were innately dull-witted (or that they looked that way). But what is interesting is that there's something it gets (almost) right. Thinking was much harder for them than it is for us—not because their brains were insufficiently evolved (whatever that would come to), but because there were then many fewer straight truths to be thought. The vast majority of our cut-and-dried truths are about artifacts of our own making, and in the pre-artifactual world, things are for the most part not cut and dried; rather, they tend to be like the horse-shaped cloud of my earlier example. If I am right about this, we are the inheritors of tens of millennia of effort and investment that, by reshaping our collective environment, have made cut-and-dried truth quite common. The much greater availability of bivalence makes many kinds of thinking *routine*, and I'll start to say what that comes to in the course of looking at the next problem area.

2.5

The hard sciences, physics in particular, purport to provide truths that are bivalent and universal: the laws of successful physics hold everywhere, and they're unequivocally true. Human intervention didn't make them true, and there's no evolutionary as-if agent to fill in for us. But if that's right, a good deal of very important truth is exempt from the no-free-lunch hypothesis.

Now I don't want to contest the way of thinking about the truths of the hard sciences that I've just gestured at here: I don't want to say that they're not *just* true; I don't want to claim that they're somehow a social construction; I don't want to deny that they've always been everywhere true. In short, I mean to concede that the laws of physics may be an exception to the no-free-lunch hypothesis.[15]

All that granted, and allowing that the hard sciences are strictly speaking an exception, it's instructive to see the ways in which the territory resembles those that the no-free-lunch hypothesis *is* true of. There are, first of all and most obviously, the nontrivial costs of designing and performing the experiments that establish an exceptionless law. Now when Congress is asked to pay for those experiments, it is told that their point is, for instance, simply to show that the law is true.[16] But that is, for our purposes, an insufficiently informative description of what the money goes for.

Successful physics replaces naive physics—that is, folk theories about the physical world that are, characteristically not fully true, but true enough to be usable in normal circumstances. (For example: 'Unsupported bodies fall.') Now when a theory or law is not fully true, but only true *enough*, its application requires judgment: for instance, judgment allowing me to refrain from drawing the conclusion that an unsupported object will fall if it is a helium balloon, or if it is a rocket, or if it is a bird. So one way of describing the triumph of the science of physics is that it replaced defeasible laws, requiring judgment in their application, with laws that are exceptionless, and so made the solutions to physics problems something one can simply calculate.[17]

That said, however, notice that applying the bivalent laws of successful physics to the unprepared world can seem, to the average user, a lot like applying the laws of naive physics: even when the law is exceptionless, its real-world applications typically *do* require judgment. In highly unstructured situations, an exceptionless law is likely to function merely as a heuristic biasing a guess. (The law of inertia is exceptionless, but when I see the runner skidding on the mud, I deploy it as though it were something like: well, he'll tend to keep going for a bit.) And even in somewhat more structured situations, successful application of the law is typically a matter of how reliable one's sensibilities are. (Maxwell's equations apply…but are Kirchhoff's laws the right approximation to use? Or is the wavelength too small, relative to the size of the system?) From the point of view of a user of the bivalent law in an unprepared situation, it is—as far as the intellectual demands being made on him go—*as though* the law were only somewhat true: true modulo the indefinitely many exceptions, true other things being equal, true but defeasible.

Controlled experiments in the hard sciences are artifacts in which a bivalent truth is persuaded to exhibit itself *as* bivalent.[18] Interfering factors are controlled, the workings of the law are made cleanly visible in the carefully arranged circumstances, and as a result, inferences made using the law can be *treated* as airtight rather than as defeasible. That is, you can infer that the result predicted will follow (which allows you to test the law), rather than that, if none of the many imponderables get in the way, the result will follow (which will not allow you to test the law).[19]

Even if real bivalence in the hard sciences comes for free, bivalence as far as the user is concerned does not. The normal way to generate bivalence for the user is to construct suitable artifacts. This often requires the allocation of substantial resources, the immediate justification for which is to create circumstances in which inferences deploying the law can be made routinely—that is, without providing occasion for judgment in the face of defeasibility.

Now there are classes of flat-out exceptions to the hypothesis that bivalence is the effect of reengineering the objects about which one is thinking. Sometimes we require hard truth, but it is, for one reason or another, not feasible, or inadvisable, to alter the objects in question. For instance, part of the process of showing a law to be flat true is showing that apparent deviations from it can be accounted for. Successful celestial mechanics requires an explanation of perturbations of the orbits of the planets; it goes without saying that we are not in a position to manipulate the planets. So here the law was exhibited in the already existing natural objects, rather than in an artifact constructed for the purpose. Or again, social scientists often need to classify human subjects or their behaviors into one or another of a short list of categories; altering the behavior to make it fit the categories would defeat the point of the research. Medical diagnoses sometimes need to be clear-cut, but it would not be appropriate to change the patient to fit the diagnosis. I will give the principled reply to the worry raised by this class of cases in section 4.6, below. Until then, bear in mind that those unretouched hard truths are less usual than they might seem at first glance. A social scientist's data points, the curves fitted to them, and much else are normally a cleaned-up idealization of what eyes and instruments registered.[20] That is, the data is, in large part, a collection of partial truths.

2.6

Mathematics is another problem area for the no-free-lunch hypothesis, if I want to allow that the mathematical facts are independent of and prior to human endeavor, and that mathematics provides us with an enormous inventory of truths that are as bivalent as they come. If I am willing to allow as much as that, do I need to allow also that mathematical truth is an area to which the no-free-lunch hypothesis does not apply?

Let me distinguish the mathematical objects in their Platonic heaven, of which there have been bivalent truths from time immemorial, from our understanding of those objects, and the truths we can manage given the state of our understanding; even if the no-free-lunch hypothesis doesn't stick to the real objects of mathematics, something like it does stick to what we understand. An example that illustrates the point very nicely can be lifted from Imre Lakatos's enormously enjoyable *Proofs and Refutations* (1976). Nowadays Euler's Theorem—that the number of vertices of a polyhedron, minus the number of edges, plus the number of faces, is 2—is just flat-out true; but it wasn't always. The original proof was persuasive and intuitive, but its conclusion was true only modulo the exceptions, and it was very hard to say up front just what those exceptions were. One very natural way to construe the problem is as unclarity in the definition of 'polyhedron'; with the right definition, the proof is airtight and next-to-trivial. Getting the definition that would let the proof go through took on the order of 150 years of mathematicians' labor. Evidently, even where the costs are not due to work done in the world outside the mind, bivalence does not come for free. And it is very suggestive that this labor, from the mathematician's point of view, looks and feels a lot like reengineering the object that is going to be the subject of one's proof.

As before, the penalty for not having achieved bivalence is that inference requires judgment. Theorems are used to prove further theorems; if your version of Euler's Theorem is only true-with-exceptions, you will need a judgment call as to whether the occasion for the use you mean to make of it in some further proof is one of the exceptions. Errors of judgment can very easily pile up, and the subject matter of much mathematics is such that errors of judgment happen easily. So mathematics is a good place to insist on full bivalence; given the way the enterprise is structured, the costs are worth paying.[21]

Notice that we also have available a story for mathematics that is analogous to the one I told about the laws of physics: that the costs lie in the application of the mathematics to the real world. To use what you know about triangles, you have to have triangular items (or approximately triangular items) to apply your theorems to, and one way to come by them is to fabricate them. I will revisit this thought in Section 6.5.

2.7

The last problem area that I want to look at now is that of logical truth. 'p or not-p' is just plain true, for any value of p; 'p and not-p' is always just plain false.[22] Philosophers have at one time and another been inclined to talk about the hardness of logic, by which they meant in part the bivalence of the logical truths. But, and here is the objection surfacing once again, if logic is there whether you pay for it or not, and if it's got that crystalline hardness, then bivalence can't be something that has to be paid for.

It is one of the harder to swallow—but also more interesting—consequences of the view we're now exploring that, while the pronouncements of logic are bivalent and universal, the way that truth is usually understood is substantially misleading.[23] It's literally true, because for any p, it's just plain true that (for instance) 'p or not-p.' But p here ranges over propositions, abstract objects which are by stipulation either flat true or flat false. Sentences and opinions—the material of real human assertion and thought—do not, if the hypothesis we are considering is on the mark, always or even often express propositions.

When bivalence isn't assured, the logical truths, and the corresponding rules of inference, start to blur around the edges. For example, modus ponens is the elementary inference rule that tells you that from p and 'if p then q' you may infer q: from 'This is a path' and 'If this is a path, I can follow it out of the forest' it follows that I can follow it out of the forest. However, the relevant categories of assertions about paths and would-be paths are not bivalent: if the path is underused, if it fades out as it crosses a field, or if it is overgrown with poison oak, it may be only partially true that it is a path; in which case it may be something that an experienced woodsman could follow out, but I could not. The antecedent may be true *enough* for the conclusion (or enough of the conclusion) to follow; but I cannot simply read this off the inference rule. Where bivalence is not (or not yet), neither is deductive logic. Rather than simply look at the syntactic form of the sentences to determine whether I can draw the conclusion, I will have to use my judgment.[24]

One natural response to the universality, such as it is, and the hardness of deductive logic is to try to account for it in terms of its subject matter: *everything* (as Frege thought), or *nothing* (as the early Wittgenstein thought). Either way, deductive logic has no subject matter of its own. But if deductive logic only gets a grip when bivalence is assured, and if bivalence doesn't come for free, then deductive logic *has*, after all, a primary range of application: the domains in which bivalence is available. And if I am right that bivalence is available when it has been engineered, and rarely otherwise, then those domains are artifactual. If deductive logic is not after all a special science, that is because its primary domain of application does not constitute the subject matter for a special science; we do not have a science of artifacts.[25] But deductive logic is not, after all, the form of correct reasoning in general.

2.8

If bivalence has to be paid for, we can ask whether it's worth our while. Sometimes, of course, the question is not really live, for any number of reasons. I've remarked that we are the inheritors of a long history of effort in this direction; bivalence in a particular domain may have been purchased long ago, and be, as far as we are concerned, free. We may have no way of bringing bivalence about. In order to come by certain sorts of bivalent descriptions of the shapes of clouds, we would have to regiment those shapes, and this is not something we know how to do.[26] Sometimes, however, bivalence is something we do not have and are in a position to effect. When it is, we need to consider what costs are worth what benefits.

I have already mentioned the extrinsic costs of bivalence: e.g., the cost of the factory that makes the subjects of bivalent sentences about Honda Civics. Note under this heading that, while bivalence in vehicle identification is worth paying a good deal for, there are limits: no one bothered to outlaw mechanics who put Rolls Royce hoods on the old Volkswagen Beetles, for example. But bivalence can also be worth nothing at all. Somewhere on the continuum between a full head of hair and a hairless scalp are heads that make 'He's bald' neither fully true nor fully false. If bivalence in this domain were important enough, there would be a straightforward response: shave everybody's head. (Here we have the Marines' solution to sorites paradoxes.) But this is a failure of bivalence we have no cause whatsoever to eliminate, and certainly not at the cost of calling out the MPs.

There are subtler, intrinsic costs as well. When I tell you that the movie playing down the street is another *Roman Holiday*, you understand that to be true in a way, but not, of course, simply true. Suppose, however, that this kind of partial truth is just not good enough for you. You, and millions like you, are only willing to pay for a full-price movie ticket if recommendations of this kind are one hundred percent true. We know only too well what is bound to happen: we will start seeing movies coming out of Hollywood with titles like *Roman Holiday II*. I would love to see another *Roman Holiday*, but I do not (and I hope you do not) want to see *Roman Holiday II*. Insisting on bivalence in circumstances like these can end up being a little like the Vietnam War, where, we were told, we had to destroy the village in order to save it.

If bivalence has costs, both extrinsic and intrinsic, and if the decision to enforce bivalence in some domain is to be reasonable, there must be commensurate benefits to be had. We have already seen benefits particular to one case or another, but the time has come to provide a more abstract, and more general, description of the point of bivalence.

Bivalence—again, exotic logics to one side—is a precondition for deductive inference. Deductive inferences can be made completely explicit. Their correctness can be checked mechanically. And they are airtight: the premises *guarantee* the truth of a deductive inference's conclusion. While constructing a deductively tight argument may take ingenuity, creativity, and even genius, once such an argument has been constructed, no further judgment is required in determining whether, in this or that case, the conclusion does indeed follow from the premises.

When, however, inference is not deductive, it cannot be made entirely explicit, correctness cannot be checked mechanically, and premises only support, but do not guarantee, the truth of conclusions. Such inferences, we saw, require a willingness to trust one's judgment as to whether the inference goes through. But judgment may be undependable, the practice of relying on a judgment call whose grounds cannot be made fully explicit may invite abuse of many kinds, and marshalling one's sensibilities may simply not be worth it when there is a way to routinize one's decisions. In short, nondeductive inference makes intellectual demands of those who deploy it which we may have many reasons not to want to impose. So we create objects about which we are able to have bivalent thoughts in order to be able to think about them deductively (rather than defeasibly), that is, in order to remove occasions for the exercise of judgment.[27]

It is easy to miss the forest for the trees, and to think that the benefits of the sort of reengineering we are considering are local and pragmatic, rather than inferential, and that the account I am developing is consequently over-semanticized. Honda standardizes its products, the objection will run, so that they can be palletized for shipping, so that its suppliers can bid on parts, so that its workers do not need constant retraining, and so on…not to make their inferences deductive. After all, when management discusses the relevant choices, can't we be pretty sure that neither inference nor deduction are mentioned? However, executing an inference is not something over and above being able to conclude, without having to stop and think twice, from the fact that Civics have such-and-such dimensions, and that the pallet dimensions are such-and-such, that a Civic will fit on a pallet. It is not as though inference were one of Gilbert Ryle's philosophical ghosts, hovering over the mundane decision to order the pallets, but ethereally distinct from it. To describe the benefit of reengineering as making available deductive inference is to redescribe the very benefits we have just mentioned, and many more like them, but at a higher level of abstraction, so that we can see what they have in common. It is precisely because deduction *is* drawing conclusions such as these that it matters—both in the business world and to philosophers.

For many problems there are two competing types of solution. One involves improving the sensibilities of the reasoners, and so the quality of the judgment calls as to whether some inference should go through or not.[28] The other involves removing occasions for judgment, by reengineering the domain of inference so as to make the reasoning deductive. The predicate '…is on my side of the street' is often vague, sentences constructed out of it are often only somewhat true, and drivers must rely on their judgment to determine whether inferences from those sentences ought to proceed. On the one hand, drivers are sent to defensive driving classes to improve their judgment; on the other, white and yellow lines are painted down the middle of busy thoroughfares, '…is on my side of the street' ceases to be a vague predicate, the relevant inferences become deductive, and drivers don't have to play chicken with each other anymore. Sometimes there are mixed cases, in which we reengineer objects in the domain so as to lighten the load, while still requiring defeasible inferences of the agents. At a red light (a condition engineered for bivalence), right turns are allowed when it's safe (a condition often satisfied to a degree, requiring judgement calls and defeasible inferences).[29]

Bivalence is required for a certain kind of clarity (not the only kind of clarity) in thought. The bivalence doctrine can be rephrased as the claim that whatever you can think is bivalent. We are in the course of discarding the bivalence doctrine as being, at any rate, not true in the main. That is not to say that it is false through and through. The truth in bivalence, which we do not want to throw out with the bathwater, is that the more bivalent it is, the more straightforwardly you can think with it. Bivalence matters—and full-fledged truth matters—when and because explicitness in inference matters.

2.9

The no-free-lunch hypothesis has been on the table for a while now, and it has grown more substantial, and more robust, as consequences have been elicited from it. But is the hypothesis *true*? In the course of spelling it out, of giving our examples and considering hard cases, we've put ourselves in a position to give a suitably nuanced answer to that question. It's certainly not entirely true. I conceded (perhaps too generously) that mathematical and hard-scientific truths might be exceptions. The relative neatness with which organisms can be classified into biological species was made to fit only with some forcing. Occasions arise, for example, in astronomy and social science research, where precision attained by altering the object of investigation would be, respectively, impossible and pointless, and we manage precision nonetheless. There were linguistic devices for getting truth on the cheap. And there are no doubt other exceptions and qualifications that will come up as we examine the hypothesis further. But after we've finished sketching the big picture, I will argue that the hypothesis is true in the main, pretty much true—true enough so that it would be a serious mistake to ignore it.[30] And if the hypothesis *is* true, or true enough, that is of course just what we should expect.

3

Deflating Deflationism

I've been suggesting that bivalence is normally a product of engineering, which we can't always afford, and I anticipated the conclusion that our claims are often enough not going to end up flat true or flat false. If that turns out to be the case, we need to consider what sort of intellectual toolkit can cope with lapses in bivalence. I am going to start in on that question by trying to say what has gone wrong with the way most philosophers have been thinking about truth.

Philosophical discussions of truth are often focused on the question of what truth is; answers to this question get described, or perhaps overdescribed, as theories of truth, and there is by now a standard menu of such theories. My own agenda is more or less at right angles to this traditional debate; I hope to put partial truth on the map alongside full truth, but I will not be trying to explain what makes a sentence or a thought true. The philosophically trained reader probably thinks of truth in connection with topics like realism and relativism, or perhaps the debate as to whether moral language really manages to say anything, or the debate as to whether truth consists in correspondence to the facts, or rather in some sort of coherence, and he may be wondering what has happened to these big and familiar questions. I am going to be doing my best to bypass the old, familiar issues; I would much rather see if we can make headway on other philosophical problems by pressing different and less over-handled questions, and I am not trying to address them.

Nonetheless, so-called minimalist or deflationary views of truth are today probably the most influential family of such theories.[1] Deflationary views of truth function as conversation-stoppers, and they tend as a matter of practice to get in the way of further discussion of truth. So while I do not want to argue here that they are mistaken, exactly, and in fact think that the view I am developing is compatible with a suitable minimalist account of truth, partly in order to make room for the view I am developing, I am going to provide a deflationary account of deflationary accounts of truth.

The rough shape of the suggestion I will be making has an antecedent in the metaethics of a couple of decades back. In *After Virtue*, a book that was much discussed at the time, Alasdair MacIntyre argued that emotivism—the view that moral judgments are not really beliefs or assertions at all, but merely expressions of the speaker's emotions—was persuasive not because it was a compelling account of our ethical or moral language, but rather because it was a perceptive description, on the part of their students, of the philosophical practice of the emotivists' immediate predecessors.[2] When intuitionists like Moore announced that they could just *see* that something or other was good, and that there was nothing further to be said about it, they really *were* doing no more than indulging in a novel mode of expression for their moralistic feelings. (Here is MacIntyre recounting Keynes's impressions: "'victory was with those who could speak with the greatest appearance of clear, undoubting conviction and could best use the accents of infallibility" and Keynes goes on to describe the effectiveness of Moore's gasps of incredulity and head-shaking, of Strachey's grim silences and of Lowes Dickinson's shrugs.') If one takes intuitionist pronouncements like these as one's model of moral judgment, and proceeds to strip away the handwaving and mystification (non-natural properties and the like), one comes away with a metaethical theory that does indeed make moral judgments out to be no more than such expressions of feeling.

I aim to tell an analogous story about how the minimalist or deflationary approach to truth became so widely accepted. Deflationism, I will suggest, was compelling not because it was a satisfactory account of truth in general, but because it captured the way truth had come to figure in the philosophical culture inhabited by the deflationists. In order to have the view I will be discussing clearly in front of us, I will begin by saying something about the spirit of the deflationary family of theories of truth, and, for the sake of concreteness, I will quickly sketch one such theory. I will then tell a short, MacIntyre-style philosophical science-fiction story. The punch line of the story will be that deflationism got off the ground because it entirely overlooked a central and indispensable function of our truth vocabulary. Having identified that function, we will be in a position to discuss alternatives to bivalence.

3.1

The deflationary or minimal approach to truth is built around what must at the time have been an eye-opening realization: that the sentence 'p is true' is true just when p is. A very natural conclusion to draw—especially in a period whose slogans equated meaning with method of verification—was that saying 'p is true' is just another way of saying p, and early versions of the view were appropriately called 'redundancy theories.' On the most widely shared version of deflationism, truth is a dummy predicate, applicable to sentences (or idealized versions of sentences), whose presence in the language is explained by the various conveniences it provides. These include brevity, a way of acknowledging that one is repeating what someone else has said, a means of endorsing sentences wholesale, and of endorsing sentences whose content one does not oneself know. (A sophisticated use of the device might be a boss instructing an employee not to reveal any ugly truths.[3]) But there is nothing more to truth than a device that provides these conveniences, and when you understand that, you have understood all there is to know about truth. There is no room for a metaphysical (e.g., correspondence or coherence or pragmatist) theory of truth, and there is nothing complicated, deep, or especially philosophically interesting about truth. The device is formally quite simple, and once you understand the device, you're *done*.[4]

In order to have one such theory on the table before us, I'm going to sketch Dorothy Grover's prosententialism. While it is nonstandard in not treating truth as a predicate of sentences or propositions, it is also the most graceful and sophisticated member of the minimalist family of theories of truth, and it nicely displays the appeal of the minimalist approach.[5]

Proforms are a category of grammatical devices of which pronouns are the most familiar. Pronouns function grammatically as nouns, and are used to stand in for (usually) previously mentioned nouns. For example:

> Once upon a time there were a Prince and a Princess. *He* lived in a turret, high up in the Department of Languages and Literatures, and *she* lived in a dungeon in the Department of Philosophy.

Proverbs (pronounced with a long 'o') are another familiar proform: they are grammatically verbs, and stand in for previously mentioned actions.

One day, the Prince submitted a change-of-grade form, and, coincidentally, so *did* she.

'Did,' here, stands in for 'submitted' (with the remainder of the verb phrase understood), in pretty much the way that 'he' stood in for 'the Prince' in the previous example. English proadjectives similarly stand in for previous adjectival descriptions.

His form had been been white with canary and pink copies attached, but when it arrived at the Registrar, it was no longer *such*.

And, likewise, proadverbs stand in for previous adverbial modifiers.

The Princess ran to the Registrar's office, waving her form wildly, and while *so* waving it, caught the Registrar's eye.

Since so many other grammatical forms have proforms,[6] we should not be surprised to find that English (among other languages) provides a pro-form for sentences. Prosentences, as we should by now expect, will have the grammatical appearance of sentences, and stand in for previous sentences.[7] And once we have the grammatical category of an anaphoric proform for sentences on hand, it is obvious that 'That's true' is an English prosentence.

The Registrar said, 'I cannot allow that form to be processed. You see, I already have a form from the Prince.'

'*That's true*,' she replied, 'but my form has priority, because it's printed on blue paper.'

Just as pronouns like 'he' are pointers back to previously introduced nouns, so prosentences like 'It's true' are pointers back to previously introduced sentences. Once you understand this, you have understood all there is to understand about truth, which is to say that the pro-sentential account of truth is deflationary. There is no more room for a metaphysical theory of truth than there is for a metaphysical theory of the pronoun.[8] Deflationary accounts of truth have been meant as conversation-stoppers, the point being that, once we know what truth is, we're *done*.

3.2

Now for a just-so story. Once upon a time, before the advent of photography made artists feel that the aspiration to realism was unambitious, works of art such as paintings were often representational, and a large part of an audience's response to such a work consisted in assessing the accuracy of the representation. It was the nature of the medium that full accuracy was very near unattainable, and so one would need to specify the ways in which, and the degrees to which, accuracy had been obtained. A painting might be said to have gotten its subject's face right, but not her expression; or to have gotten her expression mostly right, although not quite the look in her eyes; or to have gotten the look in her eyes, but not quite her character.[9] Of course, such assessments are appropriate even for photographs, and we still routinely produce them when we are shown our friends' driver's licenses.

When viewers talked this way about paintings, they were *grading* them; the practice of assessing paintings for accuracy was evaluative, and (here is where photography really has put some distance between ourselves and our predecessors) closely but not mechanically tied to a certain kind of useful- ness. That is, the point of assessing the accuracy of a painting was, often enough, to let someone else know what kind of information he could extract from it. For instance, a reasonably but not entirely accurate portrait might nonetheless allow me to recognize its subject; an extremely bad portrait might allow me to determine what the subject was wearing for the sitting; a very good portrait might tell me something important about the character of its subject. Given the difficulties of the medium, such assessments could only be useful if they were both graduated and nuanced.

Before philosophy, analytic or otherwise, came into the story, it was customary also to grade not just pictorial but verbal representations. The practice was elaborately nuanced, in just the way that the evaluation of repre- sentational paintings was. In one report of this practice, from a philosopher with a reputation of having had a real flair for it, they would say, for example, 'that a certain statement [was] exaggerated or vague or bald, a description somewhat rough or misleading or not very good, an account rather general or too concise.'[10] And one very useful part of this practice was the ascription of partial truth, as when a claim to be writing a novel would subsequently be characterized as not strictly true, but nearly true.[11]

In our own history, photography made accurate depiction seem too easy to be worthy of the attention of art. But in the just-so history I am telling, cameras never made an appearance. Instead, a kind of nervous perfectionism spread through the culture. In examinations, anything short of a perfect score became a failing grade. Any defect at all, in any product, would prompt the insistence that it was entirely worthless, and it would immediately be thrown out. And, before long, there remained only two possible grades to give paintings: 'accurate' and (when there was any flaw whatsoever) 'inaccurate.'

This cultural shift made evaluations of paintings (and, in fact, the paintings themselves) much less useful than they had been. Since paintings are almost never completely accurate, they were almost all designated 'inaccurate,' and all but the very few exceptions were no longer used. Architectural renderings, family portraits, engraved illustrations in science textbooks, and historical tableaux were all destroyed. Since it was no longer possible to qualify one's claim that a painting could be relied upon, endorsing the representational content of a painting could only be attempted for the painting just as it stood, as it were at a single go. This made it much harder to teach painting as well, because students rarely get it completely right, and the option of telling a student that he has gotten it mostly right, or has gotten some important part of it right, is always pedagogically invaluable.[12]

Finally, after some time had passed, a novel view arose in aesthetics, which the philosophers of our fictitious society called the redundancy theory of accuracy. According to the redundancy theory, when you say that a painting is accurate, you are doing no more, really, than verbally holding up the painting. You have found an odd way of repeating exactly what the painting is telling you about the world; and when you understand this, the redundancy theorists said, you are *done*, as far as understanding accuracy in painting is concerned. Many volumes had been written, addressing themselves to the question of accuracy in painting, and examining such issues as whether accuracy consisted first of all in getting (the gist of) a subject's character, or rather in faithfulness to the visual texture of surfaces in an image. In a final burst of Humean enthusiasm, the aesthetic redundantists rounded these volumes up, built bonfires in public squares throughout the country, and gleefully consigned them to the flames.

The aesthetic redundantists had been right about what judgments of accuracy came down to, but only for the practice of assessing accuracy as they found it. The very thin account worked for the very thin practice, but, as I have told the story, not for the richer practice of graduated and nuanced judgments of accuracy; it was ideology that helped conceal from artists and the consumers of their products how much they had lost. There is of course

an analogous story to be told about what happened to the perfectionists'
practice of assessing verbal representations, but for this part of the narrative
I am going to stop talking about a fictional pre-photographic culture, and
get back to talking about us.

<h2 style="text-align:center">3.3</h2>

It is no accident that deflationary views of truth became popular with the rise
of analytic philosophy. As Hilary Putnam has remarked, analytic philosophy,
in its logical positivist phase, was a program with two motors. The first was
the new logic developed by Frege, Russell, and Whitehead, and that logic
required bivalence. The second was its empiricism, which made apparently
metaphysical notions suspect, and truth was, in the early twentieth century,
such a notion. Tarski's formal treatment of truth rehabilitated it for logical
positivism, and so for analytic philosophy; but that treatment also assumes
bivalence.[13]

Now bivalence, the restriction to two truth values, when conjoined to
the practice of grading verbal representations in terms of truth, means that
there are only two grades to give out. To insist on bivalence is on a par with
adopting the stance that a very good (but not perfect) portrait is, not almost
entirely successful, but not successful at all; it is rather like giving exams and
failing any student who does not get a perfect score. The effect is to turn a
delicately nuanced mode of assessment into a standard too crude to register
anything other than the grader's full agreement, or lack thereof.

That standard is so impoverished as to be fully capturable by the minimal or redundancy approach to truth. And so, not surprisingly, we find
such accounts making their appearance almost immediately after the crys-
tallization of the analytic tradition.[14] But what is being captured is not the
practice that makes truth interesting and important to non-philosophers;
like the emotivists, what deflationists are describing is the etiolated use of
the notion that is available within their philosophical culture.[15]

Michael Dummett once pointed out that a theory of truth should make
sense of the ways that truth matters to us.[16] 'True' is a grade we give to
representations. So a successful theory of truth will be one that accounts
for the ways in which such grades are important and useful grades to give
out. Philosophers, nowadays, are for the most part college teachers, that
is, people who give out grades for a living, and so the deflationists and

bivalentists should have known better. When a student gets a perfect score, the grading process is easy. Students who get perfect scores don't need a lot of intervention. It's the middling evaluations that take all the work, and that require the sophisticated evaluative apparatus—the one that allows you to say what the student got right, what needs improvement, and how he needs to focus his efforts. And most of the evaluations are the middling ones. The very same philosophers who produce theories of an inflexible and insufficiently informative scheme for grading sentences, as if it were the only sort of scheme there could be, would find it intolerable if some university authority were to impose a grading scheme with this structure on their own classrooms!

The point of assessing the truth of a sentence is normally to provide a guide to what ranges of conclusions can be drawn from it. To take a sentence to be fully true (to believe it) is to be committed to all of the conclusions that follow from it, when it is taken together with the other sentences that one believes. To introduce terminology that I will have further use for down the road, the deployment of a sentence believed to be true is *inferentially unrestricted*. Sentences that one describes as (e.g.) not entirely true are *inferentially restricted*: there are apparently entailed conclusions that one will correctly refuse to draw. For instance, here is a rule that's pretty reliable: if it's a chair, it seats only one person comfortably. But some pieces of seating furniture are borderline sofas or chaises longues; it is true only with qualifications that they are chairs. And for such items, this particular rule may or may not be useful.[17]

To ascribe full truth to a sentence is to say that it is inferentially unrestricted: this is the least useful, and the least interesting, of the applications of our truth vocabulary. The tricky cases are the inferentially restricted cases, and here talk of partial truth is a way of gesturing at which putatively entailed inferences from a set of premises are legitimate and which are not. You can tell someone that a sentence is roughly true as a way of signaling that those inferences proceeding from it that do not involve a lot of delicacy and nuance are probably safe. You can say that a thought has *some* truth to it, meaning, roughly, that there are *some* inferences that it supports (but, of the ones you might have expected, not too many). You can say that it is officially true that someone is an Estonian, meaning, more or less, that only officially announced entailments are safe. (You may conclude that he is eligible to apply for an Estonian passport, but not, say, that he lives in Estonia, or that he speaks Estonian, or that he is descended from Estonians.) That is, partial truth talk is a way of making more explicit what ranges of inference one is willing to proceed with; at any rate, it allows one to be more explicit about what they are than simply remaining silent.[18]

The grades between true and false have to be given out thoughtfully and with caution. It is very hard to use partial-truth talk to specify exactly which inferences are being endorsed and which are not; typically the patterns of acceptable inference do not lend themselves to clean summaries. In fact we use this kind of assessment most importantly when we are unable to make those commitments completely explicit, and need to provide hints and clues that we have to hope our interlocutors will pick up on. When describing a politician's claim as a half-truth, one is sometimes in the position of being able to say just what the true half is; but probably more often one is not. After all, if we had the resources to say just which inferences we were endorsing, we would probably also have the resources to articulate an appropriate sentence whose full truth we could then endorse.

The rhetorical burden of deflationary accounts, we saw, was that, once we have the account of the simple formal device out on the table, we're *done* with truth. Actually, and this was where deflationism went wrong, we're *not* done, because, once we back away from bivalence, truth is not a simple formal device, but an evidently unformalizable and very complicated evaluative tool.[19]

3.4

Some readers will approach this project with expectations derived from more familiar treatments of truth, and it's standard philosophical practice, in the analytic tradition, to be very explicit about preempting possible mis-understandings. So before getting on with the argument, I am going to take time out to consider a number of these. Because we're still in the softening-up stage of the exposition, I'll appeal to three closely related analogies (to painting, grading, and bookkeeping) to explain why it's all right for the project we're commencing to deviate from those expectations. I mean to introduce these very ordinary, low-key comparisons as a reality check: if something sounds logically and metaphysically respectable when you say it about truth, but just plain silly when you say it about, e.g., accuracy in painting, it's time for second thoughts.

Aristotle once pointed out that there are many ways to miss a target (which is actually one way of explaining *why* partial truth comes in so many different varieties), and the remark is as pertinent when the target is understanding as elsewhere. Consequently, I'm afraid this section is going to have a bit of the look and feel of a laundry list. If you're coming to this discussion with training in analytic philosophy of language, I don't recommend skipping it, but if that's not your background, feel free to proceed directly to the concluding section of the chapter.

1.   I have been trying to let a bit of the air out of deflationism's tires, but I am not trying to work up any metaphysical—or, for that matter, anti-metaphysical—theory of truth. To point out that we have available a subtle and useful system of grading is to have committed ourselves neither to any particular metaphysical account of what is being graded nor to an account of the grades. And although I am not supplying a theory of truth (a theory of what truth *is*), nothing I have said precludes the possibility of one.

Let's supplement the analogies to painting and grading that we already have on the table with one more. Inferential bookkeeping is a primary cognitive function of truth: when we mark a sentence as true, we are registering that we are in a position to draw further conclusions from it. So let us also keep in mind bookkeeping proper—that is, accounting, where, obviously enough, the point of assigning prices in dollars, and dollar values to bank accounts, is to regulate financial transactions.

You might have thought that all there could be to a philosophical analysis of money (and ledger entries) is that it does have such and such a role in regulating transactions, and therefore there is no room for a philosophical theory of monetary value. (What something is worth is what it will bring on the market, and that's all there is to it.) But that thought is too fast, because unless we can see, for instance, why what is being exchanged on the market are items of value, we are not in a position to understand it to be a *market*, as opposed, perhaps, to a ritual or a form of entertainment. (Ask yourself why E*Trade is not just a multiplayer videogame; or consider religious rituals that have the form of financial transactions, such as the Jewish 'redemption of the firstborn.') The analogous thought about academic assessments would likewise be too fast: understanding grades to be how one keeps the academic books should not stop you from thinking about what makes the ritual of writing letters down next to names into grading.

Dummett observes that you do not understand the classification of arguments into deductively valid and invalid unless you understand what the classification is for, in something like the way that you do not understand the rules of chess unless you understand that the object of the game is to win. Generalizing his observation, if you do not understand that the point of inference is to *draw conclusions*, where these conclusions (in the case of theoretical inference) are true, or partially true, or true enough…, then you do not understand what you are doing as argument or inference. My claims about the way truth is used to regulate inference do not preempt a philosophical theory of truth, but might rather even seem to call for one.

2.   Our analogies suggest that you shouldn't expect your favorite theory of truth to rule partial truth out of bounds. *Whatever* your philosophical theory of money ends up being, it is obvious that currencies are devices of our own designing, and that they can be designed in more than one way. *Whatever* your eventual account of the distinction between genuine academic assessments and the honorary degrees awarded senior statesmen at university graduations, there are many different ways to assign grades, and indefinitely many further possible systems of grading. *Whatever* we think that our theoretical inferences are after—whatever our theory of truth—we should have a great deal of flexibility in constructing grading or accounting systems for it.

If our truth vocabulary makes up a system of grades we hand out to representations, then we should treat it that way. If you are a college teacher, you are not going to have a lot of patience for an intruding philosopher of language who tells you that you can only give out As, Bs, Cs, Ds, and Fs, because there are, metaphysically, only those five grades. And if you are a philosopher of logic, you should have as little patience for a colleague who insists that you can only give out Ts and Fs, because there are, metaphysically or logically, only *those* two grades. To vary the analogy slightly: You can't move around the tokens of one accounting system in a way that demonstrates that there could be no *other* accounting system: there is no such thing as a metaphysically necessary accounting system, and we can be pretty sure up front that any such attempt is going to beg the question.[20]

3.   The earlier analogy with painting might suggest to some readers that there really is a particular theory of truth in the background, namely, correspondence theory. (Here is the painting; there is the sitter; the painting is accurate when it corresponds to the sitter: when the ears are, in the picture, where they are on the person, when the person's eyes are as the picture shows them to be, and so on.) And it might also have suggested that partial truths are to be thought of as deviations from full truths that are very, very precise, perhaps in something like the way that contemporary museum-goers imagine realist paintings to aspire to crisp photographic accuracy.[21]

Here the financial analogy supplies a counterweight. It may be natural to think of the correspondence theory as explaining how pictures do their representational work, but it is much less natural for us, nowadays, to think of monetary representations in that way. It is not as though the balance listed on my bank statement is correct if it corresponds to a pile of bills that the bank is keeping for me. The dollar figures play a role in the regulation of financial transactions that is similar in important respects to the role played by truth (and partial truth) assignments in the regulation of theoretical inference. We are not tempted to be correspondence theorists about the former—though a century back, when a dollar bill was supposed to stand for part of a gold ingot in a federal vault, sensibilities may have differed. We should not suppose that we are (so far) committed to correspondence theory about the latter.

4. Philosophers-in-training learn very early on to distinguish quite sharply between soundness and validity: whether the premises of an argument are true, and whether the argument would go through if they were, are two entirely different questions, and (so we all were taught) have no bearing on each other. At various points in the argument to come the philosophical reflexes produced by that training are likely to prompt reactions on the order of: *But that's confusing soundness and validity!* The analogies we have in play explain why those responses will need to be muted.

Whether I have such and such an amount of money, and what I could buy if I did have that amount, are distinct questions; whether I have such and such a grading system in place, and what grade I must give to this student assignment are two different questions. Nonetheless, the design of a financial system, which determines what you can buy with what, had better take into account what sorts of resources its users are going to have, and more generally, the kinds of use to which it will be put. A trivial illustration can be lifted from a Mark Twain story built around the conceit of a million-pound note. (You ought to be able to buy anything you want, but merchants can't ever make change.) Given how wealthy we are here and now, and what we mean to use our money for, a currency system in which million-pound notes were the smallest denomination would be a very bad idea. Switching analogies, it would be a bad idea to introduce an academic grading scale without bearing in mind what sorts of performance one's students are going to manage. If you set up the grading scale so that all your students fail, all the time, that is *your* problem.

Whether I assign a candidate premise of a potential inference a designated value (such as 'true,' or 'pretty much true'), and whether the inference would go through if the premise took that value, are two distinct questions. Nonetheless, the design of our system of inference (which involves selecting the range of values with which potential steps in inference can be marked) had better take account of what sorts of inferential resources are likely to be available. If hard truths are as hard to come by as I am shortly going to argue, inferential bookkeeping that required us to restrict ourselves to flat truth and flat falsity would be a little like a country adopting a currency of million-pound notes, or a little like grading standards that ensured that no student could pass. That is, we are going to be formulating our understanding of correctness of inference *around* the reachability of the relevant inferential statuses (that are themselves to be formulated and chosen to suit that very validity concept).[22]

5. At various points in the argument, I am going to encounter the objection that what I am calling partial truths are simply falsehoods, and that sometimes it is *pragmatically* useful to reason as if they were true. This is a good time to motivate the response my account will provide. Semantic values like true and false are entries used in inferential bookkeeping. In these sorts of cases, the 'pragmatic' proposal means filling up your ledger with useless entries—with columns of zeros, as it were—and doing your 'pragmatic' reasoning off the books. Or alternatively, it is like failing all your students (or like giving them all As), but treating them very differently from one another on the basis of a system of unannounced evaluations. (The student is ecstatic to have gotten an A, but we faculty spread the word, in brief conversations in the halls, that the work was pretty weak, and that this one shouldn't really have been passed.) Isn't it better to adopt accounting methods that allow you keep as much as possible of your reasoning above board?

6. The analogy around which we constructed our MacIntyre-like science-fiction story suggests that you should not be looking for a general and formal account of partial truth. (To reiterate, an account of partial truth that is *both* general and formal; there can certainly be formal theories of one or another dimension of partial truth, and we will get to a couple of these in Chapter 7.) On the one hand, impressionism and pointillism insisted that a painting's accuracy about what philosophers used to call sense-data was more important than other aspects of realism. On the other hand, Lucian Freud is now insisting that showing bodies to be fully corporeal is a more important dimension of accuracy, when you are portraying human beings, than getting the sense-data right. You would not look for a general and formal account of partial accuracy in painting, because there are indefinitely many qualitatively different aspects of a painting's representational success

or failure which you might have occasion to emphasize. So why would you look for a general and formal account of partial accuracy when the medium of representation isn't *paint*?[23]

7.   We are anticipating indefinitely many qualitatively different types of partial truth (some perhaps taking formal analyses, and others perhaps not). That puts us in a position to anticipate a worry about my account, and to issue a promisory note to cover it. The sorts of thing I am going to describe as partial truths will include, just to start off the list, precise descriptions that are understood to be somewhat off-target, vague descriptions asserted of penumbral cases, and ceteris paribus (or other-things-equal) generalizations. Why should we regard these apparently very different items as being in some deep sense the same sort of thing? Why shouldn't we instead just start working up philosophical analyses of each of them, one at a time?

If I am right that there *are* indefinitely many forms that partial truth can take, in something like the way there are indefinitely many dimensions of painterly accuracy, then the task of analysis that the objection proposes is Sisyphean. Once we see that we cannot complete such a task, we do better off not starting in on it; better, rather, to move our analytical projects up a level of abstraction. If the many different sorts of partial truth subserve a single function, then if you do not treat them together, you will fail to understand what they are for. Equally importantly, if you don't understand their common function, you will fail to understand why, taken together, they have to belong to one's inferential repertoire (even if no *particular* form of partial truth has to belong to the repertoire). So I am going to ask you not to be distracted by the formally striking and practically significant differences between the forms that partial truths will turn out to take: one of the conclusions for which I will be arguing is that partial truth must be heterogenous (and that understanding that is understanding something very important about partial truth).

3.5

Deflationism was wrong: you should not expect a successful account of truth to be a conversation-stopper. And so I want to conclude this second warmup chapter with a suggestion as to what, if I am right, theorizing about truth—the activity, now, not its product—should be like.

Just as there are always further dimensions along which we might (and will) want to assess the representational success of paintings, so there are always further dimensions along which we might (and will) want to assess the representational success of statements. We will need to work hard at characterizing different ways in which a claim can be partially true; we will need to argue over which such assessments matter on which occasions; and of course we will get into difficult arguments over what it takes to be true enough, along one or another such dimension of assessment. Nonphilosophers often have the sense that deflationist treatments of truth, along with what analytic philosophers have so far treated as their legitimate competitors, miss a very important fact about it, namely, that truth is *difficult*. I take this thought very seriously, and while there is much more to it than I am going to try to build into my account, we can already see that truth *is* difficult.[24]

Philosophers who work on truth have been treating the construction of a theory of truth as a discovery problem: as a matter of figuring out what account of truth is already *true*. Now, the analogous attitude in the classroom would be that of taking the range of possible grades to be metaphysically fixed, and the problem of deciding on a grading scale to be the discovery of an already-existing fact. But only the most shell-shocked of students are naive enough to think of their grades *that* way. Even if you are very much a realist about how good or bad your students' work is, you will not take that to be a bar to improving your grading scheme (by changing the scale, by incorporating written evaluations, by incorporating subsidiary grades, or whatever). For the self-aware users of truth, the ongoing discussion I have been suggesting we are going to have will at regular intervals turn to how we can refine our techniques for characterizing and assessing partial truths.

In the previous chapter we considered the no-free-lunch hypothesis, which implied that a guarantee, for some range of sentences, that our grades can be limited to *true* and *false* normally requires engineering. Reengineering the objects of thought so as to make deductive, inferentially unrestricted reasoning about them possible is a design task allowing a great deal of scope for ingenuity and originality. We noticed that we cannot always execute such reengineering projects (if only because our collective pockets just aren't deep enough), and when we don't, we have to make do with partial truth. Here also, we should now expect, there is a great deal of scope for ingenuity and originality in working up new types of approximation and idealization, new sorts of hedges, and so on. If truth is a piece of intellectual apparatus that we are always in the process of articulating further, then the philosophical problem of truth isn't just a discovery problem: it's an *invention* problem.

Part II
Arguments

4

How to Find Your Match

In 1998, there was an advertisement for the American Broadcasting Corporation which ran, 'Before TV, two World Wars. After TV, zero.' The billboard was inviting its readers to make an inductive inference, whose conclusion would be something like: television prevents world wars. It was probably also inviting an inference to the best explanation, perhaps that TV viewers are too well-informed, or maybe just too over-entertained, to start world wars. As it happens, the premise of the suggested inductive inference is false: television in fact antedates World War II. But it is, I am inclined to say, *mostly* true: before World War II, television was an exotic and only sporadically available technology; it had nowhere near the influence on political developments that it later came to have. It is true *enough* for us to be forgiving about it; if the inference we are having recommended to us were any good, I wouldn't let the fact that its premise is not fully true get in the way of making it.

This kind of case, I wish to argue, is not an illusion and it is not an oddball exception: theoretical reasoning correctly proceeds on the basis of premises that the reasoner acknowledges not to be strictly true. This is admittedly a very ambitious claim, because to make it is to reject what I was calling the validity as truth preservation doctrine, that is, the idea that what it is for an inference to be correct is for it to be, necessarily, true if it has true premises. But the ambition has by this point been motivated. If the no-free-lunch hypothesis is on target, then hard truth is too expensive to be used all the time: both financially too expensive and, as our brief discussion of imposing bivalence in domains like movie-making indicates, not just financially too expensive. If that is right, partial truth should be expected to be pervasive.[1] And if that in turn is right, we might suppose that a good deal of reasoning is managed in the absence of bivalence. This chapter aims to provide an argument for that supposition. But how should such an argument proceed?

4.1

Thinking is something you do, and so the question of how to think is a practical question. I am going to be arguing against the validity as truth preservation doctrine, and for the thesis that thinking that proceeds from premises that you take to be only somewhat true, or partially true, or true in a way, can amount to reasoning, and to inference. Because the question at hand is practical, this argument is going to consist in a stretch of practical reasoning; but while the received view with regard to practical reasoning is that all of it is instrumental, or means-end reasoning, this is not my own view, and the practical argument to ensue will not have the means-end form. Since this is not the way argument on these topics is usually conducted, some orienting remarks are in order (and throughout my discussion, an account of how such an argument is supposed to work will be interleaved with the development of the argument itself).

The practical argument I will employ resembles the familiar move (sometimes called a transcendental argument) from a cognitive task or enterprise that one is in the course of performing to one or another preconditions of that task or enterprise.[2] When such an argument is run as theoretical reasoning (and the familiar move traditionally is), it's hard to arrive at interesting conclusions without using premises that beg the wrong questions. Because we cannot conclude that the preconditions for performing the task are being met unless the task is actually being performed, success in performance cannot be dispensed with, and success is hard to guarantee.[3] But from the practical perspective, the argument's force is that the preconditions of the enterprise have to be in place if proceeding with it is to make sense, and so a practical commitment to the enterprise becomes a practical commitment to *supposing*—to taking it as a working assumption, while one is engaged in the enterprise—that the preconditions *are* in place. And because one can proceed quite far with many an undertaking without knowing for sure that it is going as intended, much less needs to be ascertained before the practical form of the argument can get off the ground.

For instance, while you're playing Monopoly, you have to take it for granted that the bills don't change their denominations whenever you look away. If the numbers on the Monopoly money don't sit still, then you're not *really* playing Monopoly, and so, if it's going to make sense to continue playing, you need to do so on the working assumption that they are. (Of course, you might still have reason to go through the *motions* of playing, even if you're sure that's all you're doing.) Now, the force of the argument here is not that, because you know that you're playing Monopoly, you know that the money is not changing denominations. That would be a terrible argument, because skepticism about whether the denominations are stable would rearise as skepticism as to whether you were, after all, really playing Monopoly. Rather, its force is practical: *while* you are playing Monopoly, you are practically committed to treating the stability of Monopoly money as a fixed point in your game-playing deliberations.[4]

Here is a second example, one in which the anchoring cognitive enterprise is not merely a game. In the course of trying to develop theories about the distant past, or about distant regions in space, scientists correctly proceed on the supposition of constancy in the physical laws. The astronomer or geologist does not know that the laws of physics in the distant past were the same as they are today, or that faraway parts of the universe are governed by the laws that hold in his immediate astronomical neighborhood. But if they are not, he will be unable to make headway in developing and testing his theories, and so he goes ahead on the working assumption that they are. This assumption, adopted entirely for practical reasons, is thus available to him in the course of his arguments. I am not of course suggesting that one ought to behave like the drunk in the joke, who looked for his keys under the lamppost, rather than where he had lost them, because he was able to see under the lamppost. Once one knows that a task is not doable (in the examples at hand, because the numbers on the bills are actually changing as soon they're out of your sight, or the physical laws elsewhere are indeed different), giving up on it generally becomes the sensible thing to do—though I am willing to allow that there may be quixotic but admirable exceptions to the usually sensible way of proceeding.

The purpose of reasoning about matters of fact—in philosophers' jargon, of theoretical reasoning—is to arrive at a conclusion as to how things stand. (Not just any kind of conclusion, but not always a conclusion that is true: let's say that the aim is to arrive at a conclusion that is true *enough*.) Now, certain things must be the case if the exercise of trying to think one's way to a factual conclusion is to have any point at all, and these must be taken for granted in the course of proceeding with one's reasoning.[5] My argument will be meant to show that the satisfactoriness of reasoning with partial truth is such a precondition for figuring out how things stand.

One does not of course know that one *is* figuring out what the facts are, but—as a practical matter—while one is engaged in theoretical reasoning one must proceed on the assumption that the preconditions for doing so are in place. That is, while one is thinking about how things stand, one must take it for granted that it is all right to proceed on the basis of partial truth: that reasoning from acknowledgedly partial truths can after all be reasoning.

That you must, in the pursuit of some cognitive enterprise, suppose something to be the case does not in general show that it is. This is quite clear in the two warmup examples I have just given: maybe the laws *are* different elsewhere and at other times, no matter what the scientist has to suppose; maybe the numbers on the Monopoly money *are* changing out of sight.[6] But there are interesting exceptions to this restriction. In Monopoly, you must, while playing the game, suppose not just that the numbers on the bills are stable, but that one ought to be buying properties: Boardwalk, Park Place, and so on, and houses and hotels to put on them. A game in which the players advanced their pieces repeatedly around the board, without ever making a purchase, could remain technically within the rules.[7] But because the point of Monopoly is to win, and to win by exploiting one's acquisitions (the drawings on the cards, and so on, are not caricatures of robber barons for nothing), if you didn't take it that one ought to be buying property, you could just as well not be playing; you might as well not bother. And so here the gap, between what you must suppose and what is actually the case, vanishes. Because the content of your supposition is practical—because it is about *how to play*—showing that it is practically necessary to accept it is to show it to be correct: that going ahead and buying properties *is* how to play Monopoly.[8]

In order to show that reasoning on the basis of partial truths is the right way to reason about how things are, I will be arguing that one must, in the course of one's theoretical reasoning, take it that that's the way it's done. The pieces in play here are practical: 'inference' and 'reasoning' are honorific titles awarded to mental activity performed in accordance with what used to be called the Laws of Thought, that is, the guidelines that specify *how to think*.[9] And for that reason, showing that you must suppose that steps taken from partial truths are a legitimate way to go about thinking about how things stand has the force of showing that such steps are theoretical inference.

4.2

Let me pause to introduce a bit of terminology; this will allow me to place a claim I'm about to introduce as an instance of a very general fact.

Let's call thoughts (the things you think with, whatever those turn out to be) and pieces of them *representations*; on this usage, a sentence-sized assertoric thought will count as a representation, but so will sentence-sized interrogative thoughts, so will such parts of thoughts as names and predicates, so will larger chunks of thought that contain sentences, for instance arguments, and so will devices (visual imagery, diagrams, or whatever) that don't particularly look like sentences, or parts of them, at all. I intend to be minimally demanding about what it takes to count as a representation. For instance, we shouldn't worry too hard about whether a would-be representation really has the content it seems to, or any content at all (it can still be a representation); we shouldn't worry much about whether it's properly attributed to its putative owner (it can still be a representation);[10] we shouldn't worry too hard about whether it functions as representations of its putative type are supposed to (it can still be a representation). And with that bit of terminology on our plate, we can say: representations are only useful when they're repeatable (that is, when they can be *re*-presentations).

If you can't use a name more than once, you can't reidentify the object you're thinking about, and you can't think about it *further*. For instance, you can't think about its having this part, and its also having that part. Or again, to determine that Pascale has been all around the town today, I may bring together reports that place her at the post office in the morning, at the Metropole at noon, on the docks in the afternoon, and so on; the conclusion is not much more than a straightforward compilation of facts, but even so it depends on my being able to repeat the component representation 'Pascale.' If you can't use a predicate more than once, you can't use inductive arguments to correlate it with a second predicate (a fact I'll use further down the road). And if you can't use a sentence-shaped thought more than once—if you can't repeat a consideration to yourself—you can't construct arguments. It is this last fact that I'll take a closer look at in just a moment; but first, a delicate point that will turn out to be important later. What matters for whether a representation is repeatable is whether further representations can be *taken for*, or *used as*, repetitions of a previous representation in subsequent thought; it doesn't matter whether they 'really are,' in some more physical or orthographical or phenomenological sense, repetitions.

If our reasoning about matters of fact is to be successful, then we must be able to bring to bear on a problem at hand more considerations than just one. There are, of course, occasions on which adducing a single fact is decisive, and there are patterns of inference that move directly from a single premise to the conclusion drawn from it; but if we were restricted to such inferences, we would normally be unable to arrive at a reasoned view as to the facts in the cases of interest to us. Occasions for reasoning are likely to be those where more than one reason is going to come into play. If we are going to attempt to figure out how things are, we must do this on the assumption that inference involving multiple components is within our capabilities.[11]

Now, sometimes the effect of adducing more than one consideration is merely additive: here is one piece of evidence which, all by itself, supports the intended conclusion, and here is another, and here is yet another. (This is the kind of argument where the reasons are stacked up like so much cordwood.) But it is often enough the case that the considerations to be brought to bear in the course of one's reasoning must dovetail or interlock: no one of them, by itself, amounts to evidence at all, and it is only when they have been appropriately fitted together that they entail, or even so much as support, the conclusion in question. In a modus ponens, p and 'if p then q' interlock; p, on its own, is not a reason for q, and neither is 'if p then q'; however, the two claims together deductively entail that q.[12] Or again, if the conclusion you need to get to is 'p and q,' and you are going to get there via its conjuncts, you need to be able to check that p, and also to check that q. Inferences that deploy multiple and interlocking considerations are pervasive, and, where there is any difficulty at all to an intellectual task, they are essential; if we were unable to deploy such inferences, there would be no point in engaging in reasoning about matters of fact, because we would not normally be in a position to construct a train of thought moving from the premises at hand to a conclusion at which we hope to arrive. So, as before, we must take it for granted, in the course of our theoretical reasoning, that we have available and are able effectively to use patterns of inference that bring to bear interlocking considerations.

Using such patterns of inference requires not just having available interlocking considerations, but also the ability to recognize the elements of potential inferences *as* interlocking. Sometimes such recognition is unassisted. I may represent some claim only as 'Alice's objection,' and manage to remain aware that it, together with some further claim q, entails a conclusion r in which I have an interest. But there is only so much we can keep track of in this way, and the problem does not have to do solely with the limitations of human memory.[13] If there were some fixed, finite number of situations we could encounter, and about which we might want to reason, then if our memories were good enough, we could make up a list of the actual and possible facts—representing them, perhaps, by natural numbers—and learn the entailment relations between them by heart.

(I would *just know* that #17, together with #92, entailed #61.) But there are indefinitely many situations we might encounter, and so indefinitely many considerations that might figure in an argument that we need to pursue; the inferential relations between these considerations cannot be memorized in advance. Consequently, their inferential potentials must be made apparent to the reasoner, and so the considerations must come labeled in a way that makes evident, among other things, the ways in which they interlock. The labels standardly are sentences, of which it is a truism that we are able to formulate indefinitely many; the sentences' contents exhibit the inferential potentials of the considerations they represent.

Without any means of making sentences wear their inferential potentials on their sleeves, the recognitional capacities that make interlocking inferences accessible to us would soon be swamped. The most important devices for improving our ability to notice potentially interlocking considerations are conventions of representation that literally make visible and audible the ways in which the elements of one's prospective inference can dovetail. In many cases, these conventions have us repeat the pattern representing one premise as a subsidiary pattern in an interlocking premise, and so allow the recognition of potentially interlocking elements of an inference to be underwritten by native pattern-matching abilities; when I represent the premises of a modus ponens as p and 'if p then q,' I am easily able to match the minor premise to the antecedent of the conditional. These conventions are sufficiently general-purpose that interlocking considerations can almost always be presented so as explicitly to exhibit their joint mutual entailment of the conclusion they are being used to derive.[14]

These conventions can be used to give a name to the requirement that the components interlock: making inferential headway on the basis of interlocking considerations requires *matching*. p matches the antecedent of 'if p then q,' and from these, q follows. r does not match the antecedent of 'if p then q,' and from 'if p then q,' and r, nothing follows. So, our theoretical reasoning must proceed on the working assumption that the building blocks of potential inferences can be gotten to match.

4.3

In the course of reasoning about how things stand, it is for the most part true that making inferential headway requires matching interlocking premises to

one another. But experience teaches us that perfect matches are frequently
hard to come by, and that matching means cutting corners on accuracy.
Here are a few examples of the kind of thing I have in mind.

You might, perhaps in an undergraduate physics class, be asked to solve
the following problem: a cow of mass m_1 is standing at distance d from a
blade of grass of mass m_2; calculate the gravitational attraction exerted by
the cow on the blade. Obviously, the correct way to approach the problem
is to treat the cow as a sphere of homogeneous matter (or, possibly, a point
mass), whence, somewhat indirectly, the surprisingly titled environmental
science textbook, *Consider a Spherical Cow*.[15] There need be no pretense that
the description of the cow as spherical is accurate, or even nearly accurate;
one might say that it is approximately true, by way of saying that this is the
correct approximation to use in solving this problem, but one would not
thereby mean to imply that the cow is *almost* spherical.[16] The reason this
is the correct approach is that one does not (or anyway, one's students do
not) have the mathematical tools that would allow one to use an accurate
description of the spatial distribution of the mass of an actual cow. Rather,
one has at hand a rule which we can imagine to have the form: 'If something
is an homogenous sphere of mass m, then…' If one is to make inferential
progress, one must match a suitable further premise to this rule, and so one
inaccurately but quite properly describes the cow as a sphere.[17]

Here is a second example. Arranging a rendezvous between Jack and Jill,
I might say that Jack will be the one who looks like John Malkovich, and
that Jill has a red coat, acknowledging that neither is really true: they're true
enough for Jack and Jill to find one another under a movie marquee.[18] As
the example indicates, sometimes partial truth is a byproduct of vagueness;
color predicates like 'red' are vague, and Jill's coat is out in the indeterminate
penumbra. But vagueness is not always the problem: it is, I may inform other
members of the committee, true that John is a student—but only officially
true; I understand it to be technically true that banana trees are a kind of
grass. In cases like these, I am both aware that what I am saying is not fully
true, and willing to make that clear; but what I have said is true *in a way*,
rather than *to a degree* (or to about a certain extent), which is what talk of
vagueness suggests.

As before, my reason for advancing the sentences in the example not
bivalently, but ambivalently, is to facilitate inferential matching. The rule
I am supplying—'If it looks like John Malkovich, it's Jack'—is not true.
(It is only sort of true that Jack looks like Malkovich; if it *really* looked
like Malkovich, it *wouldn't* be Jack.) Where before the description of the

particular was tailored to suit an available rule, here a rule is being tailored to suit the available description of a particular. As before, the problem I am trying to solve is not one of uncertainty or lack of information on my part: I know exactly what Jack looks like. It is rather that we can be in the position of lacking the representational tools to say what we see. Having such tools on hand is no more to be taken for granted when the tools are names and concepts than when they are cameras, film, or brushes. When we do not have available the concept or name that will hit the bull's-eye, we may do well to choose instead a concept or name that does not quite apply, and announce it as a near-miss: since there is no well-known public figure who looks just like Jack, I settle for a public figure who does not look fully the part. If Jack and Jill are to be in a position to execute the desired inferences, I must give them conditionals which are able to match premises that their observations can supply, and so I provide conditionals that none of us takes to be quite true.[19]

Our ability to produce descriptions depends on the contents of our descriptive toolkit, so think about two contrasting approaches to building a (non-metaphorical) toolkit. The first, assembling a large collection of special-purpose tools, becomes rapidly more expensive as the number of tools increases. Acquiring highly specialized precision tools generally makes sense when there are just a few exactly repeated applications to be supported: if the bolts one needs to tighten come in just four standardized sizes, buy four wrenches in exactly those sizes. But if the screws, bolts, and so on have not been standardized, the toolbox turns into a van, or into the home hobbyist's garage, with its enormous assortment of once-used pricey power tools. Our cognitive budget is limited, and so when the world is messy, we have no alternative to adopting the second approach, that of keeping the number of tools down to what we can carry, by being willing to improvise with what we have.

Partial truth figures not just in theoretical but in practical inferences. Suppose I am interning in a museum, and have the job of sorting through the new acquisitions. The curator has told me that the paintings are to be sent on to the East Wing, and the sculptures to the West Wing. As the afternoon wears on, I find myself faced with a late Frank Stella, an object that seems to be made mainly of colored bands tensely bulging away from the wall. Neither predicate, '...is a painting' or '...is a sculpture,' quite fits: it does hang on the wall; it is compositionally directly descended from the middle-period works for which Stella became well known, and which are clearly paintings; it is intended as a solution to specifically painterly problems, and so needs to be read as a painting rather than a sculpture.[20] But it works by arranging itself in three- rather than two-dimensional space, and the medium is not primarily paint. Producing a fully true description meant to answer the question of just what this is (with painting and sculpture as the relevant contrast categories) would be a delicate matter, would probably require me to introduce a vocabulary tailor-made for the occasion, and would serve no purpose: were I to take the trouble to do so, that description would fail to interlock with the instructions given me by the curator. To do my job, I must produce classifications that match the antecedents of the conditionals I have to work with, and so I determine that this, for present purposes, is a painting, and that it goes to the East Wing; asked whether it is *really* true that this is a painting, I will shrug and answer that it's true enough.

4.4

I now want to make a large claim, which I'll call the *Messiness Thesis*: that cases like these are quite common—so common, in fact, that if one were permitted to use only perfect matches in assembling inferential connections, one would not generally have enough by way of such connections to think one's way through the inferential problems one faces. Take it for now that the Messiness Thesis is true, and that perfect matches aren't frequent enough to get by on.[21]

If the Messiness Thesis is true, one is going to have to suppose, in the course of thinking directed toward figuring out how things stand, that forcing inferential connections by forcing matches between premises is legitimate and permitted. Say that from p and 'if p then q' I can infer q, that I take the conditional to be straightforwardly true, but that what I am facing is, not p, but r. If circumstances permit, I may deliberately misrepresent the actual situation, correctly described by r, as p, making a point of remembering that p is after all a misrepresentation. It will be very natural in many such cases to think of p as true in a way, or true enough, or, briefly, as *somewhat true* or *partially true*: it is pretty much true that Jack looks like Malkovich and that Jill's coat is red; it is more or less true that the Stella is a painting; it is perhaps true for present purposes that the cow is spherical. But it is in none of these cases strictly speaking or fully true.[22]

Recall that we are constructing an argument of the form described in section 4.1. I have argued that, in the course of reasoning about how things stand, we must take ourselves to be able to assemble interlocking considerations into arguments. Because accuracy of representation often trades off with matching, that means taking forced matches to be legitimate: we must presuppose, when we are engaged in theoretical reasoning, that it is acceptable to deploy premises acknowledged to be only partially true. (I am not of course suggesting that the supposition of acceptability must extend to all partial truths, and I have not in any way spoken to the question of *which* partial truths are suitable bases for inference.) The content of that presupposition is practical: it amounts to a willingness to treat partial truths as satisfactory starting points for reasoning, reasoning whose conclusions are regarded as themselves legitimate starting points for further inference. And because of the way it is practical, we can conclude not only that it must be *presupposed*, but that it is *true*: that this *is* how it is done. So if the Messiness Thesis is true, theoretical reasoning can proceed on the basis of partial truth.

But notice that the argument we have just seen (although primarily a practical rather than a theoretical argument) itself proceeds on the basis of claims that are only partially true, or somewhat true, or true for the most part—though true enough, I am holding, for the argument to go through, and for the conclusions I am eliciting from them to follow. For instance, I claimed earlier that our inferences depend on the explicit representation of their premises' inferential potentials (in particular, of the premises' ability to interlock) in the content of those premises. That is true in large part, but it is not, as we are now in a position to see, entirely true. When we treat a claim as partially true, we bear in mind that it is suitable for drawing some conclusions, but not others; that is, we are keeping track of adjustments to its inferential status that are not explicitly represented in the claim's content. Our capacity for making these adjustments is not unlimited, and it depends on having representations from whose dictates we can deviate, but, if I am right, it is still something of which we must be able to do a certain amount.

Now, the Messiness Thesis, which I asked the reader to accept provisionally a couple of turns back, is also quite obviously only somewhat true. Perfect matches are not rare. Vague concepts (like 'red') have not just penumbral cases (like Jill's sort-of-red coat), but clear cases (like Jack's new Porsche) as well. What is more, there are regions, as it were, in which perfect matches seem to be very readily available. (Sometimes regions quite literally: in the European Union, one of the primary functions of the bureaucracy is to develop and promulgate standards that will make perfect inferential matches commonplace.) Why should we think that the Thesis is true enough for the argument we have pivoting on it to go through?[23] That useful perfect matches are not available often enough when they are needed, is, so far, merely a judgment call; certainly the handful of examples we now have on the table will not make that judgment call stick. But before I try to show that the Messiness Thesis is sufficiently true, I need to say a thing or two about the complications involved in doing so.

4.5

It is tempting simply to appeal to what one might call the *natural explanation* of the Messiness Thesis (a claim, it will be remembered, about how the pieces of inferences under construction fit together, or don't): that we are running up against the messiness or inchoateness of the world itself. After all, that the world *is* messy—that it doesn't fit into any manageable set of classifications—is just the way things are. My correspondence will not fall cleanly into the categories provided by my filing system, no matter how doggedly I reorganize it, because the letters are, as the idiom has it, all over the place: other people's choices of topic cut across my own, and letters meander from subject to subject. (Yes, it is easy enough to make my filing system exhaustive by adding categories like 'miscellaneous' and 'other,' but categories like these don't interlock with useful procedures.) Works of art are going to turn up that are neither clearly paintings nor clearly sculptures, not least because the premium the art world today places on breaking formal or stylistic constraints means that its products will shortly no longer fit my categories, whatever they happen to be. The natural world is no better: because stones come in all sizes and shapes, any reasonably small vocabulary for shapes will be useful for launching stone-related inferences only if I am willing to apply it to the many stones it does not quite fit, and the vagueness of much vocabulary attempts to anticipate this requirement. 'Lentil-shaped,' for instance, is a concept worth applying to stones; if the stones are lentil-shaped, they will end up in the lentils. A more precise concept would just put me in the position of having to apply it more imprecisely. The world, we have been told, is everything that is the case; but it is obviously also a good deal that is only sort of the case.

But things can't be as straightforward as that. We have to be careful here, because the phenomenon of messiness itself illustrates the problems of coming by clean descriptions. I have already mentioned Aristotle's remark that there is only one way to hit the target, but many ways to miss it; failures of bivalence differ qualitatively from each other in indefinitely many ways. So we should not be looking for a neat and systematic description of the phenomenon of not being capturable in a system of characterizations. Rather, we should be happy if our description of the world as messy is true enough for the argument to go forward. That said, to be messy, in the sense that is relevant here, is roughly to resist pigeonholing, and how much resistance there is going to be will depend both on what the pigeonholes are, and on what is being sorted into them.

That means that even if the messiness of the world is close to being an observation, it is less of an explanation of the Messiness Thesis than one might like. The problem is familiar from discussions of secondary qualities such as color. The world seems colored because it *is*; but the world's being colored consists in its seeming so to creatures with our form of visual perception. Likewise, the world is resistant to pigeonholing because it is messy, but its being messy just *is* resisting being shoved into the pigeonholes that, as it happens, we have. Perhaps if we had different pigeonholes, the world would not be messy, and in fact, there are evidently describable 'worlds' that would not seem messy to us as we are now. The world that Melissus, probably unreliably, reports Parmenides as taking for our own is one of these: a perfect, unchanging sphere. That makes it look to be a contingent fact about the world that it is messy, which in turn suggests that the only way to demonstrate it is by amassing observations—and this would constitute a serious obstacle to a convincing argument, since I could not hope to pile up enough observations here to do the job. The contingency also suggests that we could get rid of the messiness (and so of the practical problem that is driving the argument we are constructing) by changing our pigeonholes.

Fortunately, arguments that do not proceed simply by inductively amassing observations, and which eventuate in conclusions that we will find to be true (enough), come what may, can be compatible with the metaphysical contingency of their conclusions. So to address the first of these worries, I will give an argument to show why the world is pretty much inevitably going to at any rate start out seeming messy to us. The argument will be modeled on so-called anthropic arguments in cosmology. Anthropic arguments typically take the presence of an observer, or of a class of observations, as their starting points, and proceed by asking what it takes to have an observer, or such an observation, at hand. Just for instance: Why does space have three dimensions? You can't construct anything complicated enough to ask the question in only two dimensions, because, e.g., a digestive tract would bisect the organism. And if gravity obeys an inverse-n–1 law, where n is the number of dimensions, planetary orbits aren't stable in 4 or higher dimensions. So whenever anybody gets around to asking how many dimensions there are, the number he will come up with is 3.[24] Because this argument is meant only to set the stage for our treatment of the real—that is, the practical—problem, I will be brief about it.

Messiness, I have suggested, is an observer-dependent feature of the world; so consider what it takes for there to be an observer. Observers are functionally complex objects, and if their complexity is not to be understood as a realistically impossible coincidence, they must be engineered, either by actual designers, or by surrogates such as natural selection. Such engineering requires control, which in turn requires a fairly dense space of possibilities in which design choice can be exercised: to get a functional object that works, a designer must have had many, many options of doing things just a little bit differently.[25]

The rich variation allowed by such a space of possibilities is bound actually to appear if the design process proceeds by trial and error. Natural selection is quite clearly a trial-and-error design process, but so are, if one looks carefully, the more intentional design processes, at any rate when they are successful. A necessary condition of the smoothly engineered automobile we are used to today is the proliferation of slightly different types of automobile: there's been room for designers to try out many, many variations. A significant part of the variation in the observer's environment will be at about the level of granularity of the observer's design, and this pretty much ensures that observers will find themselves faced with variation visible to them. Organisms made out of claws and fangs are built to observe the claws and fangs of other organisms; more generally, observers will normally be attuned to variability in their surroundings at roughly the level of granularity of their top-level design.

So observers will not find themselves to be parts of worlds that are so simple that simple categories will do for full truth, and a good deal of complex irregularity will be visible to them. If the world seems messy to you, you should not be surprised: observers only arise in worlds that seem messy to them. Parmenides' world is simple enough, but, not coincidentally, contains no observers.

Now notice that this point holds even if the deep underlying structure of a world is simple and elegant in the way that contemporary physicists tend to hope that our world is. The world of human life (what sometimes gets called the *Lebenswelt*) is going to be messy even if the aspects of the world investigated by some of the sciences are not. Since it is the *Lebenswelt* in which we have to live, the practical problems presented by the Messiness Thesis are going to arise for us, whether there are clean descriptions of the building blocks or not. This is why, in Chapter 2, I was willing to be so very concessive about whether the no-free-lunch hypothesis held in the domains of the physical sciences.

4.6

On the one hand, we have a not-quite-a-priori argument for our lived world having at any rate started out messy. On the other hand, I have allowed that there are large parts of the world that are not particularly messy. We can take both of these on board by supposing that things must have changed since we began occupying the *Lebenswelt*, and there are two ways this could have happened. First, things could have changed out in the world; that is, the world itself could be neater because we have been tidying it up. Second, we could have changed our pigeonholes (our concepts, categories, and descriptive tools) to make the world (seem) less messy. These alternatives were canvassed in Chapter 2, and let me refresh your memory with a couple of new examples.

Some time back, I bought Tim Williamson's survey volume, *Vagueness*.[26] And some time thereafter, my upstairs neighbor noticed it lying around and wanted to know whether I had read it. This was a question it was hard to give a straight yes-or-no answer to: I *had* read the first chapter or so, then moved my eyes over some number of subsequent pages, without really paying much attention, and then put the book down. Afterwards, I had glanced at some of the later parts of the book, no longer remembering what had come before. In a situation like this, there are two ways to put oneself in a position to say something both informative and entirely true. One is to find a description that matches the messy contours of the state of affairs— roughly, to do much better what I took a stab at a moment ago. The other is to change the state of affairs so as to make it more easily describable, in this case, by starting the book over from the beginning, and reading it at a single go. Not solely in order to have something to say to my upstairs neighbor, I chose the second of these options.

As before, the point is that, to play their roles in inference, one's thoughts must be made for each other, but when inference is theoretical, i.e., reasoning about how things are, one's thoughts also have to be made for the things. The example exhibits one of the ways in which both of these constraints can be squared with each another: by altering the objects of one's thoughts to make interlocking inference straightforward.

For my second example, I want to take a mixed case, one in which the world has certainly been reengineered, but where it is also natural to say that we have reshaped our descriptive tools to better capture something like its underlying structure, and done so in a way that allows us to assemble interlocking inferences without cutting corners on accuracy. Some philosophers would be inclined to look to the hardest of the hard sciences here, but I want instead to take as my example advances in chronometry over the last seven hundred years or so.

Prior to the advent of clocks, there were no straight answers to questions about the time of day, and not just because it was hard to *figure out* what time of day it was. Hours were at best vague objects, minutes were an astronomer's abstraction, and there was no such thing as agreeing to meet someone for coffee at 8:10, because nothing had been done to make possible thoughts with that kind of descriptive precision. The concepts we now use for measuring time depend on a complicated mix of technology and social convention for their content and their application. The use of predicates like 'morning,' and of rules that deploy them, invite forced matches: If it's morning, it's time to start work, and (my employer insists) it's by now true enough that it's morning; so it's time to start work. With our current chronometric concepts, and the rules we have adopted to exploit them, the problems involved in such forced matches can be almost entirely avoided. From the premise that it's 9:00, and the further premise that if it's 9:00, it's time to start work, it follows that it's time to start work.[27] We have, over many centuries, changed our intellectual toolkit in a way that allows us to have, in principle, both full truth and inferential matching in the temporal domain, and have done so by exploiting already-present strict regularity (though time is puzzling enough for me not to want to try saying just what the already present regularity is).[28]

Now I want to highlight two features of these examples that I think are typical. The first is that effort and resources are required for such adjustments. (This is just a reminder of the thesis of Chapter 2.) Rereading a book in a way that makes it unnecessary to waffle about whether the book has been read costs the time and energy required to make it from cover to cover. The example is very small-scale, but even here it is clear that you cannot always address such problems in this way: you just don't have the time. In the much larger-scale chronometric example, we could not use the precise temporal concepts we now have (that is, in a rather different sense we wouldn't have had the time) if we had not managed a technological revolution in our chronographic devices. As the etymology reminds us, without clocks, there would be no 'o'clock'; our ability to tell time has depended, and depends, on the invention of the pendulum clock, on the balance wheel, on the Greenwich Observatory, and on much, much more of the same. I think the example is representative of what it takes to introduce important networks of concepts that obviate the need for forced inferential matches.[29] While chronometric observations are quite inexpensive these days, and contrast favorably in this regard with most of the observations needed by the hard sciences, clocks started out as prestige technology that only municipal governments could buy and maintain, and are cheap nowadays solely as the result of centuries of sustained investment. Moreover, timekeeping involves current costs (watch factories, atomic clocks, institutions to determine when we will have leap seconds, and so on) that fade into the background only because those costs are so widely distributed as not to fall heavily on any particular user.

So this first and typical feature of the cases we are examining sets very rough limits on how much the messy world can have been cleaned up. Because there is only so much tidying up we can afford to have done, most of the originally messy world will have had to stay as it was, and so it must now be true enough that the world that we face is messy.[30]

The second aspect of these examples that I want to emphasize is that the adjustments, either to the world or to the pigeonholes, have to be thought through if they are to have a reasonable chance of being successful. And that thinking through will have to take place in a domain that is *ex hypothesi* as yet to be navigated only via partial-truth inference, if at all. I chose to reread Williamson's book by matching a conditional premise, to the effect that if you haven't been paying attention to what you've been reading, you can't tell people what was going on, with the minor premise that I hadn't been paying attention. Both of those premises were only somewhat true: sometimes you really don't have to pay attention, and anyway I *had* been paying attention, but stopped along the way. In the early phases of the development of chronometry, assessing whether the processes being used were cyclical necessarily required many partially true judgments, e.g., as to whether two repetitions of the process had taken the same time, as to whether they *were* repetitions (given wear on the parts, changes in the temperature, the inability to measure accurately the spatial end-points of the process, and so on), and as to whether it mattered how fast the clock was moving.

Now notice that someone who does not think that what I am calling partial-truth inference really *is* inference is in the outlandish position of having to insist that the complex and difficult enterprises that produced, for instance, our chronometric concepts and the devices that make their application possible involved little or no *thought*—that clocks, railroad schedules and all of that were the cumulative effect of largely mindless activity, produced in something like the way that dams are supposed be the product of the instinctual behaviors of beavers, or anthills of ants. And on a smaller scale it is to be committed to the equally outlandish position that I did not actually think about whether to reread Williamson's book—that I perhaps just muttered thoughtlessly to myself. To be sure, to insist that, as a matter of fact, such mental activity must properly have been inference would be to beg the question, and so that is not the real use I propose to make of the premise. But suppose for the moment that denying it is a bullet which an interlocutor will not want to bite. In that case, we can proceed to make two further points.

First, if the areas of the lived world in which the Messiness Thesis no longer holds are conceded to be areas in which partial-truth inference is still (because it once was) legitimate, then it is much more reasonable to take it that the acknowledgedly partial truth of the Messiness Thesis is sufficient for the argument we have under construction. After all, the exceptions to the rule are now allowed to be areas where the conclusion of the argument is true anyway. And second, if the past is a good guide to the future, then reengineering our world and revising our pigeonholes to remove more of the remaining messiness will have to be a carefully thought-out enterprise. And as before, the thought involved will have to be partial-truth inference.

That latter point allows us to endorse and use the otherwise question-begging Messiness Thesis. The argument we are constructing, recall, is *practical*: it is about what we need to do to make inferential headway in our theoretical reasoning. And so its central claim has to be that we have no live alternative, when we are in the course of figuring out how things stand, to partial-truth inference. The anthropic argument of the previous section may have underwritten the claim that we are now faced with too much messiness simply to sidestep, but we are not in the first place trying to answer the theoretical question: is our world messy or not? We have already allowed that there are conceivable or metaphysically possible worlds containing observers to whom that world is not messy. But the mere possibility of creatures not subject to the practical constraints with which we have to live is irrelevant, if we have no way of becoming those creatures. Rather, we are asking the practical question: is there a way to cope with the messiness that doesn't help itself to (and so commit itself to the legitimacy of) partial-truth inference? The practical alternative to partial-truth reasoning in a messy world will be to take steps to eliminate the messiness.

But now, you cannot yourself understand the mental runup to those steps in the way that the opposing position is required to understand, e.g., the history of chronometry: as not being really *thought*. You are, after all, trying to figure out what to do. (Or: we are collectively trying to figure out what to do.) Arriving at a plan for achieving bivalence will require theoretical reasoning executed in the service of your practical deliberations; if what you are able to do is not inference, and its deliverances are not the deliverances of inference (if they are intellectually passive, as it were, on a par with the instinctive activities of beavers), then you are not going to be able to use those deliverances in your deliberations. You must presuppose that those cognitive steps are proper theoretical inferences, and if they are cognitive steps that proceed from partial truths, as in such domains they mostly must be, then you are committed to, and have no viable alternative to proceeding on the basis of, partial-truth inference. This *is*, it turns out, how to reason about how the facts stand; this *is* how to engage in theoretical reasoning.

5

Unity of the Intellect

What does it take to come by opinions that are worth having? I am going to argue that worthwhile opinions require a unified intellect, that a unified intellect is possible only if inference that deploys partial truth is not just possible but practiced, and consequently that you must engage in inference that deploys partial truth if you are to have opinions worth having. This will suffice to show that inference deploying partial truth is legitimate, i.e., it really *is* inference.

In Chapter 4 I laid out an argument for that conclusion, and at the time I suggested that it had the structure of what is traditionally called a transcendental deduction. Now it is characteristic of transcendental arguments that they can be cast either as having to do with the preconditions for successfully engaging in some cognitive activity, or as having to do with one aspect or another of the unity of the self. I do not want to advance here an explanation for transcendental arguments generally being in this way Janus-faced, but I nonetheless regard the ability to convert a transcendental argument given in one of these forms into the other as a test that all is in order: if the transformation does not go through, something is likely to be wrong with the argument. So although the considerations will by now be familiar, I am about to reassemble them into an argument turning on what I will call the unity of intellect. And because this will be an opportunity to put important methodological issues on the table, I will begin by explaining why it is reasonable to put an argument about what is properly counted as inference into this form.

5.1

It is something of a logical platitude that if I believe that p, and I believe that not p, I am violating a constraint of logic, namely, the Principle of Non-Contradiction; a satisfactory logic (that is, a theory providing guidelines for rational thought and inference) will tell me to do something about it: to change my beliefs in a way that avoids the contradiction.[1] However, if I believe that p, and *you* believe that not p, we are merely disagreeing; to be sure, at least one of us is wrong, but there is no logical incoherence on either of our parts, and so, as far as that goes, no need to revise either belief. Again, it is likewise a platitude that if I believe that 'if p then q,' and I believe that p, then there is logical pressure on me to conclude that q as well (or to give up one of the former beliefs). But if I believe that 'if p then q,' and *you* believe that p, there is no logical pressure on anyone to conclude anything. And generally, the constraints of logic are applied only within the mental boundaries of a person (or an entity that, like certain institutions, is modeled on persons).

This tells us that personal identity is foundational with respect to logic. Because logical constraints are imposed only on persons (and other person-like entities, but I won't continue to repeat this qualification), if there's a shape that logical constraints have to take if there are to be persons at all, then logical constraints of that shape must be part and parcel of logic. After all, a system of putative logical constraints which did not have such a shape would not apply to anyone; because constraint is a prescriptive notion, constraints that never apply are not really constraints at all. (Such a 'constraint' quickly becomes a dead letter.) So here we have a central part of the proper methodology of logic: to find out what it takes to think correctly, find out what it takes to be someone, and in particular, find out how you have to think if you are going to be someone.

Persons are not all of a kind. For instance, Bayesian inference—explicitly assigning probabilities to all your views with respect to matters of fact and updating them in accordance with Bayes's Theorem—is computationally intractable.[2] If a would-be person with roughly our capacities used Bayesian inference exclusively, it would end up not having a mind. But we can imagine someone (a creature which implements quantum computation, maybe) who would be up to the Bayesian computational task. So let's refine the claim I just put on the table: if there's a shape that logical constraints have to have, for there to be persons of some particular type, then logical constraints of that shape must be part and parcel of logic, *for persons of that type*. In this example, 'Don't be a full-time Bayesian' is part of the logic we should have, but it is not (as far as this argument goes) part of a quantum computer's logic.[3]

So we can rephrase the plan of action this way: I'm going to be repackaging our earlier argument so as to make it turn on the claim that reasoning which deploys partial truth is a necessary precondition for (one aspect of) personhood, when the persons look anything like ourselves—and even when their cognitive capacities are quite a bit greater than our own. (But I am allowing that God, and maybe other kinds of minds, could get by with only bivalence.) It will follow that inference on the basis of partial truth is part of our logic, that is, that satisfactory guidelines for reasoning will tell us to engage in it.

Use *psychologism* to mean the idea that the right way to figure out your logic is first to figure out your psychology. The founding moments of both analytic philosophy and twentieth-century continental philosophy were violent rejections of psychologism (by Frege and Husserl, respectively).[4] But the present argument is avowedly psychologistic, and since it is a recasting of the argument of Chapter 4, that argument is psychologistic as well.

In the Appendix, I will explain why some of the arguments against psychologism were mistaken. I will not here speculate as to why they were nonetheless accepted—that is, as to why, in my view, philosophy of logic took a disastrously wrong turn about a century back. For the moment, I just want to provide some initial motivational impetus for the psychologistic approach to logical questions which I am adopting here.

If you were raised in our contemporary philosophical culture, you probably think of logic as the enterprise of constructing formal systems that are supposed to model rational inference. But formal systems on their own don't tell you why you should use them (why it is *rational inference* that they model): to take the simplest possible example, when I show that modus ponens is valid, by showing that if its premises are true, its conclusion is also true, I am not yet done. I still have to explain why, given its validity, it is rational to use modus ponens: why 'validity,' in this technical sense, is tantamount to inferential correctness. And even if the explanation turns out to be a simple one (you want your inferences to be truth-preserving), it does need to be given. (In fact, the simple explanations pretty much don't work: if you *happen* to be obsessed with truth-preservingness, then you care about preserving truth, but if you aren't, the next question in line— why care about truth and truth-preservingness?—is harder to answer than you might think.[5]) Analytic philosophers have almost entirely given up on the explanatory task, and the consequences are unfortunate; with rare exceptions, they can't, and don't try to, explain why the formal results matter for inferential practice. That's just to say that they don't try to explain why the formal systems count as *logic* at all.[6] By contrast, psychologistic approaches to logic begin with the user. When you start with the needs of your client, and design inferential guidelines around those needs, you have no problem explaining why a formal model of those guidelines (if you get around to producing one) is of relevance to him: the explanation of why psychologistic logical theory should guide inference comes built in.

I do need to forestall a handful of likely misunderstandings. First, by calling my view psychologistic I emphatically do not mean that it holds the laws of logic to be empirical psychological generalizations. That was a characterization unfairly foisted on psychologistic philosophers by their opponents; it is too often accepted by philosophers who have read Frege or Husserl, but not their targets.[7] After all, a bicycle repair manual is not a list of empirical laws about the behavior of bicycles, but it would be crazy to write one without knowing something about how bicycles work. Likewise, psychologistic logicians have reasoned, a how-to manual for thinking is not an empirical theory of human psychology, but it would be crazy to try to write one without knowing anything about how human minds work. In addition, to many philosophers, not all psychology is empirical science; so, on my use of the term, Kant's first *Critique* is psychologistic (because it ties views about how to think to a transcendental psychology), but not empirical.[8] On my use of the term, a prescriptive theory that told you how to avoid mistakes you were prone to make would be psychologistic, if it had been built around empirical psychological studies that showed which mistakes were in the offing; but of course such a theory would not treat the mistakes identified by the studies as prescriptions, that is, it would not confuse its own advice with the empirical psychological generalizations.

Second, I'm not claiming that all of logic is to be derived using the method I have just announced; it suffices for my purposes if the results I am after can. Notice that even if it were true that all of logical theory were derivable from facts about personhood, we wouldn't be in a position to argue for it. Putting together an argument for that claim would require a non-question-begging demarcation of the logical from the nonlogical. But no such demarcation is available, and in my view to attempt one at this stage would be premature: first we would want an explanation of the point of (or need for) that demarcation; my own guess is that that explanation ought itself to be psychologistic; but we are not yet in a position to say why creatures cognitively like ourselves require a distinction between the requirements of logic and, say, the requirements of prudence, or morality, or convention.[9]

And third, I'm of course not claiming that all of the preconditions of one's existence amount to truths of logic. (If I exist, then I had grandparents, but as far as I can see, that fact supplies me with no novel logical constraints.) Philosophical closure on the problem this raises would require the demarcation I have just mentioned, which we do not have; but I will provide a stopgap later on.

I announced earlier that the argument of this chapter is meant to be a recapitulation of the argument of Chapter 4, seen as it were from a different perspective. That argument had a task analysis at its core: it derived the commitment to partial-truth inference by showing it to be a precondition for successful theoretical inference. But how can an argument turning on unity of the self be the *same* argument as the one I have just described? Transcendental arguments are often made to bottom out in the claim that if one or another unity condition is not satisfied, then you're just not *there*. Leaving it at that makes it sound as though the stake you have in inference correctly performed is a matter of your survival; yet surely there can be logically well-supported truths whose acceptance is not conducive to your survival (and, perhaps, precisely the contrary). So over the course of this chapter I want to be careful to exhibit the stake one has in a (sufficiently) unified intellect.

In the next chapter, I will take up the consequences of the argument we are now discussing for belief psychology and epistemology; in the meantime, I have already started using 'opinion' to cover, on the one hand, beliefs, which amount to endorsing claims as fully true, and, on the other, our various endorsements of claims as partially true. We tend to think of epistemic success as knowledge, but 'knowledge' is evidently not the right commendation to apply to, say, an epistemically successful approximation; I've also started using 'worth having' as a placeholder for whatever such commendations turn out to be. In considering what makes opinions worth having, I will however restrict myself to what a Kantian might describe as the interests of speculative or theoretical reason: the interest in coming by views about how things stand that are true or true enough, or developing resources for use in further theoretical inference, or maintaining consistency in one's opinions, or theoretical depth, or explanatory power. This means that I am putting to one side for the present pragmatic motivations extrinsic to the activity of theoretical reasoning, such as, for instance, one's interest in getting things done.

With that terminology in place, we can describe the course of our overall argument as follows: You need a unified intellect to have opinions worth having. You need partial truth to have a unified intellect. So you need partial truth to have opinions worth having. In other words, our stake in partial truth, according the argument I am about to construct, will turn out to be the stake in partial truth exhibited by the previous argument; and if the arguments are at bottom the same, that is just as it should be.

5.2

To have a fully unified intellect is to be able to bring to bear, in one or another stretch of theoretical reasoning or inference, any of one's opinions jointly with any others. If unity is so understood, I expect that no one's intellect is fully unified; accordingly, we will want to treat unity of the intellect as, roughly, a matter of degree: your intellect is unified to the extent that, for any small set of your opinions $p, q, r \ldots$, you are able to bring $p, q, r \ldots$ to bear jointly in a single chain of reasoning.

Just looking around, you might have the impression that a lot of people get by pretty well with not-very-unified intellects: they can lead happy (or at least happy-go-lucky) and even intellectually interesting lives. And whatever our stake in unified selfhood comes to, they need not even have disunified selves overall; the burden of unity may be borne, in such cases, by consistency of character and agency, or even merely by unified consciousness.[10] So we ought to ask why it would matter to us that our intellects be more rather than less unified. One way to account for our stake in a unified intellect is to ask why we bother to work on making our beliefs consistent.

Here is a familiar way of motivating close attention to the mutual consistency of our beliefs: beliefs aspire to represent the world as it is, and the world is consistent with itself, so a system of beliefs should be consistent as well. The well-brought-up philosopher will have a drawerful of equally familiar qualms. This explanation invokes the much-debunked idea of beliefs as a 'mirror of nature.' The intelligibility of the notion that the world is self-consistent is unobvious; after all, do we know what it would be for the world to be *in*consistent? And finally, the insistence that there is a *world*—that it makes sense to take everything all together as something like a single large object—may be a bit of insupportable philosophical naiveté.[11] Nonetheless, there is something that this explanation is getting right: given that beliefs are responsible to the facts, if you find that your beliefs are inconsistent, you know that something has gone wrong. Inconsistency indicates a problem.[12]

The mirror-of-nature approach gave rise to a methodology which formerly seemed like a sure-fire way of achieving consistency. First, form ground-level beliefs using some method that ensures their correspondence to the bits and pieces of the world that they are about. Then move forward from these using ironclad inference patterns. Such inferences, together with the assured truth of one's foundational beliefs, guarantee the truth of one's conclusions. Methods with roughly this shape are, probably unfairly, usually labelled 'Cartesian.'[13]

Where the Cartesian recipe went wrong was in minimizing the role that attention to consistency has to play in our theoretical endeavors. Granted, the recipe does not tell you that you can simply forget about consistency: attention to the consistency of premises and conclusions, or to the inconsistency of premises with the denial of a possible conclusion, will figure into determining whether one or another form of inference is ironclad. But (and this might seem like a very attractive feature of the method) that is as far as attention to consistency will have to go: since the world itself guarantees that true beliefs are mutually consistent, taking care of the truth of each means that their joint consistency will take care of itself.

Unfortunately, that is just not the way these things work. Treat it for the present as a brute empirical fact: no matter how careful you are about assembling your foundational beliefs, or more generally in collecting facts that are just obviously true, and no matter how careful you are about deriving further beliefs from them, you will, after proceeding in this way for a while, find yourself with a system of belief that is thoroughly riddled with inconsistency. If you have been around the block a couple of times, the observation should be solidly confirmed in your own experience (and this would be a good time to stop and check if that is correct). There are certainly more than enough publicly available instances: (i) The statement that any property at all can be used to pick out the set of items that have it was sufficiently self-evident for Frege to build it into his logic; but Russell's Paradox shows that, as it stands, it does not belong to a satisfactory logic or set theory.[14] (ii) From about the beginning of the current millennium, it became fashionable to start off epistemology papers with, 'The following claims form an inconsistent triad...';[15] epistemology as we have come to know it is thus being presented as an attempt to clean up the mess made by three all-too-obvious truisms. (iii) Drivers generally have a great deal of experience both with their own driving, and with the drivers around them; they tend to be quite convinced that they know how good at it they are, relative to others on the road; but when these opinions are brought together, it turns out that most people think they are better than average drivers.[16] Examples like these could be multiplied indefinitely, and what they show is that when one goes looking for self-evident facts, what one brings back are really just factoids.

The first wave of one's conclusions turns out to be just the starting point for a next stage in one's theoretical reasoning, during which one goes back and throws out what one had thought were observations, rejects (as it turned out, interim) conclusions, looks for further evidence that can be brought to bear, considers ways to split the difference between the conflicting claims, and much else of the same ilk. The result, if reconsideration goes well, is a system of beliefs that is more thought out, more nuanced, and has a much better chance of being true. My point here is that, *without* this second stage, one's beliefs, however carefully arrived at, are scarcely worth having. We take care of the truth by working at the consistency (and not just, as the Cartesian supposes, vice versa), and to do this we have to put ourselves in the way of inconsistency first.

The claim I am making is not that all of my pre-revision beliefs are false. When my roommate calls out, 'Where's the cereal?' and, without looking, I answer that it's on the counter, I may well be right; and I am right without having first used it in generating contradictions.[17] Often enough, however, even when it comes to mundane beliefs of this kind, I will turn out to have been wrong. I may have put it back in the pantry, or finished the box and thrown it out; I forget having done such things frequently enough. So unless I am able to check the belief against others, and unless I do a certain amount of actual checking, the belief should not be made to bear a lot of weight.

One traditional philosophical response to the phenomenon I am high-lighting is that the fault for inconsistencies is one's own; as in many other spheres, ineffective policy proposals are defended by blaming the victim. Inconsistencies, the response continues, betray not having begun with sufficiently whittled down and hedged claims, or having incautiously leaped to conclusions. Notice, however, that the response is itself an instance of the very phenomenon I have been describing: ever-more-minimal observations, and heightened standards of inferential rigor, have themselves been reactions to inconsistencies and related problems, encountered in the course of fitting together what had seemed obviously unobjectionable claims and transparently conclusive forms of reasoning. The odd philosophical vocabularies (think of sense-datum languages) that have been proposed at one time or another for couching one's completely hedged claims have never actually been usable; but even if they had, they would merely illustrate the claim we have on the table, that before being reworked to make its elements jointly tenable, the initial system of beliefs had not been in fact beliefworthy.[18] This point helps accommodate the impression that one has plenty of beliefs that are just fine. They *are* just fine—but the vocabularies used for framing them and the evidence used to support them are themselves products of the kind of revision we're now considering.

In pretty much any reasonably ambitious and interesting set of beliefs, once they have undergone a suitable amount of inferential organization, it will turn out that there are contradictions right and left, and that many of the first-pass beliefs must not have been true after all. But now, the division of one's theoretical reasoning into these two stages is an artifact of having started with the naive foundationalist method. That's a ladder we can kick away, and doing so leaves us with the following broadened version of the claim: systems of belief that have not been earned by wrestling with inconsistency are normally not worth having; beliefs that have not been cross-checked against one another are bound to come apart in one's hands.

The point is most directly made using beliefs, for which consistency is a crisp and straightforward notion, but as I will shortly be pointing out that beliefs are only a special case of a wider class of attitudes, we will want to extend the scope of the claim to include, as well, attitudes towards partial truths, including approximations and the like. Let's review an example.

The social sciences are rapidly being colonized by the so-called Rational Decision Theory (RDT) approach, which models humans and other actors as rational agents, and construes rational choice as choice that maximizes expected utility (in some more sophisticated game-theoretic variants, strategic sophistication of certain kinds is required). This is acknowledgedly an idealization. Of course people make mistakes, exhibit inconsistent patterns of preference, are not always all that bright, and are on occasion just plain crazy. The presumption is that the model is true *enough* for the purposes of social science.

The Voters Paradox is that both simple expected-utility and more complicated game-theoretic models predict that almost no one should vote; everyone will ask themselves what the likelihood is of casting the decisive vote, and almost everyone will stay home.[19] In fact many more people turn out than predicted; as we all know, about half the electorate turns out on election day—or anyway, that estimate will do for now. Notice that we are cross-checking the RDT model not against the raw facts, which would be a tedious and unwieldy task, but against a rough and ready summary that we mark as true enough for present purposes.

The Voters Paradox is so-called because it shows that something needs fixing in one way or another, and the RDT model seems obvious enough to its users for anything controverting it to be a theoretical emergency. Maybe the choice faced by potential voters needs to be reconceived; maybe the area of application of the RDT model ought to be restricted; maybe the conception of rationality being invoked is too crude; or maybe some other alteration is appropriate: the jury is still out. The point is that once you put the acknowledgedly partially true claims made by the Rational Decision Theory approach next to true-enough estimates of actual voter turnouts, it becomes clear that something is going to have to give.[20]

True, we are much more tolerant of inconsistency (or, more carefully, of its nuanced relatives) in cases of less-than-full belief. For instance, the right way to think about suspension bridges is to treat them as infinitely thin strings suspended between two points; the right way to think about strings is that if they're too thin, they won't bear their own weight. But even taking this kind of toleration into account, partial-truth representations, like beliefs, are not worth having if they haven't been, or anyway can't be, cross-checked against each other. To have putative partial truths that are worth having—that are indeed partially true to the extent and in the ways we allege—we have to have available something functionally analogous to a consistency check.

5.3

Briefly, then, your opinions need what is idiomatically called a reality check: until they have been squared off against each other, examined for inconsistencies and tensions, revised, reinvented, and so on, they will not merit having much stock put in them. To effect that, you have to be able to draw conclusions from your opinions and compare those to other opinions. So a system of opinions that is worth having must be one in which opinions can be jointly brought to bear in deriving further conclusions, and in which those further conclusions can be tested against one's still further opinions. In other words, to have opinions that are worth having requires a (sufficiently) unified intellect.

To make this consequence vivid, consider one of the many qualitatively different ways in which your intellect might fail to be unified: you might fail to cross-check your opinions, because you are inferentially compartmentalized. Compartmentalization is, to be sure, a matter of degree, and it's also a fairly egregious simplification; the crude metaphor treats the mind as a collection of boxes.[21] Still, one way to put a big idea we are arguing for is that there is nothing wrong with using egregious simplifications.

Even when there are only two compartments, the effects are deleterious. Continental and analytic philosophy address very much the same problems, but in startlingly different idioms. Occasionally you come across a philosopher who knows of discussions in the respective traditions that, as it happens, are concerned with more or less the same issues, and that even make more or less the same moves. It is unfortunate when she either doesn't notice the fact, or does notice but is unable to bring an incisive and important point that she is perfectly capable of articulating in one idiom to bear on an argument or position she's developing in the other. Such a philosopher has opinions which are worth less than they otherwise would be. If her philosophical opinions aren't simply worthless, that is because the opinions within a compartment are numerous and interconnected enough to serve as a reality check on one another.

When there are three compartments, rather than two, the damage is just that much worse. Imagine an undergraduate triple-majoring in Latin, mathematics, and recreation science. Because the subjects are, as far as she can tell, irrelevant to one another, there are no inferences in which premises acquired in different majors figure, and so there are no contradictions generated across the three sets of opinions. As before, these opinions might still be worth having, partly because the information conveyed in a classroom may already have undergone a certain amount of quality control, but more importantly, because there are enough inferentially connected opinions in each group to make the process of locating contradictions and subsequently improving her opinions possible. However, because she is trying to cover three widely disparate areas rather than one or two, other things equal, she will have less to go on in each area, and so she should be placing somewhat less confidence in her various views.[22]

These admittedly artificial examples put us on our way down a series whose limit is a mind containing a total of k opinions, and partitioned into k inferentially isolated singletons. This mind is quite clearly not made up of opinions worth having at all, and it is unlikely that there is some threshold at which opinions worth having suddenly become opinions not worth having. It is evidently true enough that the more inferentially compartmentalized the mind, the less its opinions are worth, and conversely, that other things being equal, the more intellectually unified your mind, the more stock you should put in your beliefs.

If inferential connections among a set of opinions are simply not to be had, then they will not be inconsistent. So why is this an argument for inferential connectedness, rather than an argument for avoiding it? Shouldn't we treat the triple-major whose opinions really are irrelevant to one another differently from the philosopher who fails to see the mutual relevance of her opinions? Recall the reason for our interest in consistency: We want truth from our beliefs, we think that beliefs that are inconsistent aren't all true, and we are using inconsistency as an indicator or symptom of untruth, and more generally, of intellectual shoddiness. What we find is that, when we are in a position to utilize the indicator, opinions that haven't been cross-checked are likely to be infected with substantial amounts of untruth. This is not a problem that we should imagine goes away when we confine ourselves to cases in which the indicator is unavailable.

In assessing the thought experiment, let me ask you to leave aside worries having to do with psychological state attribution. There are all kinds of objections to the ascription of opinions to the completely partitioned mind (or 'mind') at the limit of the series—its states could not be beliefs, or relevantly like beliefs; they could not have propositional contents; they do not really have an owner; and anyway, you can't count them—and these moves are part of the standard armory of contemporary philosophy of mind. But I wanted to focus not on whether there *could* be such a mind, or whether it *could* have such opinions, but on whether it would be *worthwhile* to have them. Although there could be no such mind as this, and although philosophers are trained to treat the incoherence of a description as a decisive objection to it, when the subject under discussion is idealizations and approximations, that training needs to be revisited. To use an example mentioned in passing, it is probably as deep a fact as there is about the physical world that there are no infinitely thin strings; 'infinitely thin string' is an incoherent description. Nonetheless, imagining infinitely thin strings is a very good way to think about real suspension bridges.[23]

5.4

Having a unified intellect on hand requires that any of the reasoner's opinions can figure together in a stretch of reasoning or argumentation, and we have seen that the less unified your intellect is, the less your opinions are worth. We now need to show that reasoning with partial truth is a precondition of having a sufficiently unified intellect: that without it, inferential connections within a mind are bound to be sparse. To do so, let's work our way through another thought experiment.

Consider a creature we'll call Hospitable Procrustes (or H. Procrustes, for short). H. Procrustes has many opinions (perhaps because he is very observant, perhaps because opinions just spring to mind), but his opinions are at the outset inferentially unconnected. H. Procrustes is in most respects a small-finite being like ourselves; in particular, he cannot magically foresee the future (and that is one reason he has a *use* for inference). But he is not small-finite in all respects, because we are going to grant him a highly idealized trait, that of never being at a loss for a description. H. Procrustes can come up with an entirely on-target characterization of any architectural style, facial expression, shape in the shadows on the wall, or what-have-you. There are benches; there are chairs; there are stools; but here is something that is not quite any of these, and H. Procrustes has a term for it, as he does for everything.[24] There are quaint old Victorians, and there are modernist Bauhaus structures; here is something that incorporates too many Bauhaus elements to really be a Victorian. Again, H. Procrustes has a term for it. There are vastly many ways to fall just outside the ranges of application of our architectural or design vocabulary; because the world is messy—ramshackle, inchoate, and stubbornly varied—its unregimented areas are a poor fit for the small number of terms we actually use, and of course architecture and design are just a couple of the vastly many subject matters of which this is true. Consequently, H. Procrustes uses what is by our lights a staggeringly large vocabulary to describe the world, and he correspondingly deploys an enormous number of mental representations. So (another bit of idealization) H. Procrustes has a memory sufficiently capacious, and powers of recall sufficiently fine-tuned, to be nonetheless phenomenologically unified; free association, in H. Procrustes' case, comes for free.[25]

Last but not least, H. Procrustes reasons bivalently: in his theoretical reasoning he marks the sentence-sized components of his inferences as fully rather than partially true or false, and it is only their bivalent truth or falsity that his inferences exploit. Just like his namesake, Hospitable Procrustes insists as it were on an exact fit between bed and guest, but earns his first name by offering beds in all sizes and shapes; so, unlike his namesake, some bed that he offers a guest is sure to fit, without requiring surgery of the guest.

H. Procrustes is thus starting out in the position of the hypercompartmentalized mind we described in the previous section. He has many opinions, but they are worth hardly anything at all. To improve the quality of his opinions, he will need to construct inferential connections between his representations.

Constructing usable inferential connections requires investment; free association may come for free, but inferential connections have to be *established*. Establishing an inferential connection is a more complicated process than we sometimes remember: a cursory glance at the components to be connected will not normally suffice. Take modus ponens once again, that is, the inference rule that proceeds from the premises that 'if p then q,' and that p, to the conclusion that q. Material implications—sentences of the form 'if p then q'—are true if p is false, or if q is true, or both; this might have suggested to you that the primary method of determining whether a conditional is true would be to check for the truth of its consequent and the falsity of its antecedent. But the semantics of material implication are a misleading guide to its application; a material implication whose truth has been determined in the way suggested by its semantics is useless if the intended application is a modus ponens. If you know that the antecedent of the conditional is false, then the modus ponens cannot get off the ground. And if you know that the material implication is true because you already know that its consequent is true, then you do not need the modus ponens to arrive at the consequent. Useful material implications have to be derived in some more laborious and usually roundabout way. For example, the conditional 'if p then q' could be derived as an instance of an inductively established generalization having the form 'all Fs are Gs.'

Allow another simplification, that induction proceeds by enumerating cases of items of one type copresent with or followed by items of another: not that this is the way that inductions generally work, but we can adopt the simplification without prejudice to the point we are after. If our warrant for expecting a G on the basis of having seen an F is that, time and again, Fs have been followed by Gs, we must have gone through suitably many repetitions of Fs producing the representation 'F,' and suitably many repetitions of Gs producing the representation 'G.' To get these, we must invest our attention in observing the Fs and Gs: this may mean seeking out Fs; it may mean spending money on producing them (as in controlled experiments); in any case it will mean ignoring other things.

The point holds quite generally, and even when the inferential connections are not inductive. Imagine H. Procrustes taking an interest in the

Ship of Theseus of the traditional philosopher's puzzle, and needing an advance opinion from the IRS on whether such a Ship is a deductible business expense.[26] Getting one will cost the attorney fees, the time spent on putting together the request, and the intangible cost of having used up part of one's informal quota of such questions. (Government employees will disregard such inquiries as frivolous if there are too many of them.) Putting the inferential connection in place uses up resources that cannot then be spent elsewhere.

Now, there are a vast number of (what are, for all H. Procrustes knows) possible inferential connections between possible representations. The point of endowing H. Procrustes with his overly rich descriptive abilities was to highlight that fact: H. Procrustes could go looking for inductive links between Victorians and real estate prices in the Avenues neighborhood, or between those not-quite-Victorians and real estate prices in a neighborhood-like region that only he has demarcated; he could ask the IRS whether he can deduct his Ship of Theseus, given that his business is selling props to philosophers, or he could ask whether he can deduct ships that he has transformed, by a progress of gradual replacements, into outdoor sculptures of giant demons, given that he is in some other unheard-of line of work; for him, these options are visible, as are indefinitely many more like them. But H. Procrustes' position is not deeply different from our own; each representation that he deploys is one which we could deploy, even if we do not have all of them at our fingertips at once.

Among this vast number of possible inferential pathways, very few will actually pan out into usable inferences. H. Procrustes has a name for the shape of a shadow on a wall, but shadows of this shape are not particularly helpful indicators of much else.[27] The history of science reminds us that most inferential connections which scientists have at one time or another thought up have turned out not to work: there are no interesting or important inferential connections to be established between most randomly selected empirical facts, and, for that matter, it is the unusual mathematical object that lends itself to an interesting or important proof. Statistical or probabilistic connections do not differ in this regard; it is not as though you can take two arbitrarily chosen constructs and expect to find a statistically significant correlation between them.

It follows that if H. Procrustes is going to construct the inferential connections between his representations that will allow him a unified intellect, he will need to invest his intellectual resources very selectively. If he divides his resources evenly among all of those possible connections, he will not invest enough in any one connection to make it inferentially robust. If he invests in the wrong ones, his efforts will not pan out into usable inferential links. How is he to choose his investment opportunities?

H. Procrustes cannot see the future, and so he is faced with a chicken-and-egg problem. To make his choices correctly, he would need to know both which representations *can* be linked inferentially, and which ones it will be intellectually *important* to link. That latter question is often a matter of where other intellectual investments have been made, and have paid off. Confirming that all Fs are Gs may not be intellectually important if there is nothing further you can infer from something's being a G. To know where to invest, he needs to know where the inferential payoffs are, but to know where the inferential payoffs are, he needs to have already ponied up his inferential investments.

The usual solution to chicken-and-egg problems is bootstrapping, which in this case means investing intellectual resources, initially for all practical purposes at random, in hopes of a lucky hit. One then parleys one's initial inferential winnings into slightly larger ones, and those into larger ones still, until eventually one has the inferential apparatus to support a unified intellect. In a moment, I'm going to argue that H. Procrustes will do *so* badly at bootstrapping that he's not going to end up with a unified intellect, and that his problem is being unwilling to reason with partial truths. But there are a couple of related ways out that will suggest themselves to philosophers of different stripes, and I first need to take time out to explain why they are dead ends.

5.5

Perhaps some descriptions are just more natural or more apt than others; if H. Procrustes confines himself to the apt descriptions, he will be fine. It does seem natural for philosophers to suppose that some descriptions are especially natural. But why think that our willingness to regard some but not other descriptions as apt or natural is not just a summary of our own inferential experience? H. Procrustes is starting from scratch; he can articulate any fact he is faced with accurately and precisely, and if we are going to be generous, with grace and wit, to boot. So he will either have no sense for what is natural, or will have no usable one—unless we back it up with an account of the distinction that he can use.

However, here we bump up against a discouraging and familiar bit of philosophical history. We are quite certain that grass today and grass tomorrow resemble each other in being green, but differ as to whether they are 'grue,' that is, green if observed today or before, blue if observed tomorrow or thereafter. In other words, the concept 'green' is a decent intellectual investment, and 'grue' is not: inductive predictions built around 'grue' are likely to be disappointed.[28] One philosophical diagnosis was that 'grue' was an artificial and ungainly looking predicate, or, if you like, that it was unnatural and not at all apt. And during the second half of the twentieth century, a good deal of effort was squandered on trying to cash that complaint out, by finding quick formal shortcuts that would rule out the grue-like predicates.[29] That so much effort on the part of so many philosophers went nowhere is reasonable evidence that the feature to which the objection appeals can't be articulated. If the philosophers can't figure out how to work it, we shouldn't demand that H. Procrustes be able to use it.

Perhaps, instead, what have for the past century and a half been called 'natural kinds' will solve H. Procrustes' problem. The doctrine being invoked here is that there are sorts of item whose instances have a shared internal nature or 'essence.' The traditional examples are water and gold, whose essences are alleged to be, respectively, being H_2O and having an atomic nucleus containing 79 protons. The shared essences support scientifically important inferences. And because of their underlying essences, they can do (at least part of) the work of getting *us* on track in our choice of representations, provided that we fish for them with what we might as well call essence-seeking thoughts. There are differing accounts of what these essence-seeking thoughts are like, but the idea is roughly that they pick out everything that has the same essence or nature as some initial sample (say, glasses of water, or gold rings), even when users of the term don't have even the slightest idea what the essence of the sample is. (So, users of 'water,' back before anyone knew any chemistry, had essence-seeking thoughts that picked out everything of the same natural kind, that is, exactly all of the H_2O.)

Natural kinds, however, won't help H. Procrustes, because his chicken-and-egg problem means that he isn't in a position to know, ahead of time, whether the 'water'-thought in which he invests intellectual resources, ought, for his own inferential purposes, to be a natural kind thought: that is, whether he ought to choose an essence-seeking thought, or some other kind of thought, for instance, a cultural-kind thought.[30] H. Procrustes will have *many* contrasting types of term at his fingertips. Take that other favorite example, gold. The doctrine of bimetalism was the bizarre (but, not all that long ago, quite respectable) idea that gold and silver were *naturally* monetarily valuable: that the value was an intrinsic property of the metal, like its weight or color. Bimetalists used to argue over what the natural, i.e., intrinsic, ratio of value between gold and silver was, entirely ignoring market forces. That is, bimetalist economists took it that their inferential needs were to be met by treating 'gold' and 'silver' (not coincidentally, the words for 'money' in many languages: in times past, the metals were not conceptually distinguished from money) in a way that did not distinguish natural kind terms from, e.g., cultural or economic or evaluative kind terms. In retrospect, of course, that was a mistake. But, especially given that even the distinction between natural, cultural, and evaluative kinds is available only in retrospect, why should we think of it as having been a foreseeable or blameworthy mistake? On what basis can H. Procrustes reasonably decide to allocate his resources to developing inferential pathways to and from the natural-kind concept 'gold,' rather than the bimetalists' homonymous concept?[31] The easy ways out don't work: neither natural kinds nor natural properties are going to solve H. Procrustes' chicken-and-egg problem.

5.6

The bootstrapping process evidently has two distinguishable components. To describe them, I'm going to stick with concepts, although remember that the problem of finding inferentially usable representations is more general than that. I'm also going to use a very flattened-out image of what it is to have a concept. Think of concepts as demarcating extensions in the terrain of objects: then you could, for instance, pick out a concept by drawing a line around a region of your map of that terrain; or you could, more indirectly, pick out a concept by explaining which line you were going to draw.[32]

The first component of the bootstrapping process is guessing concepts. H. Procrustes already has terms for all of them, so in his case, guessing is just picking a term. Like us, he then invests resources in seeing if the concepts he has selected can be inferentially connected. If he has picked the concepts F and G, he conducts experiments to see if Fs are always Gs, or what percentage of Gs are Fs, or he tries to prove mathematically that Fs are Gs, or he starts a court case in the hope of creating a precedent to the effect that Fs are Gs....

H. Procrustes should be expected to do badly at the initial guessing phase of the process, just because inferentially usable groups of concepts will be very sparse. And so will we. But notice that there is already a way in which he is likely to do more poorly than ordinary humans will. Suppose you are considering using the concept F as an inference trigger for G, and suppose that F turns out to be a usable choice because (to put it in the terms of our simplified picture) F overlaps with H, and H *is* a precise and reliable inference trigger for G. To us ordinary folks, it will often seem, of the Hs that are not Fs, that it is nonetheless somewhat true, or partially true, or true in a way, that they are Fs. Partial truth is a way of registering near, and sometimes not so near, misses. And that may be enough for us to draw the conclusion (defeasibly, and so with caution) that it is a G. But H. Procrustes is restricted to bivalent truth, and so he will not draw it. Already at this early stage of the process, H. Procrustes manages less in the way of a unified intellect than would competition that helped itself to partial truth.

The second component of bootstrapping is refining one's successes. Bear in mind that an operating inferential connection may start out being extremely unreliable and just barely usable. H. Procrustes' overall success will depend on what he can make of such minor successes in the first, guess-work phase of bootstrapping. But here H. Procrustes can be expected to do especially badly. There are two reasons for this that I want to pick out now. First, concepts get refined on the basis of one's inferential experience with them. And second, one refines one's concepts much more expeditiously by thinking about how one did with them than by brute force trial and error.

Under the first heading, H. Procrustes has much less in the way of usable inferential experience than we would have, if we were in his shoes. To be sure, he does have one kind of inferential experience which lends itself to improving his conceptual repertoire: since he is using the concept F to infer that this or that is a G, he may notice that not all of the Fs are in fact Gs, and that by replacing F with a more tightly demarcated concept F' he can improve the reliability of that inferential pathway. But because he never executes inferences of the form, 'It's true enough that x is an F, so x is a G,' he never has inferential experience with nearby instances that fall outside the extension of the triggering concept he has demarcated. Accordingly, he will not be in a position to extend the boundaries of the concept F so as to gather in those instances. Likewise, since his concepts have no penumbra, he does not experiment with penumbral cases, and so he cannot have good reasons to readjust his concepts to include as core cases some of (what would be for a user of partial-truth inference) their penumbras. In these ways, his attempts to build up a repertoire of tight and interlocking inferential connections, and so achieve a unified intellect, are stymied, and stymied *because* of bivalence. One improves one's inferential connections intelligently on the basis of one's experience with operating them, and a creature which uses only (what it takes to be) full truths inferentially cannot be expected to gain inferential experience with partial truths.

Under the second heading, when you redesign your inferential equipment on the basis of your inferential experience with your former equipment, doing so intelligently involves reasoning about how it did. Now everyone's initial choice of concepts for this sort of second-level reasoning can be assumed to be just as scattershot as their choice of first-order concepts. For example, an important step in a successful bootstrapping process might be the observation that, in the past, species concepts have enabled successful inferences on the basis of relatively few observations: once you have seen that a handful of robins lay blue eggs, it's pretty safe to conclude that they all do. The conclusion is that, in new domains, one should seek out species concepts, invest intellectual resources in them, and use them as bases for speedy inference.[33]

But now, consider the history of *our* concept, 'species.' At the outset, we got it wrong (of course). Philosophers will recall how Aristotle tied it to the 'species form'—roughly, a single functional blueprint—that is shared by all the members of a species. In retrospect, it is obvious that *this* concept does not properly apply to most of the species that we care about: sexually reproducing organisms come in two sexes, each of which must have a different functional blueprint.[34] If one cannot reason with partial truth, one gets stuck very early on. Nothing that early biologists applied their imperfect concept 'species' to *is* (that sort of) a species; even though partial-truth hedges were not explicitly registered, the obviously forced fit had to be, and was, accommodated by defeasible patterns of inference. Let's simplify the story by allowing H. Procrustes to register the forced fit. Because H. Procrustes reasons bivalently, he has no evidential support at all for the conclusion—again, representative of conclusions important to the bootstrapping process—that he should invest intellectual resources in species concepts.

Briefly, at the early stages, the inferential equipment which one uses to reason about one's inferential equipment will *also* be imprecise; reasoning that deploys it will have to be fault-tolerant. H. Procrustes' reasoning is not fault-tolerant, and so his bootstrapping will get stuck at this stage. Unable to think about how he is doing with what he has, the process of improving both the concepts he works with, and the inferential pathways that link them, is pretty much confined to brute-force trial and error. H. Procrustes starts out without a unified intellect, and that's how he stays.

Even if one in the natural course of things comes to have more experience with intellectual tools one understands to be legitimate than those one does not, why can't H. Procrustes, by an effort of will, seek out what he regards as heuristics, triggered by similarity to what he regards as fully true applications of predicates in which he has made inferential investments? And in that case, why won't everything proceed—albeit with somewhat different labeling—just as it does with us?

First, and returning to an issue that first cropped up in section 2.2, while sometimes similarity or resemblance can be understood independently of partial truth (as when two faces or colors resemble one another in some intuitive way), quite often these notions are just a different way of marking our reliance on partial truth: our understanding and inferential control of partial truth are prior to these latter judgments of similarity. A skateboard resembles other vehicles in that it is for some purposes true enough, but not fully true, that a skateboard is a vehicle.

Second, one is only going to do a decent job of finding usable heuristics if one is looking for them, and that requires having (something tantamount to) the concept 'heuristic.' That concept is a sophisticated latecomer; it has only become part of normal academic vocabulary over the last generation. Before he can use it, H. Procrustes must find his way to this concept as well; the odds that he will guess it at the outset are as low as the odds of picking any other concept. Imagine him investing in a nearby concept, and to keep the example vivid, think of it as our notion of divination, which does seem to occur fairly early on in many cultures. Like a heuristic, divination is a noninferential method of finding out facts; unlike the heuristics our cognitive scientists investigate, it operates supernaturally. (In the first place, we may suppose, by sympathetic magic: you can read the future off the entrails because—it is supposed—the entrails magically resemble the future.) When H. Procrustes investigates the effectiveness of divination, he will ignore what by our lights are the promising heuristics, because they obviously do not involve the supernatural, or sympathetic magic in particular. Thus the search for heuristics too involves prior intellectual investment; we have it on our agenda today only because we are and were willing and able to reason with partial truth.

Third, were H. Procrustes to explore the same inferential connections between the penumbras of his concepts that we do, that would be, for him, investing resources in establishing inferential links between *another* set of concepts; by hypothesis, he's already made his decision about which full-on concepts to invest in, and he's foregone the others. Fourth, we allowed H. Procrustes to *narrow down* a concept on the basis of his experience with it. Why can't he mimic the progress of people like ourselves just by choosing broader concepts in the first place, concepts that already include those penumbras of narrower concepts which we explore with partial truth? The costs are high: because H. Procrustes does not know *which* penumbra to include—recall that there are many ways to miss a target—his catch-all concept will have to be very broad indeed, in order to capture all of those penumbras of a narrower concept. Once again, he will have to guess which bits of it to focus his resources on: his problem has not been solved, merely relabeled.

Here is not so much an anthropic argument as an anthropic suggestion. Suppose we take our own existence to indicate that we were relatively expeditious about assembling our intellectual toolkits; had we not been, we would have been swept away by other creatures or cultures that succeeded first. So we must have rapidly refined earlier and shakier concepts and inferential pathways on the basis of highly fault-tolerant reasoning. But that was just reasoning that deployed partial truth, and, if that *is* how we arrived where we are, our confidence in our current toolkit, including the parts of it that can be deployed bivalently, should be tied to our confidence in the reasoning by which it was attained: in the first place, to our confidence that it amounted to *reasoning*. We take ourselves to have accumulated a great deal of evidence that it's worthwhile investing in species concepts, even though, in retrospect, much of that evidence was brought to bear using a version of the concept 'species' that would allow us to support that conclusion only if it was not bivalently applied. We must take ourselves also to have been thinking, more or less decently, when we drew conclusions on the basis of the forced-fit application of the concept.

I earlier promised an unprincipled answer to the question, Why isn't the existence of your grandparents a fact of logic? We now have that answer on hand: you don't have to understand your grandparents to have been engaged in theoretical reasoning, in order to understand what you will now go on to do as theoretical reasoning. But you do have to understand the past partial-truth inferences that underwrite a current full-truth toolkit as theoretical reasoning, in order to understand what you will now go on to do as theoretical reasoning.

5.7

One might complain that H. Procrustes is not a good model for real human beings, and that the lessons we are supposed to learn from him do not apply to us. The reason is that we humans exhibit differential responses shaped by a couple of billion years of natural selection. A great deal of the guesswork and experimentation has been done for us, and the results of that brute-force approach, applied over unreasonably long periods of time, are encoded in concepts we innately have (or in innate dispositions to choose concepts). H. Procrustes started from scratch, and perhaps for this reason he could not get by with only bivalence; but we do not start from scratch, and so bivalence is an option for us.

To see how this plays out, let's give H. Procrustes an innate concept, 'pasta': his concept tells him that pasta is made from wheat; that it is cooked by boiling; that it is found in a characteristic range of forms…. There are good reasons for H. Procrustes to have this concept in his repertoire: it is embedded in the inferential links encoded in recipes, and let's give him the cookbooks, also. Notice that a substantial amount of effort is involved in inventing, kitchen-testing, publishing, and reviewing these inference patterns; once again, inferential connections require real investments.

Now suppose that H. Procrustes' spouse has a particular recipe in mind, and instructs him to bring some pasta home from the corner market. And suppose that when he arrives there, he discovers that this particular market is so chic that it does not carry anything of which it is fully true that it is pasta: they have gluten-free variants, carb-free variants, 'raw' variants, strangely shaped variants, variants made out of ground Jerusalem artichokes, out of quinoa… H. Procrustes has many alternative concepts available to him, e.g., 'pasta′' (covering both traditional forms of pasta and the artichoke-based variants), 'pasta″'…; but he is not in a position to move over to an alternative concept, because he is not the one inventing the recipes, doing the kitchen-testing, publishing the cookbooks, and so on. (That is, he is not investing the resources needed to build up inferential links triggered by the concept 'pasta′'.) Because H. Procrustes is unable to say of anything on the shelf that it is true *enough* that it is pasta, he and his spouse are inferentially stranded.

It is not as though we ought to blame the cookbook writers: when the decision about what concepts to write the cookbooks around was made, no one had so much as thought of gluten-free or carb-free 'pasta.' The first point now is that the social world changes, and the concepts we need to navigate it change along with it; whatever concepts we innately have do not help us with such changes. The second is that investment in concepts, of which innateness is just an example, can anchor us to concepts whose bivalent applications are no longer usable. We can allow that if H. Procrustes (and everybody else) had the *right* concepts ahead of time, he could get by without partial truth; but to have the right concepts, he (and we) would have had to predict the future, and he is like us in not being able to do so. The third point is that because intellectual investments are socially shared, the decision about where to invest intellectual resources is not up to any one person. One has to work with the concepts one has inherited, even if they are not a good fit for one's present circumstances, because one cannot simply redo all those cookbooks.

H. Procrustes is stuck, because he must husband his scarce resources. Refining his intellectual tools to the point where they will support a unified intellect requires gradually improving them. That means gradually improving tools that, at the beginning, scarcely work at all, and which work mostly just when they are being misused. It also means working with tools that have been handed to him, and that, whatever their previous track record, increasingly work only when they are being misused. H. Procrustes can refine his intellectual tools only if he has experience misusing them, but his restriction to bivalentist inference prevents him from having just that kind of experience. He can draw on that experience only if he is also able to make do with whatever intellectual tools he has available for thinking about his experience, even if they are somewhat off-base. If everyone had always been restricted to bivalence, no one would have opinions worth having at all.

5.8

I've used the thought experiment to argue that if you don't help yourself to partial truth, you'll sacrifice the unity of intellect which makes your opinions worth having. But, like most state-of-nature stories, the case of H. Procrustes is somewhat artificial, and we should only be convinced if the conclusions we have drawn are confirmed when we inspect our own inferential activities. To do that, let's turn our attention to a family of cases which exhibit, in an especially pointed fashion, the connections between partial truth, intellectual unity, and the reasonableness of putting stock in one's opinions.

An inordinately large proportion of our inferences involve generalizations that have to be understood as containing ceteris paribus or 'other things equal' clauses. A ceteris paribus clause in a generalization means that the generalization is defeasible: that its use in an inference can be defeated by any of indefinitely many items of additional information. Almost all of our opinions about the empirical and contingent aspect of the world, when these are not restricted entirely to particulars, fall under this heading. To adapt an example of Nancy Cartwright's, the greater the altitude, the longer it takes your hard-boiled eggs to cook; however, that is true only when other things are equal, for instance, only if you are not using a pressure cooker. But it is not just the empirical generalizations: many noncontingent generalizations are also defeasible. For instance, because languages are methods of communication, their users are authorities with respect to the conventions that constitute their language, and that is not in the first place an *empirical* fact. (That is why it makes sense for linguists to rely on the linguistic intuitions of native informants, when they reconstruct a language's grammar.) However, there are many defeaters for the conclusion that you can rely on a native informant's linguistic opinions.

Let's leave to one side the point that defeasible generalizations ought themselves to be understood as partial truths: generalizations that are only true other things being equal. What are the consequences, for the unity of the intellect, of requiring full truth of the defeaters?

Here is a generalization, taken from an official timetable: that if you take the ferry, you'll be there within the half-hour. This generalization is to be understood as containing an implicit ceteris paribus clause: potential defeaters include an airplane dropping on the ferry, the police stopping the ferry to search for narcotics, a tiger's being found on the upper deck, and so on (it is obvious that you could continue the list as long as you liked). One particularly important potential defeater is, however, that, during rush hour, nothing in Sydney runs on time. Although that last statement is only partially true (it is at least exaggerated), I do not have available a fully true substitute or paraphrase for it. The defeater is important: if we ignore it, the conclusions we draw, when we deploy the generalization, are going to be much less reliable than otherwise. The claim that nothing in Sydney runs on time during rush hour is the distillate of a great deal of experience (my own and others') with the transit system (and that's *why* it's partially true). So the unavailability to us of partial truth would have the effect of compartmentalizing that experience off from the inferences deploying the generalizations in the ferry schedule.

Getting a computer to exhibit intelligence should be a straightforward task, or so Alan Turing thought, circa 1950. Human brains (he argued) are, or anyway can be simulated by, computers; human brains exhibit intelligence. What a computer can do, it is a straightforward matter to program it to do. Therefore, producing a computer able to pass the Turing Test is simply a matter of allocating sufficient programmer time.

That train of thought is defeasible by a lesson that has emerged from subsequent generations of work by computer scientists: that if it's an interesting problem, it's computationally intractable. That defeater could be brought to bear in various ways on the initial train of thought. For instance, first, one might worry that since intelligence solves interesting problems, and interesting problems are computationally intractable, intelligent human beings cannot, after all, be (or be simulated by) computers. Or second, one might object that since intelligence solves interesting problems, and interesting problems are computationally intractable, computational approaches to those problems will require ingenuity and roundabout approaches; in other words, even if computers can be gotten to exhibit intellgence, that project will not be nearly as straightforward as Turing had imagined. The point is not that I am endorsing these objections myself (in particular, not the first), but rather that they need to be considered. Even if one then goes on to discard them, a conclusion of which these are salient potential defeaters deserves to have less stock put in it when one has not given these defeaters due consideration.

Now the claim that interesting problems are computationally intractable is not flat-out true. Rather, it's true enough for many purposes. It encapsulates a lesson learned painfully and over a great deal of time, and one for which we have no fully true paraphrase or substitute. So suppose that you are reconsidering Turing's reasons for thinking that intelligent computers are just around the corner. If you are restricted to full truths, then you cannot have this consideration available to you. But then you are unable to consider the bearing of a very important potential defeater, when you are examining Turing's argument. And so you, like Turing, are likely to exhibit a confidence in your conclusions that is thereby misplaced. When you do this, you are (if you are a computer scientist, anyway) exhibiting a disunified intellect. The true-enough claim is a bridge between a great deal of important disciplinary experience, experience that is part of a computer scientist's intellectual background, and a sequence of thoughts having to do with the future of AI. When a usable summary of the experience is inferentially unavailable to you, you are unable to bring the experience to bear in a train of reasoning involving those thoughts. You are intellectually compartmentalized, and thus your opinions on the subject do not merit much trust.

The generalization that exercising, and sticking to your diet, is good for you, is of course defeasible. (Not if you have more urgent things to do; not if you can't afford your diet…) A recently prominent class of defeaters are those having to do with being anorexic or an exercise addict. Now it may be in a particular case only partially true that you are, say, anorexic; as before, you may have available no fully true substitute. Accepting that you are anorexic, or an addict, as a partial truth may bring together a great many observations, all of which are warning signs about the way your life is going; the unavailability of partial truth would segregate that group of observations off from inferences deploying the generalization with which we began. And there is a further point to be made here: in cases like these, it is precisely when the claim is partially true that it would be good to be able to take it into account. It is when you are sliding into anorexia or addiction that intervention is still relatively easy; later on, when it is a full truth, it will be too late.

Evidently, examples of this form can be produced on demand. When you are restricted to full truth, you have available only inferential moves that deploy full truths. Suppose that many generalizations deployed in inference are defeasible. They will often have potential defeaters that are only somewhat true, or true enough—for instance, because they are rough and ready summaries of lengthy accumulations of experience. There will be no fully true paraphrase or substitute available, and taking account of the defeater will nonetheless be important. If you were not sensitive to the partially true defeater, confidence in your conclusion would be misplaced. Your opinions turn out to be worth less than they otherwise would be, and the reason is that the unavailability of partial truth functions as an inferential barrier, segregating some of your opinions from others.

5.9

It's now time to address two or three objections we have had on the stack for a while. Partial truth is a way of extending the reach of other representational devices, such as generality, in a way that allows one to replace a too-large (i.e., repetition-diluting) vocabulary with a smaller one. But one might object that the usual and appropriate device with this function *is* generality, and it doesn't need extenders: don't universals allow us to abstract away from varying details to relevant constancy by subsuming the individuals under a concept or predicate? Early on I suggested that, at a suitable level of abstraction, names have a similar function, in that they allow for repeatability of representations in the face of variation in the facts. Why won't the more traditional devices, names and predicates, get the job done without forced matches, i.e., without partial truth?

The considerations that address this objection are already on hand; let's rehearse them. One is in a position to know *which* concepts, predicates or properties will precisely meet one's inferential needs only when one's inferential history is pretty much over. So one's initial intellectual investments are bound to be somewhat off-target. A theoretical reasoner equipped with the apparatus of partial truth can make do with suboptimally allocated intellectual investments, and, sometimes, work his way to concepts that allow him inferentially useful full truth. But someone who is equipped only with full truth will all too often find those initial investments useless. So universals won't do the job for you unless partial truth was doing the job for you already.

Second, why isn't the argument against making do with full truth also an argument against the adequacy of partial truth? Partial truth is just another device for facilitating thought by economizing on the number of representations in play. How can it escape the vicious circle we have identified: that you need to know where the inferential connections are before you decide how to economize, but you have to have decided how to economize before you can find out where the inferential connections are?

Selecting the representations in which you will invest your cognitive resources is inevitably something of a hit-or-miss process. The difference between making do only with full truth, and allowing partial truth, is that in the latter case you don't have to hit the nail on the head. When near-misses register, much more can get caught in the cognitive net. Let's retrieve another example from section 2.6. In its original version, Euler's Theorem was only pretty much true—which means, to someone committed to bivalence, just plain false. Call the concept that the original version deployed 'polyhedron,' and call the cleaned-up one we use today, 'regular polyhedron.' Because we were able to pick up on that 'pretty much true,' we were able to get by for what was actually a very long while, reasoning about polyhedra, exploring the inferential connections around them, and finally replacing the off-target representations with new representations selected in light of the by now well understood inferential potentials.

Metaphorically, full truth only allows you to see the facts that you're straight-on representing. But partial truth allows you to see (more or less obscurely) what's going on in the penumbra of a full truth: it lets you see a little bit around the corner. You will, to be sure, fail to see those parts of the world that are too far away from where you are looking, but the nearby bits won't necessarily remain entirely invisible to you. And that's an enormous advantage. The partial-truth visual field may be often out of focus, but the full-truth visual field is mostly blindspots.

5.10

While we are considering objections, let's also pause to discuss epistemicism, a recent analysis of vagueness as ignorance of precisely what one means, where whatever it is one *does* mean *is* precise.[35] The position is a way of holding onto classical logic: because, on the epistemicist view, our concepts have sharp boundaries, their applications are always flat true or flat false.

How *useful* is epistemicism? H. Procrustes is someone who sees the world the way epistemicists say it really is, and he consequently ends up intellectually paralyzed. Let's amend the last thought experiment slightly, and imagine that 'pasta' now *seems* vague to H. Procrustes, but that the concept in fact has sharp boundaries, just as epistemicists insist. Imagine also that H. Procrustes has been reading around in their writings, and has been convinced; let's return to the yuppie grocery store, where he stands in the pasta section, wondering what to do. He may tell himself that each of the deviant forms of pasta which he encounters either really *is* pasta, or really *isn't*. But since he can't tell, and since, for inferential purposes, he is often enough going to have to classify some of the can't-tells as pasta, H. Procrustes must allow that he is likely to be sometimes classifying something as pasta, of which it is simply not true (or anyway not simply true) that it is pasta, on the grounds that it's anyway *true enough*. Failing to draw the conclusions which classifications like this one enable will leave him, as before, too often in a state of inferential paralysis, and the general policy will condemn him to intellectual disunity, and opinions that are not worth having.

But now, if H. Procrustes is *anyway* going to have to engage in partial-truth inference, we will want to ask ourselves whether, from an epistemicist's point of view, anything has been gained from trading in genuinely fuzzy predicates for predicates that have sharp edges, but are inaccurately applied.

It is hard to see why the latter alternative is more than an alternative formulation of the vagueness it is trying to avoid, and why it is not letting the vagueness in through the back door, after all those efforts to prevent it from coming in through the front. An epistemicist sees inaccuracy and imprecision very differently: one of them is logically and metaphysically impossible. But inaccuracy and imprecision are often enough just different ways of representing the very same inferential problem. In trying to substitute inaccuracy for imprecision, epistemicism leaves you back exactly where you started.

And it is hard to see why the epistemicist's alternative is not a *worse* alternative. As a geologist of my acquaintance once put it, explaining her description of a sandstone formation as 'punky,' she would rather use a sloppy term sloppily than use a precise term sloppily. That's a thoughtful choice, but to an epistemicist, it's an unintelligible choice.

Epistemicism is widely acknowledged to be a bite-the-bullet position, one that a philosopher adopts not because it is plausible, but because it is the price of saving classical logic.[36] When you start reasoning with partial truth, you have *already* given up reasoning with classical logic: you are no longer treating correctness of inference as truth preservation, and you have surrendered bivalence. So at this point there is no longer anything to save, and biting the bullet is misguided. Remember that we are treating logical questions as practical questions: questions about how to think. To have shown that a proposed way of thinking produces worthless opinions is to have shown that it is *wrong*—provided, of course, that a better alternative is available.[37]

5.11

The point of theoretical reasoning is to arrive at opinions, and not just any opinions, but opinions worth having. If unity of the intellect is a precondition for theoretical reasoning to produce opinions worth having, then one must presuppose, while one is engaged in theoretical reasoning, that one's intellect is (sufficiently) unified. But if your intellect can only be unified enough if inference that deploys partial truth *is* inference, you have to take it for granted (again, while you are continuing to engage in reasoning about what the facts are) that inference deploying partial truth is inference, and to reason on that basis. But that in turn is just to say that the right way to engage in theoretical inference is to proceed on the basis of, *inter alia*, partial truths. Because reasoning and inference are 'how to' notions, to say that the right way to do it is on the basis of partial truth is to say that partial-truth inference *is* inference.

In his *Philosophical Explanations*, Robert Nozick famously remarked that philosophical argumentation tends to the coercive: it is as though what philosophers really wanted was an argument so powerful that if you did not accept its conclusion, you would die.[38] Because transcendental arguments characteristically work by extracting preconditions for unity of the self, Nozick's caricature comes closest to being literally true of the uses philosophers try of make of transcendental deductions. Again, I don't mean the argument we have just completed to be taken this way, and so I want to wrap up by returning to the question of what I take its force to be.

Here is a different way of putting the problem. I started the chapter by pointing out that the prescriptions provided by logic have purchase only on persons, and I concluded that, because logic is picked out in terms of its guiding function with respect to inference, if there is a shape that their logic must have for there to be persons of a particular type at all, then their logic does have that shape. I have just been arguing that unless partial truths are deployed in inference, the intellects of creatures that are limited in roughly the ways we ourselves are will turn out to be so fragmented that their opinions will not be worth having.

On the face of it these are different points. But recall that personal identity is foundational for logic because it is on persons that the prescriptions and demands of logic are enforced. And notice that logic shares with many other prescriptive enterprises the following feature: an ability to comply with the prescriptions, demonstrated by at least a modicum of actual compliance, is a precondition for enforcing them, and in fact for taking them to apply in the first place. As regards the social norms, when someone too persistently and pervasively violates them, we cease to hold him responsible to them; instead we simultaneously exempt and restrain him. We do not require logical consistency of dogs or very small children. They are simply not going to exhibit it, and, perhaps because enforcement is costly, we do not impose a demand we know to be futile.

The intellect is the aspect of one's mind doing the theoretical reasoning. So the side of logic that governs theoretical reasoning applies to the intellect. An extremely disunified intellect does not and cannot manage much in the way of worthwhile theoretical reasoning. So there is no point in insisting that such a person regiment his theoretical reasoning in one way or another; such a person will end up being exempted from the demands of the logic of theoretical reasoning. The constraints, guidelines, and so on that make up a logic must be compatible with there being something to which they can apply. So a logic of theoretical reasoning must be compatible with a (sufficiently) unified intellect.[39]

A logic of theoretical reasoning conforming to the bivalence and validity as truth preservation doctrines would not permit sufficient inferential connectedness to support even minimal intellectual unity. For creatures that are limited in roughly the respects we are, the requisite inferential connections are discovered and exploited only by reasoners who allow themselves forced matches, that is, partial truth. Therefore, a logic of theoretical reasoning for creatures who are limited in our sort of way will allow inference deploying partial truth.

So the bite of the argument we have just concluded is not that, if you don't reason using partial truth, you will cease to exist. Rather, its point is that if you don't reason with partial truth, your *intellect* will cease to exist—that is, put more directly, you won't be able to do much in the way of effective reasoning about how the facts stand, and the opinions you form about facts won't be worth much. Your stake in partial truth is just your stake in successful theoretical reasoning.

Here, summing up, is why our stake in the latter amounts to a stake in the former. We choose our initial concepts more or less blindly, and then we choose further concepts that fit our initial choices. If our initial choices are off kilter, we will end up with a grid of concepts that is systematically askew (that is, that requires partial truth for its application). Because building up inferential links between these concepts will have taken a great deal of investment, we may not be in a position to write that investment down and start over.

A painting by Howard Hodgkin can serve as an icon for our predicament. Hodgkin is known for applying pigment to already-framed canvases. One visually striking composition of this type presents the appearance of having been placed crookedly, and then painted on as though it were level. Since it now *is* hung level, the painted horizontals and verticals are askew, and the piece is appropriately called 'It Can't Be True.'[40] Given that the frame and the canvas are both integral elements of the work, and given that the paint has been applied to both, the only way to bring the paint strokes into line with the verticals and horizontals of the frame would be to start over: to paint over the whole thing. And just as we might well not want to do that, we might well have compelling reasons not to junk our investment in the network of concepts we already have, even if their applications, too, can't be true.

6

How Can We Think about
Partial Truth?

Philosophers of mind have often enough answered the question of how we think by telling us that we think with our beliefs, our desires, and so on. Implementation analyses at this level of abstraction are an important part of philosophy of mind, and partial-truth inference requires us to redo them. If the bivalence doctrine is not nearly flat-out true, what must minds contain?

The most important payoff of asking what mental states partial truth shows to be part of the mind will be a characterization of partial truth itself; it will complete the argument of this part of the book. To get there, I will first have to explain how a discussion of mental states can be a way of characterizing a semantic concept such as partial truth. The official definition of partial truth will also be an occasion to take up a question we will no longer be able to avoid, namely, what sorts of definitions are appropriate in the world of partial-truth inference. Philosophers today are trained to expect and demand definitions that amount to lists of necessary and sufficient conditions, that are consequently very sensitive to counterexamples, and that, if the definition is adequate, do not have any. But that sort of understanding of what a definition must be is part and parcel of the bivalence-driven view I am trying to dislodge.

There are a number of secondary but nonetheless dramatic payoffs that will drop into our laps on the way. First of all, that the trains of thought that make up reasoning about matters of fact are composed of beliefs, and beliefs alone, is one half of a widely held view about the metaphysics of mind called 'belief-desire psychology.'[1] To believe something is to take it to be true, a connection which is expressed in Moore's Paradox: if you say that p is true, but that you don't believe that p, you will register as having contradicted yourself. If truth can be partial, the belief side of belief-desire psychology is a philosophical error.[2] The truth can be literally incredible, and when it is, what we must do with what we are aware is other than the truth is something other than believe it. Consequently, a satisfactory philosophical psychology must allow for reasoning about matters of fact whose mental constituents are not beliefs.

Second, once we drop belief psychology, we will need to rethink our epistemology as well. Epistemology is normally glossed as the theory of knowledge, and knowledge is in turn glossed as a privileged kind of belief. For instance, so-called 'justified true belief' accounts of knowledge have it that you know something if you believe it, if it's true, and if, on top of that, you're justified in believing it.[3] But many of the psychological states involved in theoretical reasoning aren't beliefs. We don't think they're true. And their justifications will look very different from the justifications one gives for knowledge—that is, from the justifications that epistemologists have made their livings scrutinizing. Knowledge proves to be just one of a broader class of epistemic success concepts, and epistemology accordingly has a new agenda, namely, figuring out what these should be, and how they ought to work.

Two lower-profile issues will be addressed along the way. First, I will provide the promised argument that partial truth comes in indefinitely many qualitatively different varieties. And second, I will provide the reply to an objection we have had outstanding for a while: that when I qualify a claim that *p* as sort of true, I am really asserting the claim that 'sort of *p*,' and *that* claim is fully true; so we do not really need (or use) partial truth.

6.1

Let's begin with a methodological issue. I am proposing to use a position on truth, and its role in inference, to extract consequences in moral psychology; conversely, I am also proposing to use philosophy of mind to arrive at a further characterization of the notion of partial truth. Now the arguments have until this point been about how to engage in a certain kind of reasoning—that is, they have been arguments with prescriptive or advisory force. Whereas arguments about what makes up the machinery of the mind apparently concern a matter of fact. The worry then is that to take conclusions of the first sort of argument to settle disputes of the second sort would be to conflate items on the two sides of the 'is-ought distinction' (or possibly the 'fact-value distinction'). How could *advice* be the premises from which *facts* are to be derived?

It is an important and characteristic feature of philosophy that it can often be clothed in strikingly different vocabularies—so different, in fact, that two versions of what is substantively the same claim may seem to have entirely different topics. The logical positivists, who made much of this phenomenon, distinguished what they called the formal and the material modes of speech: if one said, for example, that there were objects, one would be talking in the material mode, and one's apparent topic would be the world and its contents; but one might alternatively say that our language contains a category of terms for objects, and then one would be talking in the formal mode, and making a claim apparently about our language and its grammar. I take it that something along these lines is going on here, and I'm going to recycle some of the positivists' terms (though without keeping their old meanings): I'll say that talk about truth is in the *material mode*, that talk of validity is in the *formal mode*, and that belief psychology is the expression, in what we can call the *psychological mode*, of the bivalence and validity as truth preservation doctrines. If that is correct, what I am going to be doing is not so much drawing a further and independent conclusion for a different subject area of philosophy as recasting already drawn conclusions in the vocabulary of philosophy of mind, and then recasting these in turn as points about our semantic lexicon.

Here is how the underlying subject matter can be in this way the same. Belief-desire psychology is not a view about what the components of the mind plain and simple *are*; in their enthusiasm its proponents sometimes forget this, but when gently reminded, they concede that minds contain sensations, emotions, visual and auditory imagery, subconscious proto-beliefs, and who knows what-all else. Belief-desire psychology is a view about which elements of the mind figure into reasoning or inference. These latter terms are honorifics: to say that a train of thought amounts to inference or reasoning is to say that, from a logical point of view, it was *done right* (or done close enough to right). So the apparent switch of topic really is only apparent.

6.2

To dispose of belief psychology, we first have to say more about what beliefs are, and the best way to do that is to address a further worry. It is an indication of the novelty of the view we are developing that our psychological vocabulary for less than all-out commitments regarding matters of fact is quite sparse. But it also might be understood as an objection: if mental states other than belief figure into reasoning as frequently as I say, then why don't we already have words for them?

I will presently give the principled response to this worry, but a stopgap answer is that, for our present purposes, 'belief' is also a philosophers' term of art: we don't already have an ordinary term for what philosophers call 'belief,' either. We are considering a bit of technical terminology whose meaning is fixed not by popular usage or by explicit definition, but by its recent history within the philosophical profession; belief psychology is thus the view that reasoning about what the facts are involves only beliefs, in the relevant technical sense of that term.

There are two currently mainstream ways of tying down the notion of belief. We have already encountered the first, on which beliefs are representations with a characteristic direction of fit. On the second, beliefs are picked out by their functional or inferential role.

Direction of fit entered the philosophical literature with a story, due to Elizabeth Anscombe, in which someone has sent her husband to the grocery store with a shopping list, and—let's not ask why—a detective is following the husband around and recording his actions. At the end of the shopping trip, there are two lists, the shopper's and the detective's, identical to the naked eye, but with differing directions of fit:

> if the list and the things that the man actually buys do not agree…then the mistake is not in the list but in the man's performance (if his wife were to say: 'Look, it says butter and you have bought margarine', he would hardly reply: 'What a mistake! we must put that right' and alter the word on the list to 'margarine'); whereas if the detective's record and what the man actually buys do not agree, then the mistake is in the record.[4]

Direction of fit is usually introduced as a way of distinguishing beliefs from desires: the shopping list's direction of fit is the one characteristic of desire; the detective's is the one characteristic of belief. When the world is not as the representation depicts it—when the mental state and its object do not fit each other—we can ask where the problem is to be located. If the representation is a belief, then the representation is at fault, and is to be altered to rectify the mismatch: one's beliefs are responsible for fitting the world, and not the other way around. The other way around is characteristic of desire; when things are not as your desires portray them, the problem is with the way things are, and one takes steps, if one can, to change the things, rather than the representation. The direction of fit specific to belief has been dubbed (by Searle) the 'word-to-world' or 'mind-to-world' direction of fit.[5]

Now, if this is what it is to be a belief, it doesn't look like partial truths make for beliefs, and let's just remind ourselves what sorts of circumstances will require partial truths. Bivalence, I suggested earlier on, is normally a product of engineering, and indeed, Anscombe's story only works because the shopper has been sent to a grocery store (or, if we update the narrative, a supermarket). At the grocery store, the products come in standardized units; because butter is sold in one-pound packages, Anscombe can instruct the shopper to come back with a pound of butter, and expect him to fulfill her order to the letter. Suppose he had been sent instead to a decent farmers' market. In that case, if he were to buy only what was on his shopping list, he would come back without the ingredients for a meal, because shopping at a farmers' market requires making good-enough substitutions (for instance, crossing out 'peaches' and writing in 'nectarines').

Imagine the detective following the shopper through the farmers' market: the likelihood that his list will match the husband's is very small indeed. At the grocery store, the detective was able to write down '1 lb butter,' because the butter comes packaged in pounds. But at the farmers' market, the amounts are rough and ready: how is he to record what has been bought? The weights for the stone fruit aren't accurate, and counting the number of peaches isn't very informative. Should the shiso and purslane count towards the salad greens? Was the gorgonzola-walnut loaf bread or a pastry? Do the carrots from the uncertified stand really qualify as organic? And what about the massage? If the detective is to collect the relevant information at the right level of granularity, he must make do with estimates that he and we will know are not quite true. As in our earlier examples, the detective can choose to report *something else*, and have it come out fully true; but full truth attained by changing the subject is not a way of getting by without partial truths we need. Word-to-world direction of fit is a viable approach provided the environment has been reengineered to make it available; that's the difference between a supermarket and a farmers' market. When the detective turns in his report, he may add that the entries for the trip to the farmers' market are not entirely accurate, and if he does, that part of the report will not be entirely believed.

The direction-of-fit view understands a belief as a representation such that, when there is a mismatch between the representation and the world, the representation is at fault, and is to be changed. But when a thought is acknowledged to be partially true, and is being used in inference, there is a recognized mismatch, but the representation is not at fault in any way that requires changing it. To use examples we have already seen: I will agree, if pressed, that the Stella is not really a painting, that, if you want to be picky about it, television is not a post-World War II innovation, that the path through the canyon is not properly a trail, and that the detective's entry, specifying organic carrots, is 'merely almost wholly true'[6]—but I keep the representations as they are. If a belief is a representation with mind-to-world direction of fit, then our theoretical reasoning proceeds via psychological states that are not beliefs.[7]

Second, beliefs are identified in terms of their functional role, the largest part of which is their role in inference. To believe that p, on this kind of view, is in good part a matter of one's willingness to draw—or anyway, one's being committed to drawing—the inferential consequences of p, when it is taken together with one's other beliefs and desires.

Now, recall that belief is inferentially unrestricted: that any belief may figure in an inference with any other belief. In the prescriptively oriented variation of inferential-role accounts, if you believe that p, then for any other q that you believe, and any r that p and q jointly entail, you are inferentially committed to believing r. But inferences involving partial truths are inferentially restricted, and we can illustrate this with an earlier example. In order to calculate the gravitational attraction exerted by a cow on a blade of grass at a given distance, we adopt the assumption that the cow is a sphere of homogeneous matter. When we do this, we commit ourselves to the inferential consequences of the assumption, but only for the purposes of solving the physics problem; presented with a different problem—e.g., that of preventing the cow from kicking over its milk bucket—we are not committed to proceeding here also on the assumption that the cow is spherical. Our attitude toward the statement that the cow is spherical is inferentially restricted, because we do not really believe it. On the other hand, because I believe that the cow has two eyes, I treat that as an allowable basis for inference in any other context (at any rate, in any other context consisting entirely of beliefs).

On this second way of filling out the concept of belief, beliefs are picked out largely by their inferential role. Attitudes toward acknowledgedly partial truths are inferentially restricted: if I take p to be only somewhat true, there are generally contexts in which I will correctly refuse to use it as a basis for inference. Beliefs are inferentially unrestricted: if you really believe that p, you ought to be willing to deploy that belief in any train of reasoning to which its content is relevant, and you ought not object to conjoining *p* with the propositional object of any other belief you hold. Thus attitudes towards partial truths differ in their inferential role from attitudes toward full truths. Consequently, if inferential or functional role is taken as telling us what belief is, much theoretical reasoning involves psychological states that are not beliefs.

To sum up: The beliefs invoked by belief-desire psychology are part of a philosophers' ontology, and they are picked out by the role they are given in philosophers' theories of mind. But, it turns out, the two families of theory competing to specify that role both presuppose bivalence, and so attitudes toward partial truth don't fit into either version of the role. If to believe something is to take it to be true, then if I say that it's not really true that the Stella is a painting, I should also say that I don't really believe it. If I announce that it's only somewhat true that the cloud is shaped like a horse's head, then I believe it only somewhat. And while I may use it as a premise in my reasoning, I certainly don't believe that cows are spherical at all. If it is true that, as I have been arguing, claims like these nonetheless get deployed in inference (that is, that deploying claims like these must frequently *count* as inference), my theoretical reasoning must include psychological states other than belief.

6.3

Truth is often said to be the formal object of belief: it is that at which beliefs aim. If one had an independent characterization of belief, one could define truth as that at which belief is directed. The independent characterization to be used as a starting point would tell you what you need to *do* with belief, and *that* would tell you why truth has (and has to have) the features it does.

Partial truth is the formal object of the states of mind that make up the sort of reasoning for which I have been arguing: it is that at which those mental states aim. More carefully, since utterances, inscriptions, and thoughts in the assertoric mood do not themselves literally aim at anything, partial truth is the not-fully-articulated standard, or family of standards, to which we hold them in such reasoning. We said that when a thought is acknowledged to be partially true, and is nevertheless being used in inference, there is a recognized mismatch between representation and world—but not in any way that requires changing the representations. However, if the mismatch is *too great*, along one dimension of assessment or another, we *will* change the representation. Advancing a claim as *fully* true demands *complete* fit; assessing a claim as *partially* true allows for slack...but *only so much* of it. The requirement that one adjust or discard the representation once it is *too* far out of line is what underwrites using truth vocabulary to (sometimes) register (some of) one's inferential caveats.[8]

Now that we have officially introduced partial truth, we also have an argument for a claim I have had in play for while now, that there are indefinitely many qualitatively different varieties of partial truth. We introduced the partial-truth attitudes as inferentially restricted: one does not conjoin their objects with the other premises used in a problem of such and such a type, or in a problem of such and such a different type... Moreover, as we have already observed, they are correctable in the face of mismatches, but only when the mismatch is egregious, or not merely in matters of detail, or is a technical mismatch, or an official mismatch, or a mismatch in some other designated respect... Now, the lists I just started are obviously of indefinite length. There are always further ways one could want to hedge on what further inferences one is instructing oneself or others to draw; there are always further ways to hedge on how one's representation can be out of line with the facts without calling for correction.[9] Consequently, there is no point in trying to accommodate the position I have been developing by adding on a shorter or longer list of extra truth values, and going on as before.

We now have the explanation for what looked like a missing vocabulary as well. We have one word, 'belief,' to tag a mental stand on full truth, but we don't seem to have a single term for the analogous attitude toward partial truth. That is as it should be, and thus not an objection to my account: there are indefinitely many such attitudes, often deeply qualitatively different, because there are, once again, indefinitely many ways, themselves deeply different, to hedge on one's inferential instructions, and to allow slack in correcting representations. When the category as a whole is so heterogenous, and when a list of its members is not definite enough to be completed, naming them is a thankless task.[10] And it is not just assigning names. Philosophers have assumed without much argument that analyzing belief was a worthwhile enterprise, and maybe it was; but we shouldn't make the analogous assumption about the mental alternatives to belief that partial truth requires. Because there are indefinitely many of them, the task of analysis would be inexhaustible; so we need a special reason to embark on working up a philosophical treatment of one or the other of them.

If beliefs function as crisp standards, and if we are hedging our inferential standards in ways that make them less than crisp, then there are far fewer beliefs than one might have thought. And there must be fewer yet than the focus on partial truth suggests. After all, even propositional contents that don't contain qualifications represented by phrases like 'sort of,' 'kind of,' and so on have fuzzy edges to them. Because not just vagueness, but what Waismann called 'open texture,' is pervasive, won't I be driven past the conclusion that theoretical reasoning consists not only of beliefs, but also of other, related attitudes, to the more extreme conclusion that it consists almost solely of those other attitudes, and that beliefs are scarcely part of the picture at all? And isn't that, well, hard to believe?

Not if belief is the philosophers' notion we have been considering. It's a paucity of beliefs in the ordinary-Joe sense that would be hard to believe. What the objection points out is that, on an understanding of propositions that makes them, by stipulation, bivalent, a lot of would-be beliefs don't have propositions as their objects. But if beliefs are, as the philosophers would have it, propositional attitudes, then many would-be beliefs, aren't.

Let's consider another objection, in order to raise the question of just what sort of definition we are considering here. Our official account of partial truth is that it is the formal object of the mental states deployed in partial-truth inference; that is not the sort of definition that philosophers nowadays are used to, not least because there seem to be counterexamples (or any-way halfway-counterexamples).[11] Going back once more to the example of the spherical cow, reasoning from the premise that the cow is a sphere of homogenous matter is of a piece with other partial-truth inference, as we have been explaining it, but we are, most of us, disinclined to say that the claim is partially true.

Definitions have been understood as tokens to be used in inference conducted under the bivalence and validity as truth preservation doctrines; accordingly, for a long time now, both the philosophers' definitions, and the standards to which philosophers have held them, have been tailored to the demands of bivalence-based inference. However, because the domain in which the argument of this book is conducted is, for the most part, not reengineered for bivalence, the argument is largely a series of moves from claims advanced as true enough to further claims advanced as in turn true enough. A definition meant to figure in such an argument can itself be expected to come out only true enough.

There is some precedent in past practice; the expectation that definitions preclude defeasibility in the inferences they launch is not uniform. For example, Aristotelian definitions often traced out essences. Nowadays, an essential property is understood to be a property that its possessor could not fail to have. (If the property were lost, the object would no longer exist, or would perhaps no longer be that kind of thing. Being the child of your actual parents is often held up as an example of an essential property in this sense; the idea is that if someone as similar to you as you like had been born of different parents, that person would not have been *you*.) But in the Aristotelian way of thinking, an essential property can go lacking: rationality is part of the essence of humanity, but many human beings are nonetheless irrational.[12]

Because there are indefinitely many ways to hedge on the defeasibility conditions of one's partial-truth inferences, indefinitely many inferential restrictions we can impose under the heading of partial truth, and indefinitely many ways to relax our fit requirements, partial truth is variegated and heterogenous. (I will provide an extended and formally accented illustration of this point in Chapter 7.) Briefly, it is messy, in just the ways that we have already argued make the use of partially true characterizations almost inevitable, and that is why its definition looks as it does.

6.4

Over the course of the exposition, we have put on our to-do list several variants of what is at bottom a single complaint. It is now time to address it, and I will begin by reviewing the accumulated versions of the objection. Then, because the ensuing counterargument will be a frankly clunky argument by cases, I will briefly explain its point up front. After I am done, I will recap by returning to the analogy of academic grades with semantic values like *true, false,* and *pretty much true.*

Let 'sort of' represent an item in the indefinitely long list of qualifiers that I've been claiming we use to hedge our commitment to the truth of some assertion. (Call them 'sort-of qualifiers.') The complaint is that there isn't really any difference between sort of believing that *p*, and believing that '*p*, sort of.' If I sort of believe that the cloud is shaped like a horse's head, then I believe that the cloud is sort of shaped like a horse's head.[13] To believe is, as before, to take to be true, so what is figuring into my inferences is the claim, advanced as entirely true, that '*p*, sort of.'

We saw another variant of the objection, in section 2.3, that full truth is easy to come by if only you are willing to loosen up your claims a little bit. There are many ways to do this: here, by importing the sort-of qualifier into the belief, and burying it in the belief's content.

Another version of the objection has it that '*p*, sort of,' is a misleadingly awkward way of expressing the content of the proposition that I really believe. A proposition is an abstract object that stipulates a set of truth conditions; these truth conditions are either satisfied or not. (One such way of talking about propositions, which we will see more of in Chapter 11, identifies them with partitions of the set of all possible worlds.) The surface of the sentence expressing the proposition, and so the presence of sort-of qualifiers, is irrelevant. In principle, if necessary by introducing new vocabulary for that very purpose, the proposition could be expressed without sort-of qualifiers at all. And this means that although I may not have an elegant or graceful way of saying what proposition it is that I fully believe, what I believe is fully and not partially true.

All of these variants on the objection share the following thought: that where I claim we are deploying a partial truth, it is possible to locate a full truth on the premises. Bear in mind, before we proceed to meet this concern head-on, that we already have two piecemeal responses on our plate: first, that some variants of the objection fail to preserve the content of the partial-truth claim, and thus substitute an inferentially irrelevant claim for the one that was needed; and second, that one of the points deflationists make about the uses of full truth applies to partial truth as well: namely, that while truth is often dispensable in single cases, where one is able to state the allegedly true claim oneself, truth vocabulary is required when one is affirming classes of claims, or claims whose contents one does not oneself know.[14]

Truth is the formal object of belief, and partial truth is the formal object of the attitudes that figure into partial-truth inference. To figure out what semantic assessments need to be in play in the trains of thought we're considering (and, in particular, whether they can be restricted to just plain *true* and *false*), we can ask whether the reasoning can be recast as moving from belief to belief. Beliefs, once again, are part of a philosophers' ontology, and their defining features are their direction of fit and their inferential or functional role. So the question we are considering is whether psychological states in such trains of thought can be gotten to *behave* like beliefs.

Full 'mind-to-world' direction of fit means that the facts serve as a standard guiding crisp correction of a putative belief. We saw in the previous chapters that the inferential functionality of full belief consists in, *inter alia*, clean matches that trigger deductive (as opposed to defeasible) inference: a would-be belief that is unable to serve as an inferential match for other beliefs is not playing the functional or inferential role of a belief. The family of objections we are considering proposes a range of substitutes for partial truths. Will the psychological states that represent them behave as beliefs?

Let's begin with direction of fit. The milder version of the objection was that when *p* is sort of true, '*p*, sort of' is fully true. Now full-fledged word-to-world direction of fit means that (a relevant aspect or part of) the world serves as a standard for the representation: if I notice that the world is other than the representation has it, I am to change the representation. Having a standard to apply means that its user can *apply* it as a standard: that it is clear when the standard is met.[15] Once I hedge the claim that *p* with a sort-of qualifier, I am assuming greater (usually, significantly greater) responsibility for determining when correction is warranted; the standard is no longer crisp. But if we grant that the 'sort of' used to hedge assent to the original representation preempts crisp application of the standard, we have to grant that a standard whose threshold of success is that '*p*, sort of' places the very same responsibility on the shoulders of the user.

Perhaps there is a representation, call it *s*, that is available in principle, and that expresses precisely the proposition picked out by '*p*, sort of' without using any sort-of qualifiers. But then we have no reason to suppose that *s* is framed in the same terms or concepts as the initial '*p*, sort of' representations. There are, after all, often large conceptual shifts in removing an unqualified rendering; think of the sciences and their Kuhnian revolutions. And if that is the case, we have no reason to suppose that the user of the initial representations is equipped to recognize the (crisply delineated) mismatch between *s* and the way the world is. So the in-principle-possible alternative representation does not enable crisp correction, but rather, in what is probably the usual case, completely disables it.

Briefly, converting claims advanced as partially true into putatively fully true ones, by building sort-of qualifiers into the content of the claim, does not produce the object of a psychological state that behaves like a belief, as far as direction of fit goes. And notice that this point applies to the most aggressive version of the objection as well, on which what we can do with our representational stand-ins for a proposition is irrelevant to whether the proposition *itself*—the bivalent-by-stipulation abstract object—is true or false. (I will return to the stance adopted by the aggressive version of the objection in the recap, below.)

Turning now to inferential role: as we saw in Chapter 4, my represen-tations must repeat, if I am to think with them; when I am constructing arguments, I must be able to match claims with parts of other claims, if I am successfully to traverse the arguments. The function of partial truth and sort-of qualifiers is to tag forced matches. The objection to partial truth had it that my representations can incorporate the qualifiers that I have argued are marks of forcing. To reproduce the inferential behavior of beliefs, such representations must repeat, and the matches go through, without forcing, and so the substitutes envisaged by this family of objections must enable clean, deductive matches.

There are two sorts of cases to consider. First, it might be thought that if I believe that 'p, sort of,' and I also believe that 'if p, sort of, then q,' I have a match: the qualified belief that p matches the qualified antecedent of the conditional. (Call this the *direct* case.) Second (this is a more complicated inference pattern, but one we must often enough allow ourselves), if I believe that 'p, sort of,' and I believe that 'if p then q,' and finally, I also believe that in cases of this kind it is permissible to conclude that q, then my inference can proceed unobstructed. (Call this the *mediated* case.) So perhaps I believe that this is sort of a path, which matches the appropriate part of my belief that, if this is sort of a path, I can follow it out of the forest. Or perhaps I believe that when it comes to paths in Point Reyes, I can match 'sort of a path' (in the minor premise) to the 'path' in the conditional. (If I don't believe that I can, then surely I had better not!) In either case, forced matches are unnecessary. If forced matches are unnecessary, then the practical argument for the legitimacy of forcing matches does not go through. And if that is correct, then there is no reason to insist on partial truth, and so bivalence suffices, and so metaphysics that presupposes bivalence is fine as it stands. Thus the objection.

Let's begin with the direct case. *Sometimes* a 'sort of' does match another 'sort of.' Recall the intern in the museum basement, sending anything that is a painting, or anyhow, sort of a painting, off to the East Wing. An art critic wandering around the East Wing might come to believe that everything there is a painting, or anyhow, sort of a painting, and might quite correctly use his belief in his inferences: asked by another museumgoer whether the Calders are in this wing, he might reason that they're not paintings, or even sort of paintings, so they must be somewhere else. When he does this, his representation both contains a qualifier, and here, at least, functions inferentially as a belief.

But often enough one sort-of qualifier does *not* match another: after all, there are indefinitely many qualitatively different variations on partial truth. Remember the cow of which I had occasion to say that it was approximately spherical. Now I might have a rule lying around to the effect that if something is approximately spherical, it rolls. But suppose I am trying to solve the problem of escaping from the cow who is now chasing me around the field. Suppose I believe that things don't roll uphill. And suppose I were to conclude that I could escape by heading uphill. If I did, I would be making a mistake, because here I don't have a real match between the premises. In the one case, the force of 'approximately' is that this is the right approximation to use in solving a toy physics problem. In the other case, the force of 'approximately' is (let's say): spherical, but with a few dents.

The example is crude, and most actual mismatches of this kind will be somewhat more subtle, but the point holds in the more subtle cases also; when it comes to the kind of qualifiers we are considering, surface similarity is not much of an indicator of an inferential match. To reiterate, representations have to repeat if thought is to be possible, but that repetition is not a matter of the physical or phenomenological shapes, as it were, of the representations—even when it is the shapes that give our recognitional capacities a handle on the connections between them. Repetition is a matter of inferential usability, and the recurring shape of a '*p*, sort of' may not (and mostly, I think, will not) signal what is for the purposes of inference a repeating representation.

There are two main ways of handling this practical problem. One is to gloss the force of the 'sort of' explicitly, in something like the way I did a paragraph back, only more so. (In Chapter 7, I will survey a handful of formal techniques for doing this in special cases.) If we do this, we will occasionally recover robust matching, but at the cost of overly detailed and collectively unmanageable representations, and only on rare occasions: the more idiosyncratic detail I build into one belief, the less likely it is that I will have other beliefs that are good inferential matches. The second is to register, along with the primary premises of your inference, the fact that matching in such a case is permissible. E.g., the art critic might think to himself that the 'sort of' in his judgment about the Calders really does come to the same thing as the 'sort of' in his generalization about the contents of the East Wing.

Now this latter device moves us from the direct case to the mediated case, in which the use of additional bridging premises tells you that in the inference at hand you can match the primary premises. In our earlier examples, such bridging premises might have been: that it's safe to rely, for purposes of picking someone out of a crowd, on the distinctive features of a well-known actor, as long as there's *some* resemblance; that treating objects as spheres or point masses is acceptable for the purposes of calculating the gravitational forces between them, if they are not too distended; that for purposes of display, rather than conservation or transportation, the way a work of art has to be read is more important than its shape.

When we consider the mediated case, we find that bridging premises tend to fall into three categories. First, they may be instance-specific judgments, to the effect that the inference will go through. ('This time, it's safe to treat the cow as a sphere.') Second, they may be general but still fully true claims about when it is pragmatically permissible to use premises of this kind. ('When such-and-such conditions are satisfied, then, for every ϵ, there is a Δ...') And third, they may be general, untrue but usable claims to the same effect.

So, first, if all you have is the instance-specific judgment, it would be an overstatement to call it a further *premise* (if by that you mean something that captures an independent reason for proceeding). John Searle once pointed out[16] that in assembling a practical syllogism (with the premises, say, that I want to get to the party, and that riding with so-and-so will get me to the party, and the intended conclusion that I should ride with so-and-so), the conclusion only follows other things being equal, and that it would be a mistake to try to make the inference deductively tight by adding the further premise, 'Other things are equal.' That would be not a genuine assertion (*what* other things? equal to *what*?), but merely an expression of my sense that the conclusion is the right one to draw. The instance-specific bridging premises we are considering are much like that. Rather than assuming part of the inferential burden, which is what each of the interlocking premises in an inference properly do, they register how very much of the inferential burden still rests on the reasoner.

Second and third: I want to acknowledge that one does on occasion come across fully true bridging premises. But even when they are available in principle, they are likely to depend on powerful, technically sophisticated treatments of approximation techniques, and so are exotic in practice, and consequently too rare to matter. And even if there actually is an argument whose premises are true, no ifs, ands or buts, and whose conclusion is that it is all right to treat the cow as a sphere, freshmen are trained to choose the approximation without having or giving the argument—and so, without having to decide whether it is true, or merely another approximation. The proof would take more math than they have, and in any case, the semester is too short.

This means that while one is able to provide, every so often, a bridging premise to support the use of an acknowledgedly untrue premise in inference, that bridging premise is typically not flat true. Take, for example, the train of thought that led me to reread Williamson's book (section 4.6), one of whose premises was that if you haven't been paying attention to your reading, you won't be able to assess it: this is at any rate not entirely true, because there is a lot of reading for which inattention suffices. (Sometimes the fact that you found it hard to pay attention tells you all you need to know.) Or again, take the bridging premise which we can imagine supported my telling Jill that Jack would be the one looking like Malkovich: that when it comes to picking someone out of a crowd, close to the face of a well-known actor is good enough. This is only more or less true; there are actors of whom it does not hold (though not coincidentally it's difficult to think of examples offhand). In both of these cases, it's hard to come up with fully true substitutes for these premises: reading matter, and faces, are just too variable. But if most of the bridging premises invoked by the objection fall into the third category, and are themselves not fully true, then the objection requires further bridging premises to make the application of the partially true bridging premise possible: we are embarked on a regress.

As before, we can allow that there is a representation, call it s, available in principle, which expresses precisely the proposition picked out by 'p, sort of' without using any sort-of qualifiers. As before, the large conceptual shifts often involved in removing an unqualified rendering mean that we have no reason to think that s is framed in the same terms or concepts as the initial 'p, sort of' representations. So we have no reason to think that the user of the initial representations is equipped to recognize matches between s and representations couched in terms of the vocabulary and conceptual repertoire that required the sort-of qualifiers in the first place. So the in-principle-possible alternative representation does not enable crisp matches, but rather, in what I expect is the usual case, completely disables it.

Putative beliefs whose contents contain sort-of qualifiers often enough don't function as beliefs. Their contents can't be directly matched, because, for inferential purposes, the sort-of qualifiers they contain don't count as repetitions of each other; another way to say this is that from the point of view of one 'sort of' the other 'sort of' is only sort of true. The mediating premises that might be brought to bear for the most part just generate further instances of the same problem. Sort-of qualifiers imported into the contents of a claim can provide the appearance of inferential matching, but not the substance, and so putative beliefs into whose contents the sort-of qualifiers have been imported are unable to play the theoretical role of beliefs, and since beliefs just are occupiers of a theoretical role, that is just to say that they're not actually beliefs at all.

As before, the point as we have it holds for the most aggressive version of the objection, the one that insists that whether the proposition picked out by the hedged assertion behaves like a belief is irrelevant to whether it is true or false: a proposition that cannot be represented in a way that permits crisp responsiveness to failure of fit, or matching that allows for deductive rather than defeasible inference, does not figure as the *object* of belief. But we now need to take up the question of why that matters, and why it is not to the point to insist that, out in someone's Platonic heaven, the bivalent proposition is *there*.

I want to be concessive as regards what the objection we've been considering actually claims. I'm willing to allow that '*p*, sort of' expresses a proposition, and that such an abstract object is, by stipulation, entirely sharp-edged. I'm willing to grant that, however it is you think propositions are structured, a sort-of qualifier is not part of that structure (or mimicked by it). I'm happy to allow that there *could* be a way of representing such a proposition under which flat-out truth or falsity would be the right semantic values to assign to it.

All of that is, however, irrelevant to what semantic values we should assign to the claims we in fact advance, given the system of representations we have available to advance them, and the ways we have to hedge and qualify those claims so represented. Recall our analogy of semantic values with academic grades. Semantic values (such as *true, false, pretty much true*, and so on) are assessments used in inferential bookkeeping; consequently, we must make choices about what ranges of values to use that enable the bookkeeping to get done. *True* and *false* are appropriate and sufficient grades when the tokens being moved around in inference amount to beliefs: that is to say, when they *behave*, or can be gotten to behave, like beliefs. And I've argued that in the type of inference we're considering, they can't.

To respond by insisting that there *are* fully true or fully false propositions behind the scenes is on a par with a student who has received a C+ complaining that he couldn't have gotten such a grade, because under *his* preferred grading scale, he would have gotten an A. Those of us who are in the business of handing out grades have all heard such complaints: that if the student had taken the course pass/fail, the C+ would have been a pass;

that by the grading standards of some other, less demanding course, the exam would earn an A. (I must admit that no student of mine has appealed to a Platonic realm of abstract objects in which a less muddy version of a paper resides, one which is worthy of an A; but that's only because the students haven't yet heard of epistemicism.) Such complaints are irrelevant, given that the course in question *does* have such and such grading standards, given that the course *is* being taken for a letter grade, and so on. If there are good practical reasons to use the semantic values that are being used, it does not matter that there are other imaginable systems of assessment: at any rate it does not matter once it has been argued (as it has in Chapters 4 and 5) that they are impossible to implement.

6.5

If knowledge is true belief with additional bells and whistles, and if many of the steps in our theoretical reasoning are not beliefs and do not purport to be true, then the concept of knowledge has relatively limited application within our investigations into how things stand. When you introduce into an inference the premise that the cow is a homogenous sphere of matter, the question of whether that is something you *know* simply does not come up. Nonetheless, some partial truths and approximations are inferentially appropriate, and others are not. So we need ways of distinguishing the good from the bad, and it is not just that 'knows' will not do: whatever are plausibly the ingredients or components of knowledge will not do, either. Think of how you would justify your use of the premise that the cow is a sphere, and how different that justification will look from one you might produce for a claim you were advancing as fully true: say, that the cow will shortly be herded off the hillside for the winter.

Game theory can make a suggestive model for epistemology. One thing that game theorists do is look for successful strategies; in this discipline, games are problems for which you try to find solutions. But another thing that game theorists do is look for solution concepts, that is, for conceptions of what success, or a solution, would be. The most famous solution concept is probably Nash equilibrium, but the literature contains, I am told, on the order of 150 of them. There's an ongoing and lively debate about these in the field, in the course of which new solution concepts get proposed, criticized, tried out, emended, and so forth.

Epistemology's etymology proclaims it to be the theory of knowledge. Knowledge is a success concept for theoretical reasoning, but it is taken far too much for granted, and for the most part is treated as though it were the only possible success concept. Epistemology has been preoccupied for far too long with trundling out one analysis of knowledge after another, where it should instead be devoting at least as much time as the game theorists do to coming up with new success concepts.[17] It is, after all, a bad idea to get stuck on the first concept you think of, because, as Chapter 5 has reminded us, our initially chosen representations are mostly just stabs in the dark.

One could treat the various analyses of knowledge that have been proposed not as competing attempts to analyze a single success concept, but as themselves alternative success concepts, suitable for different sorts of application. However, while it is a very interesting question what circumstances would call for, respectively, justified true belief, counterfactual-based tracking, Bayesian tracking, etc., these already available benchmarks are not suitable for assessing avowedly partial truths.[18]

If one task for epistemologists is to come up with new success concepts, another is to say how to go about satisfying them. We should not assume that the correct order of investigation is to arrive first at the precisely rendered success concept. Epistemologists as a group behave as though you had to concoct the right set of necessary and sufficient conditions for counting as knowledge before getting on to ask how easy the success concept is to apply, and how often it *will* apply—how *useful* the concept will be. On the contrary, we've been claiming that you should only expect to be able to tighten up the concepts and names you're working with after many passes over the inferences in which it is involved, during which you figure out what's going to be useful, and what isn't.[19]

Triangles are easy to study; you can prove many and elegant things about them. Unfortunately, the real world doesn't contain any triangles, and there isn't much you can prove about the thick, jagged, and crooked near-triangles it does contain. So the right strategy has two phases: first, study the triangles (if you were Plato, you would tell people first to study 'Forms' or 'Ideas'); then see how you can adapt those results to the close-enough objects in the actual world.

Plato said that the close-enough objects 'participate' in the Forms: this was a promissory note to be redeemed by the second phase of the research project, a phase that was never successfully implemented. If you can only have full-fledged knowledge of Forms, Plato seems to have concluded that you should concentrate your intellectual efforts on them, and not bother with the real world. But this was a mistake. If knowledge is possible, for the most part, only of the Forms, and not of the real world, this shows not that one should abandon the real world, but that knowledge is overrated.

Part III

The Competition

7

Logics of Vagueness

I began by suggesting that the bivalence doctrine has been taken for granted by most analytic philosophers, and that allowing partial truth on board will require rejecting the older model of rationality, on which deductive inference provides our central and paradigmatic form of it. In doing so, I put aside two closely related objections. The first is that I have unfairly mischaracterized at least the last couple of decades of analytic philosophy, during which work on vagueness has become a recognized subspecialty with an extensive literature.[1] The second is that almost all of that work has extended the older model, rather than displacing it with a deeply different approach; that is, much of the subspeciality has been focused on constructing formal treatments of vagueness (for convenience, I'll call these *logics of vagueness*) that are recognizably continuous with the traditional bivalence-driven deductive logic. That is (the objection runs), we are already well on the way to a unified formal treatment of what I have been calling partial truth (or as much of it as is reasonable), and while some of the theories do drop bivalence, they do not involve the sort of radical departure from the tradition that I take that to involve, and which I have been recommending.

I will begin by surveying three representative formal approaches to vagueness. (Just three: to keep the discussion manageable, we have to pick and choose.) I'm aware that this is the stretch where I'm most likely to lose readers, and if you happen to be one of them, you'll be able to pick up the thread again in section 7.4. That said, I will do my absolute best to give an accessible presentation.

Then I will argue for three modest but important points. First, once the formal treatments are put side by side, it becomes evident that even vagueness is not an homogenous phenomenon: the various logics of vagueness model different sorts of subject matter. This observation will allow me to respond a second time to an objection we encountered earlier on, that partial truth is really too many different things to constitute a theoretically unified and interesting category.

Second, since different logics of vagueness model different subject matters, it is unsurprising that the different logics of vagueness are suitable for different uses. My discussion of that point will provide a response to another objection we have had pending for a while, to the effect that sensitivity to context can be used to preserve bivalence, and so forestall the need for partial truth. Since one of the logics of vagueness we will consider models context-sensitivity, we will be able to ask *when* it is usable.

Third and finally, I am going to argue that logics of vagueness reproduce the dilemma which has framed our discussion throughout: that, normally, you can either pay the costs of reengineering the domain of application to match the formal model you intend to use, or you can, as you reason, compensate for the imperfect fit of your model to the domain. You should not expect a free lunch, and replacing bivalence-driven classical logic with alternative logics of vagueness is not a path between the horns of the dilemma, or a way of avoiding that choice.

7.1

Sorites arguments consider cases like this one: if you pull just one hair from the head of a man who isn't bald, that won't push him over the line, and that's true no matter how many hairs he has. If you keep on pulling hairs out, one by one, and repeating the argument that just one hair won't make the difference, you end up, paradoxically, with someone who has no hair at all, but who, according to the repeated argument, isn't bald. The name of the game in vagueness is to provide something to say about the sorites paradox (defaultly but not necessarily, an explanation of why sorites arguments aren't after all sound and valid), and because theories of vagueness get constructed with solutions to the sorites as their finish line, it is easy to get the impression that the tail—the quirky paradox—is wagging the theoretical dog.[2]

I will elsewhere take up the question of what motivates the apparently obsessive preoccupation with the paradox, and whether that philosophical motivation can be coherently sustained. Right now, we just need to sort out some of the labels. Because the vagueness literature is focused on the sorites paradox, it tends to contrast clear cases and full truth with fuzzy boundaries and properties that fade out (in something like the way that baldness fades in as you remove hairs, or being a heap fades out as you remove grains of sand). As we've already seen, much partial truth doesn't have anything like this look and feel; as should be by now apparent, the position this book has been working up does not take the sorites paradox as a point of reference. I'm going to allocate the terms 'vague' and 'vagueness' to the phenomenon discussed by the sorites-preoccupied literature.[3] I'll continue to use 'partial truth' as my more inclusive generic contrast to full truth. On this way of talking, vagueness is one type—or rather, as we'll presently see, several types—of partial truth; not all partial truth is vagueness.

Let's take up our first representative of formal work on vagueness. A sorites argument's natural home is a domain with the structure of a spectrum: colors that edge imperceptibly over into other colors, or predicates like 'bald' or 'heap,' which occupy a stretch within a series, but a stretch without clear termination points (e.g., a maximal number of hairs on a head, or a minimal number of grains of sand). So the first approach is to treat partial truth as a matter of degree, and the semantics for these formal systems usually use the closed segment [0,1] as a model of the spectrum: the color can be 0.7364 red, the head 0.341 bald, the collection of grains of sand 0.982 a heap.[4]

Within the approach, substantive details vary, and in order to have a concrete example on the table, I'll describe Dorothy Edgington's reinterpretation of the probability calculus; this has the advantage of deploying an elegant and already debugged formalism. Her term for the degree of truth of a proposition is 'verity,' and with that substitution (for 'probability'), the rules are familiar:

1. $0 \leq v(A) \leq 1$ (where $v(A)$ is the verity of a proposition A)
2. $v(\text{not } A) = 1 - v(A)$
3. $v(A \text{ and } B) = v(A)v(B/A)$
   (unless $v(A) = 0$; then $v(A \text{ and } B) = 0$)
   (B/A means the verity of B on the hypothetical decision to count A as definitely true—as when it is unclear that a shade of near-pink is red, but *if* we are to count it as red, then we had better count a slightly redder shade as red also. This is 'conditional verity,' the analog of conditional probability.)
4. $v(A \text{ or } B) = v(A) + v(B) - v(A \text{ and } B)$

The rules are supplemented by a definition of validity: An argument is valid if and only if the unverity (1 minus the verity) of the conclusion must be smaller or equal to the sum of the unverities of the premises.[5]

Since in this business the finish line is a solution to the sorites paradox, let's use Edgington's as an illustration of what the machinery does. A sorites argument has something like this form:

1. A million grains of sand make up a heap.
2. If a million grains of sand make up a heap, then 999,999 grains of sand make up a heap.
3. 999,999 grains of sand make up a heap.
4. If 999,999 grains of sand make up a heap, then 999,998 grains of sand make up a heap.
5. 999,998 grains of sand make up a heap.
   $\vdots$
n. Zero grains of sand make up a heap.

On Edgington's account, each of the even-numbered premises has a verity extremely close to 1, but not quite 1. So each has a small positive unverity. Summing up a million or so of these small positive unverities gives you a number greater than 1. The conclusion is obviously just plain false, and so its unverity is 1. But the argument is valid, on her definition of validity, even though it has a false conclusion: validity is verity preserving, but we didn't have full verity—actual truth—in the premises. The argument to the sorites conclusion overlooks the tiny (but accumulating) departures from full truth at each step.[6]

7.2

A second sort of logic of vagueness takes '[v]agueness [as] ambiguity on a grand and systematic scale.'[7] We explain 'p is definitely true' (sometimes written Δp) by saying that p is true in all precisifications—all of the ways the language could be made completely precise. We explain 'p is indefinitely true' (sometimes written ∇p) by saying that p is true in some precisifications, but not all of them.

Take as an example a color, say, red; red bleeds away into orange, purple, and pink, and it's hard to draw principled borders around it, but a car is *definitely* red if it comes out red no matter where plausible borders are drawn. And it comes out indefinitely red if, on some plausible precise borders, it would count as red, and on others, it wouldn't. (In other words, complete precisifications are the analogs of possible worlds, in standard semantics for modal logics: a sentence is definitely true if it is true on all its complete precisifications, in the way that a sentence is necessarily true when it is true in all possible worlds.)

It's natural to think of precisifications as being put in place incrementally. For instance, we might start off with an imprecise determination of 'red,' one which settles that the paradigm cases, like sports cars, are red, but leave almost everything else up for grabs. At the next step (and there are of course different ways one can take such steps: formally, the precisifications are partially ordered), we perhaps settle that some of the more orangish items also count as red, and that some of the more purplish items don't, but leave the rest unassigned; at the limit, we put in place a precise delineation of the concept that counts everything up to exactly *these* shades as red, and everything beyond as not. In such stepwise precisifications, we add content, but we don't change content we already have. And in doing so, we preserve 'penumbral connections,' entailments that ought to hold even when the concepts and terms in play are vague; for instance, if one shade is less reddish than another, then if we designate the one shade as red, we have to designate the more reddish one as red also. (Recall that in Edgington's alternative treatment, this bit of functionality was implemented by conditional verities.)

As before, the official finish line is a solution to the sorites paradox, and let's modify our sample sorites argument to make it match our present example:

1. This sports car is red.
2. If this sports car is red, then this second sports car, which is *almost* the same shade (but slightly less red), is also red.
3. This second sports car is also red.
4. If this second sports car is red, then this third sports car, which is *almost* the same shade (but slightly less red), is also red.
5. This third sports car is also red.

$\vdots$

n. The blue sports car over here is red.

In each complete precisification of the concept 'red'—every way of drawing precise borders at precise shades—it has precise cutoff points. That means that (in each precisification) there's some shade of off-red such that the next shade over *doesn't* count as red. That in turn means that in each complete precisification, one of those even-numbered premises is false (though it's a *different* false premise in each precisification). No wonder the sorites argument has a false conclusion.[8]

Colors that fade out into other colors, heaps, and progressively balder men are examples which don't adequately exhibit the differences between the degree approach to vagueness and the precisificationist approach, and so let's briefly look at a less toy example, namely, precisificationism itself. There are many different ways to fill in the details of such a view. Trivially, but it's useful to know this, the precisifications can be called many different things (including 'sharpening,' 'specification,' 'extension,' 'regimentation,' 'interpretation,' and 'refinement').[9] Another such choice: where we introduced 'definitely' as meaning, 'true in all complete precisifications,' the more standard ('supervaluationist') precisification of precisificationism uses *true*: it's true (or 'super-true') if it's true in all complete precisifications.[10] Yet another choice is between alternative validity concepts: An argument can be valid when, if the premises are true per the supervaluationist ('super-true,' i.e., definitely true according to other versions of the view), the conclusion is definitely true (i.e., 'super-true'). Or an argument can be counted as valid if, in any precisification in which the premises are true, the conclusion is true.[11]

The plethora of possible precisificationist theories doesn't have anything like the structure of a spectrum, and so the example shows how precisificationism handles cases for which degree theories are an awkward fit (e.g., by giving us a way of considering what's definitely true of precisificationism, and what isn't). Spectrum and precisificationist theories evidently have different if overlapping natural homes. Vagueness about color is well handled by both; underspecified theories of vagueness are at best an awkward fit for spectrum theories, but a much better fit for precisificationist theories.

7.3

The last of our representative treatments of vagueness differs from the two we have seen in that it attempts to model the dynamics of a conversation.[12]

Think of conversations as having scores, abstract objects that figure in the management of a conversation in something like the way that the score of a baseball game (including not just total runs, but a count of innings, strikes, etc.) is deployed, e.g., to determine when it's time to switch off at the plate, when a batter gets walked, when the batter is out, and so on. One component of a conversational score would normally be used to manage vagueness, and David Lewis, who originated the proposal, seems to have thought of it as a standard (or list of standards) of precision. For instance, if I insist on the vague statement that France is hexagonal, I am tacitly adjusting the standards of precision for our conversation, making them low enough, if I get away with it, for my utterance count as true (flat out true, simply true); you are then entitled to assert that Italy is boot-shaped, which will count as true (flat out true, simply true) by the same standards of precision.

Lewis offered in passing what amounted to a treatment of sorites arguments, the idea being that, unlike baseball games, conversations are cooperative endeavors, and so are subject to a 'rule of accommodation': if a small adjustment in the score is required by a move my conversation partner has made, then the score is thereby adjusted. So when we march down a sorites sequence, the standards (for flatness, or baldness, etc.) gradually get higher and higher (or lower and lower). And counterintuitive though it may seem, that is entirely legitimate. But once we leave that particular conversation, the standards as it were snap back to their default settings; you can 'create a context in which [a sorites conclusion] is true, but that does not show that there is anything whatever wrong with…claims that we make in more ordinary contexts. It is no fault in a contex that we can move out of it.' That is, Lewis's 'solution' to the sorites paradox is that one does end up drawing the paradoxical conclusion, but only temporarily, so no real damage is done.[13]

As one of a series of rapid-fire illustrations of conversational score-keeping, Lewis's discussion of vagueness failed to spell out his suggestion that a conversational score might contain a component that sets standards of precision. But Stewart Shapiro has since then worked up a candidate vagueness-management component of such a score.[14] Shapiro's idea is to adapt precisificationist model theory to that role, and to explain how he does this, I'm going to simplify it a bit. (So what you're about to get is a stand-in for his proposal, but one which will be easier to follow, and which will give you the idea.)

Think of a *tree* as a structure like that in Figure 1. v_1 is its *root* or, in these discussions, its *base*. v_1 is connected to further *nodes* v_2, v_3…below

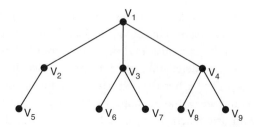

Figure 1 Trees can be used to represent stepwise precisifications of a language. V_1 represents the vague natural language. V_2, V_3, and V_4 represent alternative partial precisifications of V_1. V_5–V_9 are alternative fully sharp precisifications

it (v_1's *children*); these in turn are connected to further nodes below them; the nodes with no further children are the tree's *leaves*. (Yes, the tree is upside-down; sorry, that's the convention.) Trees capture a pattern that we encounter frequently in everyday life. For instance, a tree might be used to represent the structure of this book: the book as a whole being represented by the root of the tree, the chapters by the next layer of nodes down, and the book's sections, by the leaves.[15]

In the precisificationist model of vagueness we encountered in section 7.2, a vague natural language is at the base of the tree; its children are alternative incremental further specifications; the leaves, at the very bottom of the tree, are fully precise versions of the language. (Once again, this is a simplified special case.) On the precisificationist way of thinking, a claim in that language is definitely true if, standing at the base of the tree and looking down at its leaves, you can see the claim to be true in all of them.

Since the point of Shapiro's appropriation of precisificationism is to track vagueness-related adjustments in the conversational score, think of stages of the conversation as being tied to locations in the precisification tree. As the conversation progresses, we move from node to node. At any node, we will assess sentences by whether they come out true in the subtree below our present location.

Two more bits of machinery, and then we're done. Recall that in the logics of vagueness we've already surveyed, penumbral connections and conditional verities were ways of keeping track of conceptual constraints that our vague claims and thoughts have to honor. (In supervaluationist model theory, penumbral connections are preserved as we sharpen up the language.) Now, Shapiro thinks, the very phenomenon that gives rise to sorites arguments—that if you apply a sorites-inducing predicate to one of

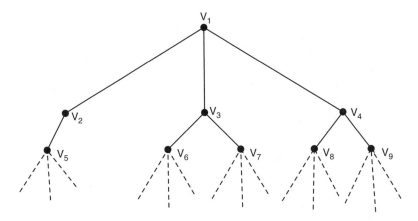

Figure 2 Tolerance means that precisification trees get sharper and sharper, without ever reaching a completely sharp bottom

two sufficiently similar neighbors, you can't refuse to apply it to the other— is itself such a penumbral connection. (Call it 'tolerance.') This means that a tree that represents the progressive sharpening of a vague language cannot have completely sharp leaves; a fully sharp precisification would violate tolerance, by saying of two extremely similar cases that, say, 'red' applied to one of them, but not to the other. So the trees that we're using as our stripped-down stand-in for Shapiro's model typically have no bottom: they get more and more precise, but without ever getting fully precise. (See Figure 2.)

Because precisificationists relied on those completely precise leaves, that entails appropriately changing the method of semantic assessment. A sentence comes out *forced* at a particular node of the tree when, for every node below it, there is a further precisification (i.e., a node lower down in the latter's node's subtree) which is precise enough to make the sentence come out true, and does so. That means that you count a claim as true if, looking down from your current position in the precisification tree, you see that, whichever way you sharpen up the claim, it will eventually get sharpened up enough to make it true. (See Figure 3.)

As before, the finish line is a solution to the sorites paradox, and here Shapiro replaces Lewis's with an idea of Diana Raffman's.[16] Changes in the vagueness-management component of a conversational score amount to changing the conversation's current location in the precisification tree.

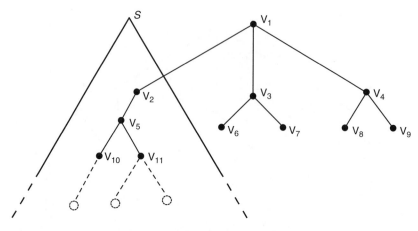

Figure 3 A sentence p is forced at V_2 if any path downward through its subtree S will eventually sharpen p up in a way that makes p true

Normally, a conversation will traverse the precisification tree incrementally, via the step-by-step accommodation-driven adjustments envisaged by Lewis. Sometimes, however, as a matter of brute psychological fact, subjects will not accept one more step down a sorites sequence, and when they do not, tolerance requires that their new judgment back-propagate. That is, when the subject finds himself unable to agree that, say, this next, slightly hairier person is bald, he retracts his judgment that the previous individual in the sorites sequence is bald as well, and so on an indefinite number of steps back up the line. (So, unlike Lewis's 'solution,' you never get all the way down to the absurd end of a sorites series.) In Shapiro's rendering of the conversational score, this is jumping to a new location in the precisification tree; neither the point from which the jump is made nor the new location in the precisification tree will generally be precisely predictable from earlier stages of the conversational score.

Spectrum-based, precisificationist, and conversational score theories of vagueness are not the only approaches. Others construe vagueness as involving truth-value gaps or a finite number of additional truth values.[17] In addition, my own opinion is that there is not much weight to be put on the distinction between 'how true is it?' and 'how far from the truth is it?'; so I regard discussions of 'truthlikeness' or 'verisimilitude' as further alternative formal approaches.[18] The claims I'm about to make extend, suitably adjusted, to these alternatives; but it's time to consider what to make of the fact that there *is* this range of alternatives.

7.4

One of the hallmarks of work on vagueness is the notion that a treatment should be general and uniform: vagueness is *one* kind of thing. I have presented partial truth as heterogenous, and including approximations, idealizations, vagueness, representations that are—a bivalentist will want to say—useful although false, and much else besides.[19] It's time to take up an objection we encountered in section 3.4: the many forms of partial truth behave differently; why think of all of them as one sort of thing?

If the point of the objection is that we do not need a theory of partial truth (because it is not one kind of thing), but we do need a theory of vagueness (which is), and that that's the closest we're going to get to what I'm looking for, then the objection is not well motivated. Even our abbreviated survey of logics of vagueness makes it clear that vagueness itself is not one kind of thing. Spectrum-based treatments work well on domains structured like spectra, and not, I suggested, on domains (such as precisificationist theories of vagueness) that are not. Over the remainder of the chapter I will work at showing how precisificationist techniques work best on domains that map cleanly onto its model theory, and how using conversational scorekeeping to manage vagueness is a good way of running *some* kinds of conversations.

The natural homes of these techniques overlap but are not identical. Rather, you should expect that, for just about any such representational device, there are probably phenomena that fit it closely, or anyway, that can be brought to fit it decently with a sufficient outlay of resources. But there are equally phenomena that—just because they fit some *other* representational device closely—fit this one badly.[20]

The variety of treatments indicates that even vagueness is indefinitely many substantively different sorts of thing: that the heterogeneity of partial truth reappears in microcosm as the heterogeneity of this particular subtype of it. But if vagueness is itself varied in this way—if what turn out to be substantively different phenomena are usefully thought about under that one heading—then we should not balk at the suggestion that, substantive differences among them notwithstanding, the various phenomena that I've been classifying as partial truth are usefully thought about together.

7.5

I have been claiming that we normally face the following choice: to pay the costs of reengineering a domain to permit deductive reasoning about it, or to be willing to reason with thoughts that we take to be inaccurate, and only partially or somewhat true. Logics of vagueness might seem to provide a third option, that of nonclassical but nondefeasible inference about unengineered domains. We may need to surrender bivalence, but if we are willing to give up the letter of the validity as truth preservation doctrine, we can sidestep the engineering (and its associated costs) while nonetheless retaining the spirit that animated classical logic.

Against this, I am going to argue that, even if logics of vagueness give us alternatives to bivalence, they will not generally allow us to sidestep the choice between approximation and engineering. The engineering they require will typically end up costing *more* than the engineering needed to produce bivalence. Consequently, these methods will be *less* frequently usable than the standard two-valued logic.

To use the real numbers between zero and one as a model for partial truth, you need a domain that has near enough that structure, and you need enough of a handle on coordinating those numbers with items in the domain for the exercise of reasoning with them to be more than make-believe. The requirement is not that you need the impossible precision suggested by the real numbers; nonetheless, unless there is a pretty good fit—a fit you can make out in your application—you are not really using the logic, but just going through the motions.

There *are* domains that satisfy these conditions, and color, which is not by coincidence a favorite in discussions of vagueness, happens to be one of them. It is not just that orange comes somewhere on the spectrum between red and yellow; we can sensibly talk about a reddish orange being around 0.79 red. In the history of those domains, however, we will generally find engineering of the kind I have been arguing characterizes the bivalent case. For colors, what makes such talk possible is the 'Pantone Book,' for some time now an essential tool for graphic designers. The Pantone Book organizes and provides samples of 1,024 colors, referred to professionally by Pantone number (although Pantone also supplies mnemonic names—like 'Mauve Mist' and 'Blue Grotto'—in six languages). Pantone boasts that, prior to its 1963 500-color product, 'there was no common language or frame of reference for specifying color'—an exaggeration in some respects

(Munsell's *Atlas* dates to 1913), but true enough when it comes to the kind of frame of reference that would be needed to make use of a degree-oriented logic of vagueness.[21] Color designations by position on the color spectrum are not simply a philosopher's fantasy; you can pick up your phone and specify the colors in your printing job, or for the fabrics in your new line of sportswear, by Pantone number. This is possible because Pantone licenses manufacturers who can reliably and accurately meet its color standards. The standard-setting, licensing, and manufacturing that ensure the requisite consistency of color are expensive: Pantone operates its own printing facility, an ink laboratory, a textile laboratory, a color standard laboratory, and an electronic color systems laboratory.

Degree theories of vagueness reproduce the dilemma of Chapter 2 in slightly modified form. Do we pay the engineering costs of coercing the domain into the spectrum-like shape presupposed by the formalism, and of coordinating our descriptions with points on the spectrum? When costs of this kind remain unpaid, invoking this sort of logic of vagueness is, with occasional exceptions, a bit like going out to play with your imaginary friend. Because the real numbers are *very* fine-grained, our budgets will generally run out before we have finished the reengineering; when that happens, we can treat the spectrum-like representation as an idealization or approximation.[22] But doing that is to treat the representation of vagueness as itself only partially true, and this was the other horn of our dilemma: inferences from claims about degrees of truth will then have to be treated as themselves defeasible, and their use will require intelligence and judgment, with all the costs and consequences we have seen that to entail.

7.6

The point is not confined to degree-theoretic logics of vagueness. Recall that the motivating idea of precisificationism is that, by tightening up a language, i.e., making it more precise, you arrive at versions of it from which vagueness has been eliminated; for instance, our vague predicate 'red' might be allocated a range of colors between Pantone 19–1764 ('Lipstick Red') and Pantone 18–1852 ('Rose Red') as a precisification. It is definitely true (or true, depending on how you tighten up generic precisificationism into a precise theory) that a color sample is red if it's red on *any* precisification.

Let's put this proposal side-by-side with a passage from the history of French public transportation, engagingly written up by Bruno Latour. Between about 1970 and 1987, various French governmental bodies and Matra Transport invested heavily in a project called Aramis, a futuristic light rail system intended to deliver the conveniences of an automobile and a subway rolled into one. Aramis was originally conceived as

> the programmed metro seat. The traveler merely goes to the station. He sits down, punches in the program, and opens up his newspaper. When the thing stops, he looks up, puts away his paper, and there he is, where he wanted to go. It's point-to-point, with no connections, no stops at intermediate stations.[23]

The label 'Aramis' started out vague; building it meant firming it up into a detailed, precisely specified object—turning it, in fact, into a blueprint. That never happened: when Aramis was terminated the blueprint was still incomplete. But along the way, a small handful of possible precisifications were tried out (not nearly all of them). Seeing what is involved even in such an uncompleted precisification is a valuable reality check on the notion that precisificationist logics of vagueness are the preferred method for representing vagueness across the board.

Notice that the model-theoretic ideas underlying the precisificationist approach seem initially appropriate here. Because 'Aramis' was a vague name, important claims that invoked it were vague also. Conducting his post-mortem, Latour wisely refused to answer the questions on everybody's minds: Was Aramis technically feasible? Was it economically viable and socially acceptable? In the spirit of precisificationist logics for vagueness, we could say that these are sentences that will come out true on some precisifications of 'Aramis,' but not on others; there was no point in trying to give a definite answer.[24]

Latour's history tells us that canvassing precisifications of a vague concept in realistic cases can be very expensive indeed. Coming up with the small handful of partial precisifications of 'Aramis' involved building mock-ups, prototypes, and experimental installations; developing a new kind of electric motor; ordering custom chips, ultrasound receptors, and station equipment; designing protocols for the cars and implementing them in software, and much, much, more of the same, totaling on the order of half a billion francs (at a time when the franc was worth a good deal more than its final pre-euro value). Applying precisificationist apparatus, in a concrete case of this kind, involves engineering the objects one is reasoning about, in a way that gives the apparatus traction on the domain; a systematic survey of the possible precisifications of 'Aramis' would be unimaginably expensive.

Precisifications of our color language differ from precisifications of the vocabulary centered around 'Aramis.' Even before paying the costs of producing the Pantone Professional Color System, we have a pretty good idea of what more precisely specifying the colors would be: roughly, drawing different lines on the color wheel. Consequently, when we talk about 'all possible precisifications' of a color vocabulary, we are not just talking through our hats.[25] When we talk about precisifications of 'Aramis,' however, we are not in anything like this position. It is not just that we do not know what the precisifications *are*; it is that, before producing them, we don't know what it *would be* to be a precisification of 'Aramis.' Among the different versions of Aramis were a short-distance intra-airport shuttle, a four-seat automatic taxicab on tracks, a relatively conventional commuter train capable of splitting at branch points in the line, and a World's Fair showpiece using non-cutting-edge technology—and there was almost always someone on hand insisting the the proposed specification was no longer *really* Aramis.

The problem I'm after now isn't that what it is to be (an) Aramis is itself vague. It's rather that when we have to make the gesture of quantifying over 'all precisifications' without knowing what we're talking about, the appearance of putting a powerful and elegant mathematical tool to work is just that: an appearance.[26] Sometimes we understand the domain well enough to understand what we mean (as with colors), but often (as with Aramis) we don't.[27] Because we do not want our quantificational gestures to be empty and blind, precisificationist models are usable and useful primarily when the range of possible precisifications is, whether vague or not, well understood, and there is a usable (even if vague) criterion for being an allowable precisification. Like degree-theoretic logics of vagueness, precisificationist logics of vagueness have preferred domains of application.

Here's how the choice looks in a case like this one. If you do *no* engineering work on the objects in the domain about which you want to reason, you are only pretending to use the precisificationist logic of vagueness. If you do *too much* reengineering, you will fall into a trap we examined when we were considering the decisions of filmmakers and curators.[28] Perhaps Aramis could have been made to conform to the precisificationist model bureaucratically, by specifying the space of precisifications ahead of time. But much like enforcing analogous constraints on movies and paintings, that would have turned it from the highly innovative engineering project it was into mere selection among already well understood and predefined alternatives. Is there a happy medium, a level of engineering on which the precisificationist representation turns out to be an idealized approximation of your engineering problem? In that case, to reiterate, it must be treated as partially true, and the inferences it recommends will have to be regarded as defeasible. My own best guess is that our ability to coordinate the representation with what it is representing will remain too loose to allow us effectively to manage the defeasibility of those inferences, and that a precisificationist treatment is inadvisable in Aramis-like cases.

7.7

The issues that determine when our third logic of vagueness is and isn't usable turn on the ways that the abstract object serving as the vagueness-management component of a conversational score is *complicated*. Recall that conversation partners are supposed to be treating a precisification tree for a language in roughly the way that baseball teams treat scoreboards. They have to keep track of their location in the tree, even though some changes of location are unpredictably timed jumps with unpredictable landing points. Each node of the tree contains a great deal of information: in the standard supervaluationist semantics, a node amounts to a stage in the specification of an entire language, and even if not all of that is necessary for running a particular conversation, the parts of it that are will still be formidable. And remember my earlier caveat: what I described was a good deal simpler than the model that it takes Shapiro most of a book to put in place.

I'm not suggesting that Shapiro has come up with the only possible vagueness-management component of a conversational score. However, I do think that the level of complexity is about right. Anything plausibly able to do the job will have to be just about as complicated as this—and perhaps a good deal *more* complicated.

Conversational scorekeeping does differ in at least two ways from score-keeping in games like baseball. First, there is no visible scoreboard posted over the playing field: conversation partners have to keep track of the conversational score in their heads. Second, adjustments to conversational score are (almost always) tacit: when I raise the standards of precision, in Lewis's story, I do so by making a conversational move that presupposes higher standards; but I do not announce that I am hereby raising the standards by such and such an increment. After all, if the scoreboards *were* visible, and the adjustments in score explicit, Lewis would have had no call to write a paper introducing the notion of a conversational score; were they explicit, every competent user of a language, and every philosopher of language, would already have known about it.

Let's bring these two differences to bear on the model. Human beings are cognitively limited creatures, and only in exceptional cases can we expect them competently to manipulate solely mental representations of an abstract object of such complexity. Having a conversation, on this account, is a bit like playing a game of chess without the board—only harder, because the precisification tree is much more complex than a chessboard. Moreover, because the moves are tacit, and because jumps, in particular, take one to locations in the precisification tree that are not predictable from the previous state of play, we have very little reason to suppose that conversation partners will be able to track the conversation's traversal of the tree.

If this is what a conversational score that permits vagueness management has to look like, then we have every reason to think that this sort of vagueness management is bound to be a shaky, sloppy enterprise for creatures cognitively like ourselves. What one has said and committed oneself to is determined by an invisible scoreboard, one which in any case registers a score complex enough to swamp human cognitive capabilities, and one which is adjusted tacitly, from moment to moment, in ways that are not deterministically computable from the previous state of the board and what one can observe in the course of the conversation. This means that conversational scorekeeping makes much better sense on some occasions than others. Not all conversations are genuinely cooperative, good-will endeavors; for instance, people negotiate, and when they do, they try to get away with things. In noncooperative conversations, the device we have just described is ripe for abuse.

If you are a teacher, just imagine managing your grading this way. Over the course of a semester, you assign letter grades to students. However, what you *mean* by those grades changes from lesson to lesson and week to week: one day, a B means that the work is good but not perfect; the next week, it means that the student is doing substandard work, and is in real trouble. The space of possible assessments that a particular grade can express is unimaginably large: too large for anyone to survey, and not explicitly spelled out. The changes to what grades mean are unannounced, forcing the students to try to infer them from your casual remarks and demeanor, along with their prior speculations as to what the grades had meant before. A system like this is an invitation to arbitrary grading, bullying, and exploitation; it would generally and correctly be regarded as unfair.

Letters of recommendation, in the academic philosophy business, are unfortunately written to exploit the faults of the conversational scorekeeping model. Think of the job market as using an invisible scoreboard, one very important element of which sets the standards for interpreting the vague (and not-so-vague) descriptions of job candidates. Every year, the letters are further inflated, and those of us who serve on search committees are familiar with the difficulties of extracting usable information from them. The problem is not just that the code is constantly changing, and that the way it is changing is neither announced, nor something that it's possible to calculate straightforwardly. Rather, it's that these letters are intended to take advantage of those facts.

Think of it from the point of view of a placement committee: you want to place all your candidates; you cannot write different letters for all the institutions to which a given candidate is applying; you need to sound enthusiastic to get your candidate hired *anywhere*; but you do not want to foist someone you think is a dud on influential and important colleagues at another producing institution. Consequently, these letters are meant to be read differently by different audiences. Those hiring departments that are closer to the center of the profession have a better sense of the updated score; they will read the enthusiastic hyperbole of three years back as meaning, 'No, we're not really recommending this candidate strongly.' But the placement committee is counting on peripheral departments and their more naive readers mistaking that very same letter for a strong recommendation. The institutional deceptions that make the philosophy job market go around trade on the weaknesses of the conversational scorekeeping model; we would do a lot better to run this part of the business differently than we do.

The scorekeeping treatment of vagueness is not restricted to conversations between distinct and possibly antagonistic persons; we can imagine it internalized, and used as a model for managing vague thoughts. So notice that the problem does not stem merely from having shysters for conversation partners. We have argued that our inferential apparatus is often the product of extensive investment. The history of that investment constrains the shape of the inputs to effective inferences. Since investments mature slowly, those constraints can be treated as fixed in the course of any particular inference. Thus, to trigger a link that will carry you to a further conclusion, you require a premise tailored to the role, one with content matching the trigger condition of the link. But now, on the conversational scorekeeping model, the content of an utterance changes from moment to moment, without any visible sign. How are you to match the fluctuating content of a potential premise to the trigger condition of the high-value inferential link that will get you a conclusion worth having? Important inferential clients typically need either fixed and very specific contents, or deviant contents carefully assessed for suitability and inferential fit. But conversational scorekeeping is an especially ineffective way of tracking deviations from those very specific targets; if you were to try to concoct an inferential procedure meant to assure confusion and failure, you could very well come up with this one.[29]

For the most part, partial truth vocabulary does better. Sometimes making good use of one's inferential capital requires you to force imperfect matches. Partial truth vocabulary leaves the content of the description it is hedging intact, so that you can see the match you are near; it allows you to register, out loud, that the match is not perfect; it permits you to assess the satisfactoriness of an imperfect fit explicitly. This is much, much better than a set of conventions that leaves everything unspoken.

However, the conversational scorekeeping approach to vagueness management is suitable for informal contexts, and for conversations in which not much is at stake. If I can only erratically track our conversation's location in a precisification tree, or for that matter can only inadequately represent the tree itself, that is fine when diverging understandings of what we are saying do not matter. When decisions about an investment portfolio, or academic grades, or a business venture, or almost anything of consequence are in the offing, the scorekeeping model is inappropriate, but that does not entail that it is not frequently a good model for what we do. *Conversation* can be important, even when the *content* of conversation is unimportant (for instance, when the point is to exhibit friendly interest, or to reassure someone), and that is why, abuses to one side, Lewis's abstract description captures something that we recognize ourselves as doing.

Even if it is not a good general theory of vagueness management as we practice it, conversational scorekeeping does present us once again with the practical choice we described in Chapter 2. We could treat the model as an engineering and implementation proposal, in which case we could consider ways of ameliorating its shortcomings. For example, we could design scoreboard software. We could carry on the conversation in a way that creates a paper trail; businessmen use email for this purpose, and diplomats are trained to take extensive notes on their conversations. Or we could designate participants as umpires or as monitors of particular elements of the score.[30] Alternatively, we could treat the conversational scorekeeping model as an approximation or idealization—briefly, as partially true.

7.8

We have encountered a recurring form of resistance to pressure on the bivalence doctrine, expressed as the objection that the context-sensitivity of our utterances preempts the need for partial truth. What we say is always flat true or flat false, and what I have been presenting as partial truth is really a matter of the shifting contexts that make the same sentence true at one moment, untrue the next. That is, what to the layman seems like neither full truth nor full falsity is just a zone of permissibility in which the sentences one utters might come out one way or the other, depending on context: but they *will* come out one way or the other, and not anywhere in between.

The truism that how we understand a sentence is properly context-dependent lends plausibility to the view. However, it is not enough to adduce the pervasiveness of context sensitivity to show that partial truth is a philosophical illusion: after all, why shouldn't a sentence, interpreted with due attention to context, come out partially true? Sustaining the objection would take a systematic account of the relevant sort of context-sensitivity, one that shows how apparent partial truth inevitably turns out to be context-sensitive full truth or falsity.[31] The opposition construes partial truth as vagueness, and let's allow that for the sake of the present argument. Then if context-sensitivity is going to be used to keep bivalence afloat, the objection must deliver a systematic treatment of vagueness, one which shows how shifts in context support, across the board, true-or-false semantic assessments of putatively vague utterances. The only account in play that can plausibly purport to do this job is the conversational scorekeeping model.

Now, the use to which the objection is forced to put the model requires that scorekeeping *always* work to resolve apparent partial truth into either full truth or full falsity. But we have just been considering when it is and isn't satisfactory; that is, we have just seen that it isn't always usable. So conversational scorekeeping won't do the job of supporting the objection from context-sensitivity.

Recall that we have the option of treating the scorekeeping account as partially true. To do so, we would need to be told what problem the model was being used to address, because once again, there is no such thing as an approximation's being good enough, *tout court* (as opposed to: good enough for something in particular). That has not been on the agenda of philosophers of language. Rather, it has been suggested to us that conversational scorekeeping is *what is really going on*, and that it gives us flat truth and flat falsity when we have truth values at all—a proposal we were considering as support for the objection that we do not need to surrender the bivalence doctrine (or anyway, to revise it more than allowing truth-value gaps). All of *that*, we have now seen, just won't do.

<h2 style="text-align:center">7.9</h2>

Partial truth, I have argued, comes in indefinitely many qualitatively different varieties. Some of these, at any rate, are amenable to formal treatment, and logics of vagueness are examples from one smallish part of the territory of partial truth. As we can now see, they provide inductive confirmation for the account we have under development; they are instances, and not, after all, competition.

Thinking about them has extended our understanding of the tradeoffs we first took up in Chapter 2. You don't fix the problem of fit by giving up hard truths for hard verities, or hard super-truths, or generally, for other semantic values that figure into formally explicated guidelines for inference. On the contrary, the more filigree a formal system has, the harder it is to fit to a messy subject matter. And so because logics of vagueness are more elaborately articulated than classical logic, except in special cases, you are replacing the previous version of the problem with a harder and more expensive version of the same problem.

Early on in motivating the approach I am taking to partial truth, I used a handful of analogies to postpone an inevitable question: is there a logic— where what is meant is a formal or mathematical logic—of partial truth? We are now in a position to give the properly considered answer to that question. '*The* logic of partial truth' is a failed definite description, because there are different formal treatments suitable for differing subject matters and applications. The argument of Chapter 6, to the effect that there are indefinitely many qualitatively different forms of partial truth, should have led us to expect this outcome.

We have just seen convincing illustrations, albeit not the *best* illustrations. The usability of logic for one application or another is a consideration that is largely alien to the tradition with which this chapter has been concerned. In this tradition, logic is thought of not as a how-to guide of any kind—not as a user's manual for your intellect—but as, to put it crudely, the science of the consequence relation.[32] Thus, observations about the uneven fit of the various logics of vagueness to a subject area typically prompt the response that these too can be represented; in the ensuing treatments of what has come to be called higher-order vagueness, questions as to the usability of those representations do not arise. I hope to discuss the lessons of higher-order vagueness elsewhere, and for now will ask you to recall the psychologistic frame of the present investigation: a representation of the correctness of inference that cannot be used for the effective regulation of inference is not doing its job.

Be that as it may, the logics of vagueness we have surveyed were meant to solve the puzzle of the sorites, and not to be used for any practical purpose. This is why the formal treatments of different varieties of partial truth that are most instructively geared to concrete applications are found not in the writings of philosophers and logicians, but scattered throughout the sciences.[33]

Part IV
Applications

8

The Quinean Turn

If it's true, or true enough, that truth comes in flavors like *true enough*, then we need to rethink our metaphysics, almost from the bottom up. I'm going to try to substantiate this claim by giving a four-chapter history of one strand of twentieth-century analytic metaphysics. I will explain how the series of moves that made it up served as a frame for much further work in the field, and suggest that the work it framed was well motivated only if the framework was itself well motivated. Then I will argue that the framework in question presupposed the bivalence doctrine (again, that truth comes in only the two flavors *true* and *false*), and was not well motivated if the doctrine is not true. By focusing on a handful of defining points in that history—Quine's views in this chapter, Davidson's in the next, and two methodological moments in the work of David Lewis in the following chapters—we will be able to get a sense for how deep reliance on the bivalence doctrine went and still goes, and how much will have to be revamped or discarded once the bivalence doctrine is rejected.

Cynical readers may expect that they're about to get something of a Moscow show trial. But while this is going to be history in the service of a judgment, I mean the verdict to be fair. Any history as brief as this one (like any history, no matter how exhaustive) will leave out a lot of the small stuff; while it is characteristic of history to dissolve into a welter of detail, and of historians to complain that inattention to detail has made their predecessors' histories untrue to the course of events, the inclination to insist on too much detail is, recall, part of the mistake I am hoping to correct: partial truth is, after all, a way of filtering out unwanted and unmanageable detail. I'm not trying to be exhaustive about the large-scale morphology of the history of analytic philosophy, either, but I *do* claim to be describing a part of it that is central and structurally important enough to make the point I am in the first place after: that dropping the bivalence doctrine has large consequences for metaphysics.

8.1

There is something that should probably be called the Mystery of Analytic Metaphysics—the mystery being that there ever was such a thing as metaphysics in the analytic tradition at all. 'Analytic philosophy' was a label invented to underscore the ideological (and stylistic) ground common to two philosophical movements, logical positivism and ordinary language philosophy, and each of these movements had dedicated itself with great fanfare to the repudiation of metaphysics. Their techniques had slightly different foci: The logical positivists' most famous talking point was that the *vocabulary* of metaphysics could be shown to be literally meaningless.[1] On the ordinary language view, the problem was not so much the vocabulary; rather, metaphysics, without exception, involved committing something like a *grammatical* mistake (though not normally a mistake about the grammar-book grammar).[2] On both views, metaphysics was word-salad nonsense. So how did it happen that, within a generation, analytic philosophers—the very students, and students' students, of the early logical positivists and ordinary-language philosophers—could be found taking vigorous stands on such unmistakably metaphysical topics as, just for instance, the individuation of events, or again, transworld identity?[3]

I don't think that I'm alone in taking the enabling moment to be a pair of papers: W. V. O. Quine's 'On What There Is' and 'Two Dogmas of Empiricism.'[4] But before I try to explain how that moment happened, I need to say something about why Quine's predecessors had thought that what *they* were doing wasn't metaphysics. Logical positivist doctrine divided meaningful claims up into two distinct and non-overlapping kinds. First, there were empirically verifiable statements, those that could be checked by observation or experiment…especially, and in the first place, scientific theories, or important parts of them: these were *synthetic*. Second, there were the *analytic* statements, those that were true by virtue of the meanings of the words…especially, and in the first place, logical and mathematical statements. Clearly (thought the logical positivists) the former weren't metaphysical; and the latter weren't metaphysical either; so if everything you said was one or the other, then you weren't saying anything metaphysical at all.[5]

Against this background, Quine made three simple but striking moves, which I will collectively call the *Quinean Turn*. First, he pointed out that you could use the formal logic developed by Frege and Russell to make explicit the ontological commitments of your scientific theories: rewrite the theory in the formal notation, and look at the quantifiers, together with their bound variables, to find out what your theory says there is. The quantifier-variable combinations

$$(\exists x)\ldots x \ldots$$

and

$$(x)\ldots x \ldots$$

rendered back into English, read respectively as:

There exists something [call it *x*] such that...it [i.e., *x*] has such-and-such true of it...

and

Everything [call any such thing *x*] is such that...it [i.e., *x*] has such-and-such true of it...

To be, the slogan went, is to be the value of a bound variable. Since you believe your (best) scientific theory, you can simply read your ontology— your inventory of what the world contains—off your theory. For instance, if your best physical theory, suitably rewritten, quantifies over electrons— if it contains bits that read '$(\exists x)$ *x* is an electron, and...'—then you can conclude that *there are* electrons: electrons exist, or anyway, that's what your theory says. This procedure had the merit of making ontology every bit as respectable as logic and as physical science, which for the logical positivists were jointly the gold standard of respectability.[6]

Second, Quine jettisoned the analytic/synthetic distinction—that is, he denied that you could explain and maintain the distinction between, on the one hand, sentences that were true by virtue of the meanings or definitions of the words, and, on the other, sentences that were empirically true, i.e., that had to be checked by observation or experiment. At the time, his arguments for rejecting the distinction were notoriously thin, and really amounted to no more than a rhetorical question: What makes you think that you really have a distinction you can use? But no one had ever thought to ask, and the rhetorical question was enormously compelling.[7]

Third, Quine added a caveat to the proposal that you could just read your ontology off your scientific theory. Ever since Russell had formulated his Theory of Descriptions, it had been obvious to analytic philosophers that the logical form of a sentence—for present purposes, its canonical transcription into logical notation—might not be its surface form.[8] If the quantifiers and variables that seemed to carry an ontological commitment could be correctly paraphrased away (in something like the way that Russell had shown definite descriptions could be paraphrased away), then you weren't really ontologically committed after all.

Quine's first move, by itself, did not trespass the bounds of empirical theorizing. (That was why it looked so respectable.) But the second move disposed of that boundary: it removed, as it were, the glass ceiling that had kept theorizing from being promoted to metaphysical topics. To see how this went, consider a question which 'On What There Is' discussed in passing: Do mathematical objects, such as numbers and sets, really exist? Paradigmatically metaphysical, it had been rendered off-limits to the logical positivists by the analytic/synthetic distinction: mathematical statements were, they thought, analytic, and to ask about the existence of, say, numbers was either to ask a trivial arithmetical question, or to be exhibiting deep confusion about the status of our arithmetical definitions or conventions. But with the distinction removed, there was a straightforward way to address and answer it. Do our (best) scientific theories quantify over numbers? If they do, then we are ontologically committed to the numbers—according to our (best) theories, they exist. And if not, they don't.

To be sure, it wasn't *quite* as straightforward as that, because there was still Quine's third move. Numbers would turn out to really exist only if they couldn't be paraphrased away.[9] So in order to settle the matter, philosophers would have to argue about what paraphrases—or *reductions*, and here we see why debates about what can be reduced to what have been such a persistently recurring theme in analytic philosophy—were or weren't legitimate and successful. Quine had given analytic philosophers a recipe for argumentation, along with permission to turn the arguments on formerly forbidden metaphysical subject matter, and with the alacrity of unhappy dieters convincing themselves that the triple-fudge chocolate depth bomb really *is* a permitted food group, analytic metaphysicians were off and running.

To underscore my claim that the Quinean Turn set the agenda for sub-sequent work in analytic metaphysics, let me adduce Exhibit A: Hartry Field's *Science without Numbers*, published just over thirty years later, and widely discussed at the time. The book tried to show that central parts of physics could be reconstructed without quantifying over numbers or other archetypally mathematical entities like sets.[10] Field's project made sense to his readers and to himself because Quine's framework was being taken entirely for granted. A metaphysical question—whether abstract enti-ties, specifically numbers and sets, exist—was to be settled by determining whether or not they are quantified over by scientific theories we believe, physical theories in particular; arguing about that is mostly a matter of arguing about whether apparent quantification over numbers can or can-not be paraphrased away; so Field, who didn't like abstract entities for all the usual reasons (you can't see them, you can't kick them…), was arguing that a paraphrase is available.

Let me introduce a new theme at this point. Any metaphysics owes an answer to the question: why take it seriously? I'll call this the *Question of Seriousness*. When Quine introduced his ontological criterion, it was clear enough why you were supposed to take the ontological commitments of your theories seriously: those theories were supposed to be empirically well supported and predictively powerful science, the kind of theories that put men on the moon and mushroom clouds over islands in the Pacific. Consequently, their pronouncements could be delivered with imposing *gravitas*.

8.2

Once you've decided to let your theory (of whatever) tell you what there is, the obvious and urgent question becomes: what makes you think you've got the *right* theory? Maybe your evidence is no good; maybe you don't have enough data. The philosophical and skeptical version of the more practical worry is that, no matter how good your data is, and no matter how much you have, maybe it *still* isn't good enough: maybe the data leaves the correct choice of theory indeterminate. Perhaps unsurprisingly, then, the principled indeterminacy of theory in the face of evidence proved to be another pre-occupation of analytic metaphysics, and, perhaps surprisingly, it came to the fore when Quine eventually took a shot at filling in the missing argument against the analytic/synthetic distinction. I want to discuss that later episode so as to bring out the role played in it by the bivalence doctrine.[11]

In Quine's thinking about the analytic/synthetic distinction, analyticity had been the side of the contrast that, to borrow Austin's locution, wore the trousers: analytic truths are true solely in virtue of the meanings of the words, and synthetic truths are the truths that aren't analytic. Since the point of the argument was to be that meaning was too obscure a notion to work with, Quine proposed translation as a fair substitute: everyone who believed in meaning would agree that it was what successful translation preserved. If it were to turn out, Quine reasoned, that there was no such thing as a uniquely correct translation (or if correct translations did not end up equivalent, 'in any plausible sense of equivalence however loose'), then there would have been no meanings, and so no meanings for sentences to be true solely in virtue of, and so no content to the notion of an analytically true sentence, and so no distinction between analytic and synthetic. And to show that there were no uniquely correct translations, he proposed a famous thought experiment.

Imagine a linguist doing fieldwork on a hitherto uncontacted tribe. The linguist's task is to construct a bilingual dictionary and a grammar, together amounting to a translation manual, for the natives' language. What the linguist has to go on is, on the one hand, the natives' utterances, and on the other, the circumstances in which those utterances are made. For example, if natives face-to-face with rabbits consistently exclaim 'Gavagai!' the linguist might hypothesize that 'Gavagai!' should be translated as 'Rabbit!' Quine claimed that if you thought about it, you would see that no amount of evidence could dictate a unique translation manual. The linguist would be free to translate 'Gavagai!' as 'Undetached rabbit-part!' or 'Lo, rabbithood again!' or any one of an indefinite number of startlingly different expressions—provided of course that he made compensating adjustments in other parts of his dictionary and grammar.

Now, 'if you thought about it' had better mean: if you came up with an argument. It is not as though I know in my bones that I could go on and produce an alternative dictionary and grammar for a given language, and you shouldn't think you know, either. *Would* the compensating adjustments all fit together? Maybe, maybe not: if you visit the reference section of your library or local bookstore, you will not actually find pairs of bilingual dictionaries, for any language, that diverge in the way Quine says they can. Briefly, this pivotal claim does need an argument, and Quine never quite gave one. But he did indicate what the *form* of such an argument would have to be, and let's consider for a moment how it would go.

To assemble an indeterminacy argument, you need, first of all, a way of describing the data (here, linguistic data) to which the theory (in this case, the translation scheme) is held responsible. Quine described his imaginary linguist's data in terms meant to sound like in-period Skinnerian behaviorism: his lengthy presentation is full of phrases like 'pattern of chromatic irradiation of the eye,' 'ocular irradiation,' 'stimulatory situations,' 'speech dispositions,' 'verbal stimulations,' 'observable behavior, vocal and otherwise,' 'overt behavior, notably the wincing instinct,' etc. More tersely, the linguist had to work with, on the one hand, stimuli,[12] and on the other hand, behavior. But this was Pretend Science—it should have been recognized as such even during behaviorism's heyday—and it is philosophically important to be honest about that: it is not as though anyone ever had a behavioristically acceptable vocabulary in which to describe the stimuli and the behaviors.[13]

Quine's way of sidestepping this difficulty was to assume that a linguist would quickly recognize assent and dissent in his native informants. (The linguist is then supposed to try out 'Gavagai!' in front of, and away from, the rabbits, and note whether his native agrees or disagrees.) Of course, this is a fudge:[14] if indeterminacy of translation were as deep a phenomenon as Quine had insisted, the correct translation of 'Yes' and 'No' would be as indeterminate as anything else. But what Quine was doing was supplying behavioristic-sounding surrogates for the truth values of sentences, and so determining what was really going to count as the evidence for the linguist's theory. His indeterminacy claim accordingly amounted to this: that your informants could fix all of the truth values for all of the (anyhow, assertoric) sentences in the language (this being the data able to do the determining), and that you could *still* produce alternative translation manuals (these being the theories choice between which the data would leave indeterminate).

Quine never gave the argument for that last claim,[15] and so, as I've already remarked, he never finished up the argument against the analytic/synthetic distinction. But we can say this much about it: for the argument to tell us anything about whether translation is indeterminate for *us*, we have to be able to suppose that the linguist could be in the position of having the truth values for the natives' sentences (the natives' assents and dissents) without *already* understanding the rest of the language.[16]

Allow, as I have been arguing throughout this book, that truth comes in indefinitely more versions than two. Any intelligent informant will respond to many, perhaps most, suggestions of the sort that Quine wants his linguist to advance with *qualified* assent. 'Gavagai?' Well, in a *way* (it's a toy rabbit). 'House?' Sort of (a mostly glass-walled cottage on the grounds of a study center is an odd borderline case). 'Boat?' Yes and no (depends how you think of it—it might with equal accuracy be described as a large manned buoy).[17] 'Mother?' Well…(there's a complicated story involving two previous marriages). These qualified responses have to be part of the data to which the linguist is responsible. It's not just that there's no principled ground for excluding them, and it's not just that without the qualified responses, there isn't very much to go on. It's that if you don't know what counts as a partially true (in one way or another) use of a sentence, or application of a description, or of a name, you don't understand the language and you don't speak it.[18]

Bear in mind why it was truth values that Quine substituted for behavior in his thought experiment. It's not just that they seemed well tamed to a logician. The idea that the meanings of sentences are given by their truth conditions was what remained of the logical positivist sentiment that meaning is the method of verification: find out under what conditions you hold it true, and you know what it means. There's a lot of truth to that; if you don't know under what circumstances a sentence would come out true, you probably *don't* know what it means. But as the examples above suggest, if you don't know under what circumstances a sentence would come out *partially* (somewhat, or mostly, or in a way, or technically…) true, you don't know what it means, either. Without allowing the truth-qualifying usages into the linguistic data, it's not going to be possible to reconstruct, in your translation-manual-under-construction, what you know when you know a language.

I'm willing to stretch my sense of the plausible, and allow for the sake of the argument that one could come to understand straight assent and dissent without already understanding most of the rest of the language. But I'm not willing to stretch it as far as supposing that anyone could understand the qualified truth values—the ones I am claiming are most of the data—without already understanding a great deal of the rest of the language. And if that is right, Quine's thought experiment is beside the point. It is irrelevant to whether a unique translation is fixed by how we assess the truth of sentences of a language that some sparse and especially uninformative subset of those assessments does not rule out alternative translations.

Moreover, even if somehow we could collect the partial assents and dissents, without already having settled what the correct translation of the language was, there is a further problem. Recall our earlier complaint about the raw behaviorist version of the problem: that Quine wasn't in a position to construct the behavioristic version of the argument (that is, the version he really wanted), because he wasn't in a position to give an adequate description of the behavioristic data to which the theory was to be held responsible. A very similar complaint can be fielded against the version of the thought experiment that takes the data to be truth conditions, once we allow that we have to include the conditions under which a sentence is, in one way or another, partially true. As I have argued, we qualify our truth claims in indefinitely many ways, most of them qualitatively different from one another. Consequently, we have no clean way of giving a general characterization of the data to which the translation manual is to be held responsible, when the data consists of subjects' elaborately nuanced qualifications to their own agreement or disagreement. So there is no way to construct an argument showing that, given the linguistic data, the theory of meaning (the translation manual) remains indeterminate.

How did these difficulties with Quine's never-quite-completed argument go unnoticed for so long? Over and above analytic philosophers' century-long willingness to take bivalence for granted, there are Quine's rhetorical strategies, which should not pass unremarked—and let me apologize in advance for my own excursion into a rhetorical mode, that of post-colonial studies, with which I'm usually rather impatient. Quine's thought experiment is an odd mix of Robinson Crusoe and mid-last-century scientism, and this turns out to matter for the way it goes down. It plays on the fantasy of natives who are a bit simple-minded and rather eager to please, and who don't try to give intelligently qualified answers to the questions they're asked.[19] It also draws on a picture of what goes on in a behaviorist's laboratory, where the subjects (very often animals) are induced to generate responses that neatly fit the investigator's coding scheme. (The pigeons peck at the right button or the left button; the human subjects pull one of three levers.) Behaviorism is a defunct research program, but it's still worth remembering what Vicki Hearne called its dirty little secret: that to get the animals to cooperate, you have to starve them down to 80 percent of their normal body weight. Even when it's animals, you get a data set of straight yes-or-no answers only by coercing your subjects; when it's people, you hide the arm-twisting from yourself behind condescending self-delusion about the 'natives.' It's not, it turns out, mere coincidence that 'Jungle' is what Quine calls the language he sends his imaginary linguist out to interpret.

The point we want to take away with us is this. Once you stop thinking that bivalence is uniformly present, you can't give the missing argument to the effect that there is, in principle, always more than one translation manual for a language. But recall that Quine's thought experiment, and the claims about it that such an argument would support, were his belated attempt actually to argue against the analytic/synthetic distinction. And recall that the rejection of that distinction was one of the pivotal components of the Quinean Turn, which was itself the birthing moment of analytic metaphysics. If taking bivalence for granted was a mistake, then analytic metaphysics was born in original sin, and founded—as Prichard once said of moral philosophy—on a mistake.

There is a secondary moral we might want to bear in mind as well. The not-quite-there argument for the alternative translation manual is exemplary of the ways that analytic philosophers articulated and supported their worries about the indeterminacy of theory in the face of evidence. If that is correct, those worries need to be rethought: not only don't we have any good arguments against the analytic/synthetic distinction, we don't have any good arguments for indeterminacy, either. Now, it's not that I'm claiming to have done away with the worries; there is something deep going on in them, and we will not want to hastily discard the insights buried in the treatments we can now deem unsatisfactory. But arguments for indeterminacy that presuppose bivalence will have to be retooled or replaced: the most influential of them is quite clearly no good at all.

8.3

We identified, as the very beginning of analytic metaphysics, the idea that if you *have* a theory, and you *believe* your theory, and your theory says that such-and-such *exists*…then you do, and ought to, believe that such-and-such exists. But once you have taken on board the notion of partial truth, there's an equally direct rebuttal: who says you believe your theory? Quine took the theories in question to be *scientific* theories, so let's consider those.[20]

Newtonian mechanics is regarded today as an approximately true theory. An approximately true theory is likely to leave out pieces of what you take to be the correct ontology, as for instance when Newtonian mechanics implies that there are no black holes. Newtonian mechanics tells you that there is such a thing as the mass of an object (where we distinguish the rest mass and relativistic mass). In the practice of Newtonian mechanics, you end up quantifying over—i.e., on the Quinean view, implicitly committing yourself to the existence of—either point masses (of which you don't think there are any) or rigid or elastic bodies with highly idealized properties (you don't think there are any of these, either). The theory quantifies over the precise momenta of precisely located objects (again, there aren't any, and you know it). And, although this is a little trickier, on some ways of staring at it, the theory tells you that there is absolute space, an inertial frame in which Newton's laws of motion hold. (The theory of relativity tells you that there isn't a preferred frame.) Briefly, if you think a theory is only approximately true, you get to be selective about how much of the theory's ontology is *your* ontology. (But the example also makes it clear that there need be no veil of approximations; it is not as though you cannot ever see past the partial truths to the full truths.)[21]

Calculations having to do with particle scattering are generally too difficult to do exactly. Instead, one uses perturbation techniques: first, one solves a base case (typically, the trivial case, in which the particles don't interact at all); then, one corrects one's result incrementally. Each term in the expansion series is represented by a Feynman diagram. (Leave aside complexities having to do with divergent terms and renormalization.) Feynman diagrams describe particle interactions in terms of the exchange of virtual particles, and virtual particles—although they are mentioned, and although they are quantified over—don't actually exist. (It's not just a matter of tone of voice, or of being *called* 'virtual': they're exempted from the relations between momentum and energy required of particles generally.) The moral of the story: when you're in the business of approximation, you may need to introduce 'entities' that you quantify over, but to which you're not ontologically committed.[22]

One of the founding moments of twentieth-century evolutionary biology was the Hardy-Weinberg Theorem, which says that in an infinite population, in which individuals mate randomly and there is no selection, migration, or mutation, gene frequencies remain stable from generation to generation. It goes without saying that no biologist believes that there are any infinitely large populations. Moreover, on a plausible understanding of what is intended by 'population'—namely, a group of organisms that mate with each other—and trivial assumptions having to do with the spatial distribution of organisms, the notion of an infinite population is, like other idealizations we have already seen, incoherent. (The chances of organisms mating with each other drop to zero with sufficient distance; in the intended sense, infinitely many organisms cannot make up a single population.) The point of appealing to an infinitely large population is to eliminate the effects of drift, i.e., sampling error; when the population is, as sometimes gets said, 'effectively infinite,' drift can be neglected, and the Hardy-Weinberg Theorem is true enough.[23] What a scientist's theory quantifies over is not a particularly good guide to what the scientist thinks exists, if the theory involves idealizations—and what powerful theory does not?

Another example: It is a fairly widespread view that 'species represent biological realities,' but 'the higher-level categories of the Linnaean hierarchy' do not; 'their definitions,' a standard textbook tells us, 'are arbitrary.'[24] A recently proposed clade-oriented reform to procedures of biological classification has been resisted on the grounds that in a domain in which theories of phylogeny are in flux, a theory-driven classification method will give rise to erratically fluctuating classifications. To be usable, classifications must be stable and familiar. So we should stick with the old ways of naming taxa, even though that normally involves talking as though those taxa exist. Here we have practitioners of a science who are happy to have their patterns of quantification diverge from their ontological commitments; insisting on identifying these, one of them tells us, 'is based on a fundamental misunderstanding of the difference between a phylogeny (which is real) and a classification (which is utilitarian).'[25] If the scientists' own attitude to their quantifiers is explicitly only sometimes ontologically commital, the philosophers should know better than to treat the quantifiers as telling us what the commitments are.

Once you allow partial truth into your scientific theorizing, your bound variables are no longer a particularly good guide to what sorts of entities exist, and Quine's recipe will produce, not a list of what there is, but a list containing a certain amount of what there isn't.

8.4

Instrumentalism (in the philosophy-of-science sense, rather than the practical-reasoning sense of the term we encountered earlier on) is the view that theories are merely calculating devices that allow us to 'save the phenomena'; they are aids to prediction, and not meant as true descriptions of unobservable entities. Other philosophers have helped themselves to instrumentalism and its relatives to block the Quinean Turn.[26] And, earlier on, I identified a central function of our partial-truth vocabulary to be that of narrowing the inferential consequences of statements. This might suggest that the story I'm telling should be understood as just another variant of instrumentalism: when I call a statement 'partially true,' I'm giving you instructions about what it's safe to infer from it, but really, there's nothing that justifies calling these claims partially *true*, as opposed to just plain false but inferentially usable. To prevent my account from getting stuffed into the wrong pigeonhole, I'm going to take time out to explain why insisting on either the instrumentalist or the contrasting realist classification would involve too much forcing: even if there is some truth to one or the other, there is too little for the classifications to be intellectually useful.

Recall some of the differences between our former illustrations. There is something of a spectrum, with truth-qualifiers that more naturally take instrumentalist interpretations at one end, and truth-qualifiers that more naturally take realist construals at the other. I treat the cow as a sphere because it gives me useful results, but I'm not committed to cow's being shaped anything like a sphere! However, that television is a post-World War II technology is pretty much the way things were, modulo some hard-to-spell-out fuzz at the edges which we can ignore. Truth vocabulary is much less strained at the latter end of the spectrum, and it's important not to let one's account be shaped by just the former range of cases.

If there are indefinitely many qualitatively different forms that partial truth can take, and if partial truth is a way of hedging one's inferential commitments, then, since there are indefinitely many ways of doing that, there ought to be indefinitely many qualitatively different ways of hedging one's specifically ontological commitments. So you shouldn't expect to have to choose between across-the-board realism (the idea that our scientific theories tell us what's *really out there*) and across-the-board instrumentalism (again, that they're devices for calculating results, but we don't need to believe them *at all*). And that's borne out by our examples, in which the theories' users are fully realist about some aspects of their theoretical descriptions, but not about others: as when you know perfectly well that the population you are considering is not infinite, and in fact, you even happen know exactly how many members it has.

One of the alternatives comes up frequently enough to be worth talking through, as a way of substantiating the claim that we are not forced to choose between instrumentalism and realism, and that there are indefinitely many intermediate positions to put on our map. Back in the days before calling stores 'factory outlets' was merely franchise branding, people went to outlets to purchase clothes that were cheaper because they were irregular—that is, because they were, in one way or another, not manufactured to spec. An irregular does not conform to its official type description; if we think of the design specifications for a style of clothing as the 'theory' of it, many, even most, of the items in the outlet fail to conform to the theory we use to think about them. Nevertheless, factory outlets shelved and priced irregulars, that is, classified them, by styles (that is, by their type description). Because irregulars deviate in indefinitely many ways from the specification, there was no point in replacing the 'theory' with a taxonomy of defects; it would not have made sense for the Levi's outlet to have a shelf for the jeans with the nonstandard zippers, and another for the jeans sewn with off-color thread, etc. However, when you say that an item is irregular, which is tantamount to saying that its official specification is almost but not entirely true, you are not suggesting that the item does not *exist*. After all, you are in the factory outlet precisely because the irregulars are there on the shelves.

There are important theoretical domains in which many or even most of the items are, so to speak, irregulars. Just as in the factory outlet, entities mentioned by one's theory of the domain are known not to conform fully to the description the theory gives. Just as in the outlet store, where the items are shelved by style rather than by defect, the irregular theoretical entities are picked out and inferentially engaged via the concepts they do not quite instantiate. Just as in the outlet store (where there is likely to be something wrong with the product, but maybe something you can live with), when reasoning about the entities you are considering, you have to bear in mind the ways they deviate from their theoretical characterization. (Inspect carefully before you buy!) And finally, just as in the outlet store, you can save a bundle: the hedged ontological commitments of a partially true theory can sometimes lower inferential costs dramatically.

Recall that in section 2.4 we considered species, understood as reproductively closed populations, as a case of bivalence produced without human intervention, and recall that we also qualified that observation: bivalence itself can be something like a matter of degree, and there are borderline cases of reproductive isolation. There are of course many competing species concepts, but this one is embedded in a theory that is too powerful, at least when it comes to sexually reproducing organisms, to just throw away. There are many ways a would-be species can be reproductively isolated *enough* for the theoretical machinery to be useful, while falling short of full compliance with the requirement. To pick an illustration almost at random, 'it may well be that *Quercus macrocarpa* [one species of oak] exchanges many more genes with local *Q. bicolor* [another species of oak] than it does with *Q. macrocarpa* in Texas.'[27] That is, many of the items to which we want to apply this species concept are irregulars; it's not that, because the theory isn't fully true of them, they *aren't there*, but rather, that something *almost* conforming to the theory's characterization *is* there.

Memes are, paradigmatically, psychological contents that are copied from mind to mind, that mutate (by being miscopied), and that, because they give rise to a greater or lesser number of copies of themselves, are acted upon by forces of selection. Memes allow one to adapt a great deal of the explanatory apparatus of Darwinism to cultural evolution, and while opinions differ as to the promise of the concept, its enthusiasts certainly think it is worth exploring.[28]

But many memes are irregulars. Dawkins, the originator of the meme concept, mentions stiletto heels, which are not psychological contents but artifacts; it is more straightforward to think of the replicators as being the shoes, rather than the accompanying preferences, and so on. Again, the replication of memes is normally understood to be mimicry-based copying; I hear the tune, it runs through my head; I whistle it for others to hear. But irregular memes could bypass the copying: imagine an idea that, given the proper setup, students will figure out for themselves. Such an idea might normally be taught, not by presenting it for memorization, but by assigning a problem set. Then the meme would spread by creating the conditions for its being reinvented on a regular basis. Overall, my estimate is that, for any way of tightening up the meme concept, many items you will have good reason to apply the theory to will be irregular instances of the concept.

Finally for now, computers are devices that can be modeled by Turing machines. (That itself is a simplification in various ways—commercial computers are descended from von Neumann architectures, for instance—but not in ways that matter to the present point.) Turing machines have infinitely large memories, discrete states, alphabets of discrete symbols, and deterministic transition functions; they compute recursive functions. No actual device fully conforms to this model. Parity bits, and more generally error correcting codes, are in wide use because cosmic rays and the like produce nondeterministic and unintended jumps from state to state; because imperfections in magnetic media produce memory errors; because analog implementation of a digital system means that, rarely but every so often, the computational state of part of the system (represented as a voltage) fails to be discriminated and preserved. Many, perhaps most, of the applications to which computers are now put do not amount to computing recursive functions.[29] Certainly there are other models of computation; most familiarly, finite, pushdown, and nondeterministic automata. But the traditional theory of computation is too powerful to give up. We're not about to deny that computers exist; you can find them on every other table top. But they are, all of them, irregulars.

In none of these cases is the instrumentalist spin appropriate. Recall the just-so story I told in Chapter 3: to grade paintings for accuracy in an articulate and discriminating manner, one that takes account of the niceties and fine points, is not to be antirealist about what the paintings depict. (Nuance, subtlety, and marking gradations are not antirealism!) Why should it be antirealism when what we are grading is sentences? If the truth of scientific theories is not always all-out, but partial, idealized, and approximate, the contrast between realism and antirealism is perhaps quite often an intellectual distraction.

9

The Davidsonian Swerve

The direction initially set by the Quinean Turn was altered by three subsequent swerves. Each of them was an application of the recipe Quine had provided, each of them set the agenda for a library-swamping volume of writing by other philosophers, each of them modified the program in important ways, and once you have relived these three moments in intellectual history, you are no longer just reconsidering history: you are looking at analytic metaphysics as it is being practiced at the beginning of the twenty-first century. In this chapter, I'll discuss the first of these, Donald Davidson's revision to the Quinean program.

9.1

As we have already seen, metaphysics in the Quinean mode often turns on establishing the logical form of one or another family of expressions. Davidson produced an elegant, influential, and Quine-inspired argument to the effect that we quantify over *events*, and therefore events, although unlike other, more tangible objects, nonetheless belong in our ontology. A sentence like, 'The ship sailed longingly but impertinently toward the horizon,' entails the shorter sentences, 'The ship sailed,' 'The ship sailed longingly,' 'The ship sailed impertinently,' 'Something sailed longingly and impertinently,' and so on. The only transcription able to capture those entailments cleanly was, Davidson claimed, this one: There is something which is a sailing, and which was done by the ship, and which was done longingly, and which was done impertinently, and which was done toward the horizon. With this representation, we can drop conjuncts to get the requisite implications—but now we have bound variables (those instances of 'something…which…') ranging over events, and so, it turns out, events exist.[1]

The argument for an ontology of events makes sense only within the framework put in place by the Quinean Turn: we proceed by reading our existential commitments off a canonical transcription of our statements into a regimented logical notation. And Davidson's work served in turn as a framework for a great deal of further work in metaphysics, work which is consequently well motivated only if Davidson's work is itself well motivated. Under this heading, consider Exhibit B, Stephen Yablo's paper on 'Identity, Essence, and Indiscernibility,' which tries to work up, roughly, a model-theoretic account of event identity; again, what is important for our purposes is that the project only makes sense when *both* the Quinean Turn, and Davidson's subsequent application of the Quinean method, are in the background and being taken for granted.[2] If events aren't an already accepted part of your ontology, you have no reason to go looking for their identity conditions. Or as Exhibit C, take Davidson's own further work on causation. Having convinced himself that events were part of the furniture of the universe, he decided that this meant he owed criteria for individuating them. (Here he was following Quine, who had announced that there was no 'entity without identity.') Casting around, he came up with the following candidate: events were individuated by their location in the causal network, that is, events *a* and *b* were identical just when they had the same causes and the same effects. Without a theory of causation to back up his criterion of event identity, this wouldn't have stuck, and so Davidson produced one; it had, for our purposes, two relevant features. First, causes and effects were made out to be events, as required by his proposed identity criterion. And second, the causal relation was understood as entailing the existence of an exceptionless underlying law linking the cause and the effect. Our interest is not in the plausibility of this move but in its philosophical motivation; the reason for insisting, however implausibly, on the exceptionless law was that it made the causal connections between events crisp enough to serve as individuating conditions. In short, what made this account of causation a reasonable next move was a sequence of prior moves that included, first, the Quinean Turn and, second, Davidson's own subsequent application of Quine's recipe for doing metaphysics.

But, and I'm going to call this the Davidsonian Swerve, notice that the Quinean program has been importantly modified: whatever those facts about our impertinent sailboat belong to, it is not some theory that will ever be taught in a physics class, and they are not continuous with anything that Quine would have acknowledged to be *science* at all. Instead, they are data about our language, to be reconstructed, Davidson thought, by a theory of meaning. So while the Quinean recipe's mixing directions remained in the cookbook, the type of theory it used as its main ingredient changed dramatically. In Quine, you were to be drawing on primarily physical theories, that is, theories whose object was the world out there. Davidsonian theories instead had as their object *us in here*, specifically the languages we speak.[3]

9.2

Davidson's account of a theory of meaning was an appropriation of the Quinean thought experiment we rehearsed in section 8.2, and to explain how the bivalence doctrine was embedded in the Davidsonian Swerve, we will need to explain what Davidson did with the idea of radical translation. His blueprint for a theory of meaning adapted Tarski's blueprint for a theory of truth, and I will use a toy illustration from Carnap to explain the spirit of the proposal.[4]

Tarski had proposed a success criterion for a theory of truth (for a given language): it would have as theorems all the 'T-sentences,' i.e., sentences of the form

T_1: 'Snow is white' is true (in English) if and only if snow is white.

or

T_2: 'Heute ist Sonntag' is true (in German) if and only if today is Sunday.

or, more generally,

T: 'p' is true (in L) if and only if p.

—where the left side of a T-sentence gives a quote-name of a sentence in the object language L (the language you're talking *about*), and the right side gives a translation of that sentence into the metalanguage (the language you're doing the talking *in*).

Here's how he proposed to construct theories so as to satisfy that success criterion. Consider a tiny language, which we'll call *micro-German.* Micro-German contains only two names ('der Mond,' 'der Titisee'), two predicates ('ist kalt,' 'ist blau'), and two logical operators ('und,' 'nicht').

You can build sentences out of these in the obvious way (obvious, that is, if you're a German speaker, but I'll still spare you the explicit definition of the syntax), for instance:

- 'Der Mond ist kalt.'
- 'Der Titisee ist blau.'
- 'Der Titisee ist kalt und der Mond ist nicht blau.'

Now here's how you construct your theory of truth for micro-German. First, you specify the denotations of the names:

1. 'Der Mond' denotes the moon.
2. 'Der Titisee' denotes the Titi Lake.

Then you specify the denotations of the predicates:

3. 'ist blau' denotes the property of being blue.
4. 'ist kalt' denotes the property of being cold.

Then you specify how sentences get truth values:

5. An atomic sentence is true when the property denoted by the predicate holds of the object denoted by the name.
6. A compound sentence made by conjoining two sentences, with an 'und' in the middle, is true if and only if both of the conjoined sentences are true (false otherwise).
7. A sentence made by adding a 'nicht' to another sentence is true if and only if the latter sentence is false.[5]

...and we're done, since it's a very simple language. You can now demonstrate, as theorems of this tiny theory for a tiny language, that, for instance:

1. 'Der Titisee ist blau' is true (in micro-German) if and only if the Titi Lake is blue.
2. 'Der Mond ist kalt und der Titisee ist nicht kalt' is true (in micro-German) if and only if the moon is cold and the Titi Lake is not cold.

...the proofs, such as they are, being left as exercises to the reader.

The logical positivists had considered truth a reprehensibly metaphysical notion; it was Tarski's treatment that made it once again philosophically legitimate. Davidson, following Quine, was less worried about truth than about meaning, and in fact was willing to take truth as a primitive: 'Truth,' he said late in life, 'is one of the clearest and most basic concepts we have, so it is fruitless to dream of eliminating it in favor of something simpler or more fundamental.'[6] That meant, he decided, that he could stand Tarski-style theories on their head—that is, treat the T-sentences as data points, and treat the theory as explaining, not truth, but the semantic features of the language.

What this means is that, in Davidson's use of a theory with Tarski's preferred structure, the T-sentences end up being a canonical form of representation for the data that Quine's field linguist was off collecting. Take our theory of truth for micro-German. The T-sentences it produces are data that can be checked against native speakers' utterances. (*Do* they say, 'Der Mond ist kalt' pretty much just when the moon is cold?) But now, and this was Davidson's driving idea, once we have an adequate theory of meaning for a language—i.e., one which allows us to prove all its T-sentences— we have a theory that exhibits the metaphysics implicit in that language. For example, the theory of micro-German explicitly tells you that there are objects (the items named by 'der Mond' and 'der Titisee'), and more ambitious quantifier-laden languages, such as our own, will exhibit what sorts of things we quantify over, thus allowing us to apply the Quinean procedure to them.[7]

We can give an initial estimate of the angular displacement imparted to analytic metaphysics by the Davidsonian Swerve if we briefly consider the train of thought with which Davidson meant to address the Question of Seriousness. Metaphysicians often tell us they want to know what kinds of things make up (the basic structure of) the world, and why should a theory of *what we mean* tell us *that*? As we've just seen, because a theory of meaning explains meaning on the basis of truth, in reconstructing your understanding of another's language, you have to take truth as primitive. The T-sentences are the data to which your theory of meaning is responsible, and so you have to be able to come up with the T-sentences. But because truth is a primitive, there's not going to be any theory-driven way of telling what makes a sentence true. So you'll have to *just tell* what a speaker of the language takes a sentence to be made true by, matching salient facts about the circumstances of speakers' utterances (the right sides of candidate T-sentences) with the utterances themselves (the left sides of the T-sentences), and taking those facts to be what make the utterance true. To do that is to presume that the speaker is *right* about those facts.

So interpretation—construction of a theory of meaning for speakers of a language—requires adopting the Principle of Charity (that is, taking the speaker to be mostly correct, and, though I haven't given this bit of the argument, mostly consistent). But now, since that is how *you* are going to be interpreted yourself, *you* will come out being mostly correct (and mostly consistent) yourself. So you can take the *deep* features of your understanding of the world (those captured by a theory of meaning for the language you speak) to be (at least almost entirely) correct.[8] In short, you are supposed to take the metaphysics produced by the Quinean recipe seriously, not because science used to put men on the moon, but because you cannot, as a matter of methodology, be interpreted as being *very* wrong. This may be a better or worse answer than Quine's; it is in any case quite different.

9.3

What happens to this ingeniously conceived project once we have given up the bivalence doctrine?

The data for a theory of meaning, we saw, are the T-sentences: these capture what a speaker of the language understands when he grasps the truth conditions of the sentences in his language.[9] When we drop the bivalence doctrine, we have to expand the data set to include partial-truth T-sentences. This is a point we made while discussing Quine's never-quite-completed argument for the indeterminacy of translation: if you don't know when sentences in a language are, in various ways, partially true, you don't speak or understand the language. A Davidsonian meaning theory is meant to capture what it is a speaker knows, in knowing how to speak a language, and so it must capture his mastery of its partial truths, as well as the all-out truth conditions of its sentences.

What, then, would partial-truth T-sentences look like? We can gesture at their general shape. For instance, we might write down sentences like

PT₁: 'Snow is white' is pretty much true (in English) if and only if snow is pretty much white.

as typical instances. But because there are indefinitely many (qualitatively different) truth qualifiers to be accommodated, we can't do better than the gesture, and this means that Davidson's project inherits two of the difficulties that, we found, undercut Quine's thought experiment.

First, with partial-truth T-sentences in the mix, you are no longer in a position to give a clean and comprehensive specification of the theorems which your theory of meaning must reproduce if it is to be counted successful. You can't say what your data are, and if you can't even do that, you certainly can't show that your theory of meaning reproduces the data.

Second, Davidson's interpreter is no better off than Quine's field linguist: he could not know what the partial truth values of a speaker's sentences are without already understanding the workings of the language and the contents of the sentences in it. That means that the program of constructing a theory of meaning held responsible to data that are independent of it is not one we can execute.[10]

Third, even if the partial-truth T-sentences were specifiable, there would be no way to produce an axiomatized, Tarski-style derivation of them, and here's a special case that shows why.[11] With bivalence in place, we saw (in our tiny theory of truth for micro-German) that you can specify the truth value of a conjunction as a function of the truth values of the conjuncts. But you can't do this with partial truth in play: p may be pretty much true, and q may be pretty much true, yet 'p and q' may be scarcely true at all. For example, it may be true enough that trucks are safer (because they are, modulo rollovers), and true enough that an El Camino is a truck (because although technically a car, it comes with a truck bed, and so is functionally a truck). But the conjunction is not true enough, because a way of hedging its truth that accommodates both of the conjuncts' very different qualifications is only weakly true—as displayed by the foolhardiness of drawing the obvious consequence of the conjunction. (In the next chapter, I will return to the point that partial truth is not well-behaved under conjunction.)

Fourth and finally, once you allow partial truth, you no longer have the option of treating truth as a primitive. When you characterize a claim as true enough, or true in a way, or almost entirely true...you need to be able to explain what you mean by that. These explanations, we have seen, proceed case-by-case, can themselves involve a great deal of subtlety and nuance, and as we are seeing, they are the occasion for a great deal of clarificatory theorizing. Whether or not full truth is what we understand the best, complacency is not an attitude we can reasonably adopt toward partial truth.[12] Once we take partial truth on board, we have to drop Davidson's direction of explanation: we cannot take truth for granted, and go on to use it to reconstruct first meanings, and then metaphysics. But recall that it was that direction of explanation which allowed Davidson his answer to the Question of Seriousness. (Once more: because you take truth as primitive, you also have to be able to take it that your informants are mostly right; so there is no methodological alternative to the Principle of Charity; insisting that the Principle of Charity has to be applied to yourself as well answers the Question of Seriousness.) Once we give up bivalence, we have to give up Davidson's reasons for taking the metaphysical output of his variation on the Quinean recipe seriously.

9.4

We pointed out that if you don't believe your scientific theory is true (e.g., if you regard it as an idealization or approximation), then you're not necessarily committed to its ontology. There is a similar objection to be made to the exercise of reading your ontology off a theory of meaning for your language, and I will use as my illustration Michael Thompson's recent treatment of the metaphysics of action.[13] The illustration is in many respects quite close to Davidson's own most celebrated attempt at ontology. First, the subject matter is close: Davidson thought of actions as a special case of events (and, not accidentally, called his first collection of papers *Essays on Actions and Events*). Second, like Davidson, Thompson holds his metaphysics responsible to the inferences that competent speakers of a natural language must take to be legitimate; that is, the metaphysics is to be elicited from the logical form of their utterances.

There are two important differences we need to highlight on our way in. First, Thompson substitutes Anscombe's way of picking out intentional actions for Davidson's: an action is intentional if the sincere agent must not refuse an answer to the question, 'Why did you do that?'—an answer that adduces the point (and not merely causal antecedents) of the action.[14] Second, Thompson focuses on a different family of linguistically built-in entailments than did Davidson, those encoded (in English) using grammatical aspect.[15] Action descriptions can be either perfective ('I baked the cake') or progressive ('I'm baking the cake,' 'I was baking the cake'), and these grammatical forms carry different implications. From the perfective 'I baked a cake,' it follows that at some point there *was* a cake. From the imperfective 'I was baking a cake,' it doesn't follow: perhaps I was interrupted by a phone call, and never got back to the baking.

Now, Thompson argues, what sounds like the present of 'I walked' isn't really that: 'I walk' means that I habitually walk. (What you might call the theatrical present is a relative of this usage: when the host of the cooking show, breaking the eggs, says, 'Now I break the eggs,' she means that this is the point in the recipe at which one generally breaks the eggs.) That there is no present form of the past perfect is a feature of the logic of our discourse about action. Let *atomic* actions be actions that have no parts that are themselves actions. If there were atomic actions, then there could be a present-tense form of the past perfective form. That is, and taking blinking to be among the likeliest candidates for an atomic action, you could say something on the order of 'I blink,' and not with the 'habitual' meaning; that is, you would thereby mean that you are performing the blink *now*, but also that it's *over and done with*. (Your claim would not, as Thompson puts it, 'span the present, reaching into the future.') Therefore, atomic actions would violate the logic of our action discourse. And therefore, all actions are composed of smaller actions; any action has further actions as its parts.

I think that Thompson's argument does a good job of eliciting the metaphysics implicit in grammatical aspect. But notice that this metaphysics has consequences that are strictly incredible. We are faced with an infinite regress, downward, in the composition of intentional actions, entailing that any action is composed of infinitely many infinitesimally tiny actions. The most important objection to that conclusion is that intentional action is, in the Anscombian rendering that Thompson is taking over, what gives 'Why?'-questions a grip; consequently it involves the exercise of some sort of attention and control. But human beings are small-finite creatures, and so there could not be that much attention and control to go around. That the ontology is unbelievable is good evidence for a weaker claim I expect to be simply granted: that we *don't* believe it. (And not because we have some other preferred ontology.) But, and here is the extent of my agreement with Thompson, we use the implicit ontology anyway.

The unbelievable ontology does not have to be believed, if the theory built into the rules of grammatical aspect is understood to be only approximately true. And that is evidently the right way to take it. Our grammar implicitly presupposes that the following conditionals are true across the board: if an action is now being performed, its planned progress is not yet over. (Of course, the action *itself* might be over at any point; actions, we have already reminded ourselves, can be interrupted.) If it is not yet over, then there must be a subsidiary action that is yet to be performed. But the former conditional is only true for the most part: I mentioned blinking as a likely candidate for an atomic action, and I think it actually is one. For those of us who are sufficiently literate to read a street sign at a glance, reading is sometimes an atomic action; I can imagine a battlefield use for a radio report deploying a present perfective of 'fire.' Because momentary actions—actions confined to the specious present—that we have cause to mention are relatively rare, our grammar, quite reasonably, does not bother to accommodate them; the historical processes that form a grammar will not necessarily clutter it up for the sake of a few oddball cases. And as far as the latter conditional goes, there need be no subsidiary intentional actions to be performed, even when an action stretches perceptibly into the future. Suppose that a competition diver is so thoroughly trained that, once she has launched into her dive, her muscles execute the movements of the dive in a way she can no longer control: she cannot abort or modify the remainder of the dive. (Although of course she can still, say, be shot out of the air by a lurking sniper.) Then the remainder of the dive is not a subsidiary intentional action, and not composed of distinct, smaller actions, but, as it were, an anticipated side effect of having started the dive.

The entailments that Thompson has located in our grammar (in our logic of action) are *true enough*: almost always true, when the actions we are concerned with are those we have cause to mention in day-to-day discourse, even if they are not true of oddball but everyday actions, like blinking; of oddball but exotic actions, like that of the overtrained diver; and of the very small actions at the edges of our powers of monitoring and discrimination. The logic of our grammar embeds an elegant and very usable approximation to what our actions are like in fact.

But, just because it *is* an approximation, we do not have to be committed to its ontology, and it is neither surprising nor worrisome that we find the nether reaches of it strictly incredible. Thompson acknowledges that the regress to even-smaller actions is likely to seem unpalatable, and gestures at theories of vagueness as one way out; his idea seems to be that somehow the regress will just fade away. That is in the spirit of our approach—vagueness is after all a form taken by partial truth—but probably unworkable in the letter. The expectation that a formal theory of vagueness can be cooked up to cleanly supplement Thompson's account is an instance of the widespread mistake of supposing that the right approach to the lack of fit between a representation and a messy world is a more elaborate representation. Better to think of it this way: the theory implicit in grammatical aspect is a good fit for what we regard as the practically more important or central cases of action. As we approach the threshold of our abilities to monitor and control our actions, the fit of the theory becomes worse, and in this neighborhood inferences made using it are no longer just defea*sible*, but typically defeat*ed*.[16]

Approximations are usable and informative in some circumstances, and misleading and unusable in others. If we were somewhat different creatures than we are—if many more of our day-to-day actions were like blinking or reading street signs (voluntary, but over and done with in the specious present, and without any voluntarily controllable parts), or like the rigid action of the diver (voluntary, and with perceptible duration, but, after initiation, without any subsequent voluntary parts)—we would have to have a different grammar, and a different logic of action. We should not assume that a metaphysics extracted from a theory of meaning goes very deep. Even a relatively small adjustment in what Wittgenstein called forms of life may sweep it away.[17]

I suggested in Chapter 2 that we are often faced with a choice between truth that is partial, on the one hand, and engineering our way to full truth, on the other. And in my view, the metaphysics of actions does present us with that choice. The question is not what actions already are, nor just what a satisfactory and approximately correct representation for them might be, but what actions are *to be*. The control structures that shape and produce our behavioral outputs are in principle (and not just in principle) open to redesign. I hope to discuss this issue further on another occasion.

9.5

Like physical theories, theories of meaning may be partially true (and they may embed theories that are partially true). Where you are not committed to the full truth of a theory, you cannot read your ontological commitments off your theory. Once the bivalence doctrine is rejected, what Davidson called the method of truth in metaphysics stops working. The Quinean Turn was founded on a mistake, and the Davidsonian Swerve inherited that mistake.

Davidson thought that Tarski-style theories of truth could be reappropriated as theories of meaning, that you could read your metaphysics off the theory of meaning for your language, and that methodological considerations would give you an answer to the Question of Seriousness. That's just been shown to be untenable, because the project can't accommodate partial truth: Davidsonian metaphysics presupposed the bivalence doctrine.

As with Quinean indeterminacy arguments and their successors, I'm not saying that you couldn't rethink *something* like Davidson's thoughts, in a way that took account of partial truth; I think that there is something deep— although very slippery—in them that one would want to save from the wreckage. But you would have to rethink them from scratch, they wouldn't come out looking anything like Davidson's ambitious constructive project, and at best you would end up with a *different* set of systematic philosophical views, one in which what is worth preserving in those thoughts would be expressed.

We've seen that, once you surrender bivalence, a great deal of the history of analytic metaphysics looks to have been a mistake. Gilbert Harman used to promote the counterintuitive view that it is often rational to go on believing what you came to believe for bad reasons, but those of us who regard this advice as bad advice treat identifying the mistaken presuppositions of our philosophical projects as normally being reason to surrender those projects.[18] That the topics in question are specifically philosophical gives this conclusion even more bite: in philosophy, the motivating frame for a problem is needed to determine what would count as a solution to it (and what would count as a *better* solution to it). Once you strip away the presuppositions that give a philosophical enterprise its point, you are no longer in a position to decide whether the theories you come up with are any good.

But still, Quine and Davidson have already slipped past the threshold of philosophy's specious present into, well, history. And so you may be thinking: that was then, this is now. Even if bivalence was an indispensable presupposition of past metaphysics, we haven't yet shown that our results matter in the same way to the metaphysics of the early twenty-first century. So in the next two chapters I will turn to two influential and contemporary metaphysical views (both associated with David Lewis), and to research programs derived from them, namely, the so-called Canberra Plan, and modal realism.

10

The Lewis Twist: Mind Over Matter

As I write, a great deal of metaphysics is modeled on or framed by yet a further modification to the Quinean Turn (that is, to Quine's recipe for generating an ontology, discussed in the previous chapter). I will call this modification the *Lewis Twist*, and it comes in two stages or versions. The first already has a name, the *Canberra Plan*, and in this chapter I will use David Lewis's treatment of the metaphysics of mind to introduce and illustrate it.[1] In the next chapter, I will proceed to the doctrine with which Lewis had by the end of his life become identified: modal realism, or the view that possible worlds—ways things might have been—really exist, in just the way the actual world does. The methodology of the second stage of the Lewis Twist doesn't yet have a name, and I'll call it the *Reverse Twist*. Since I am using Lewis's work as the locus classicus for both of these methodological moments, it's worth registering that he never took time out to distinguish them. As in our earlier discussion, the object of the exercise is to support the claim that, once partial truth is added to the mix, analytic metaphysics will have to be rethought from the ground up.

Analytical functionalism is the name is now standardly used for Lewis's expedition into philosophy of mind, which will be my primary illustration of the Canberra Plan. Philosophy of mind concerns itself with such items as beliefs, desires, sensations, etc., and there is no shortage of philosophical difficulties with these. You might have wondered how to determine what the contents of minds are. You might have wondered if it's possible to account for the ineffable feel of a sensation, or for the way that beliefs and the like are *about* things (their 'intentionality'). In certain philosophical moods, minds and mental states can become enormously strange items, too strange to be real. How *could* such odd objects be an integral part of a fully physical or natural world? It's a symptom of the perceived difficulty that Descartes invented a special kind of substance (unextended but thinking substance) to be a bearer of these features, and that popular conceptions of the mind have likewise, for as far back as the history goes, tended to identify minds with immaterial souls. A physicalist (someone who follows Quine in making the physical sciences the final arbiters of his ontology) might end up concluding that we don't have minds, because such things couldn't exist. Lewis understood the problem to be one of showing how the psychological subject matter can fit into the physical world, i.e., how it is that, despite appearances, it really just is physical after all. The claim that's supposed to cash this out is that psychological facts supervene on physical facts, and I'll call this the *Mind Over Matter* thesis.[2]

The Canberra Plan, we will see, is a program of assembling opinions held by the populace into theories of a philosophical subject matter, and then deriving ontologies from those theories. The populace, however, treat their opinions as only partially true, and this sort of partial truth, I will argue, prevents us from producing a unified theory from the scattered opinions. But if there is no theory, then a Quinean cannot read an ontology off it. The lesson I will draw is that partial truth requires us to be more cautious about what it is to have and use a theory than recent philosophy has too often been.

10.1

The Canberra Plan was born out of another formative moment in the early history of analytic philosophy, Russell's Theory of Descriptions.[3] Definite descriptions are constructions like 'the Saturday farmers' market,' or 'the only farmstand to carry organic raspberries,' and while it is a task for another occasion to account for why the Theory of Descriptions *was* such a formative moment, because I will in due course have a use for it, I am going to explain one problem it was meant to solve.

It's natural to think that the meanings of sentences are built up from the meanings of their parts, and it's also natural to think that the meaning of a name is its bearer—the item for which it stands. But now, what about names with contingently existing bearers, that is, names whose bearers might not exist? There might not actually be a Saturday farmers' market, in which case, it seems to follow that the expression, 'the Saturday farmers' market,' is meaningless; and since the meaning of a sentence containing such an expression is supposed to be a function of the meanings of its parts, it seems to follow that sentences containing the expression 'the Saturday farmers' market' would in those circumstances be meaningless. But surely we *understand* what those sentences mean, whether there is a Saturday farmers' market or not.

Bertrand Russell proposed that you could analyze sentences in which definite descriptions appear so as to eliminate what, on the face of it, looks to be a complex name. The idea was that definite descriptions carry with them a presumption that there is something that satisfies the description, but only one of it, and that this presumption just has to be made part of the content of the expression explicitly. For example, and taking a very straightforward case, one in which we are attributing properties to the items picked out by definite descriptions,

The Saturday farmers' market will go on, rain or shine.

was to be rendered as

There is exactly one Saturday farmer's market, and it will go on, rain or shine.

or, more elaborately, and glossing the uniqueness clause in the standard way,

There is a Saturday farmers' market (call it x), and for any Saturday farmer's market (call it y), y is identical with x, and x will go on, rain or shine.

(Henceforth, let's abbreviate that by allowing ourselves a quantifier that means 'there exists exactly one,' to be written $\exists!$)

On this rendering of definite descriptions, if there is no farmers' market on Saturday our claim about the Saturday farmers' market turns out to be false rather than meaningless: the meaning or sense of the expression has been distinguished from the bearer of the expression. The upshot is that definite descriptions are safe: you can use them without worrying that the meaningfulness of sentences that embed 'the Saturday farmer's market,' say, is contingent on whether there really is a farmer's market on Saturdays.

Lewis proposed to extend Russell's treatment to very complicated descriptions, complicated enough to be full-fledged physical or psychological theories.[4] Unlike Russellian descriptions, where we are introducing one term at a time, such theories might contain arbitrarily many theoretical terms (terms for the items making up the subject matter of the theory, and contrasted with other terms for other items): for instance, a psychological theory contains terms for the many different kinds of psychological states. Like Russellian definite descriptions, a theory, Lewis thought, implicitly claims to be uniquely satisfied. His idea was to use the uniquely satisfied theory as a term-introducing device, and so to let the theory tell you what its terms mean. To do that, he thought, is to produce a conceptual analysis of its theoretical terms, one that is firmly anchored in vocabulary that does not belong to the subject matter of the theory, and thereby to resolve one's philosophical difficulties with the theory's subject matter.

Let's see what this comes to by walking through Lewis's attempt to work up a philosophical picture of the mental. To demonstrate the Mind Over Matter thesis, one first characterizes the psychological subject matter by collecting platitudes or commonplaces about the mind: popular views concerning the mental that together amount to an implicit theory of the mental (conventionally referred to as 'folk psychology'). Now at this point, I need to register a reservation of my own, which the reader might or might not share. It is not at all clear that Canberra Planners are really collecting ordinary people's platitudinous beliefs. After all, if they were, wouldn't their lists be made up of such proverbs as 'Birds of a feather flock together,' or, as I suggested a moment ago, claims about immaterial souls? Whereas instead, Lewis and his followers pointed to claims along the lines of: 'People avoid pain,' or, 'If someone has a desire for something, and he has a belief that doing such-and-such is a way of getting it, then, other things being equal, he's going to do such-and-such.' I've already suggested that *these* 'platitudes' are not folk doctrine at all, but the projection onto the mind of a theory of practical rationality, one that is, as it happens, too crude to be plausible, and one that is held in the first place by philosophers, and by ordinary people only insofar as they have somehow absorbed views invented by philosophers.[5] Nonetheless, in the service of exploring the Canberra Plan, let's put these reservations to one side, and accept that the deliverances of folk psychology are the sort of thing that the Planners say.

Second, one conjoins the platitudes, so as to produce a single long sentence: the folk theory of the mind, rendered explicit.

Third, one replaces the philosophically puzzling theoretical terms in that long sentence ('pain,' 'desire,' 'belief,' and so on) with bound variables (and binds them to those 'exists exactly one' quantifiers which we introduced a few moments ago); that is, for instance and very crudely, one might replace

...and if someone has a desire that p,...and he has a belief that if q happens, that will cause p to happen, then he will come to have a desire that q...

with

$(\exists!F)(\exists!G)$ ...and if someone has an F that p,...and he has a G that if q happens, that will cause p to happen, then he will come to have an F that q...[6]

The result is called the theory's *Ramsey sentence* (or more precisely, its 'modified' Ramsey sentence, since we have added the unique instantiation requirement).

Fourth, one is at this point in a position to define such entities as beliefs and desires; they are simply occupiers of slots in the ramsified theory. Belief, for instance, is the sort of thing that is related to all the other theoretical entities mentioned by the theory, in the way that the theory says. Here is why that is supposed to demonstrate the Mind Over Matter thesis. In the course of ramsifying the folk psychological theory (i.e., of replacing psychological terms with bound variables), you have deleted all of the psychological terms. Let's suppose, just to keep things straightforward, that the nonpsychological vocabulary that remains is physical vocabulary. Then the resulting Ramsey sentence characterizes a pattern or structure in solely physical terms; when you proceed to define a psychological term (such as 'belief' or 'desire') as the occupier of such-and-such a slot in that pattern or structure, you are giving a physicalist definition of it.

Fifth and finally, once such a definition is on hand, you can ask what actually occupies the slot it picks out. Lewis thought that, when we are talking about human beings, the roles of mental states are played by neurological states of human brains. Were we discussing robots or space aliens, the occupiers of these slots might turn out to be something else entirely.

Abstracting from the example, this, then, is the Canberra Plan. Identify the platitudes and commonplaces about a subject matter of interest to you. Conjoin them into one long sentence. Replace the theoretical terms with variables bound by (unique-instantiation) existential quantifiers. Define the theoretical terms as the occupiers of the respective slots in the theory: that is, proceeding down one's list of n theoretical terms, the kth theoretical term is equivalent to a definite description, namely, the thing or property that, together with the respective 1 to $k - 1$ and $k + 1$ to n other things or properties, uniquely instantiates the theory. Scout around for what satisfies that description. And you're done.

10.2

Let's pause to compare the philosophical motivations for this methodology with its predecessors. First, it puts us in a position to apply the by-now-familiar Quinean ontological criterion. Ramsification of the theory puts the quantifiers up front, and so makes its existential commitments completely explicit. Indeed, Lewis took out time to reiterate Quine's view about those commitments: 'we have reason to think a good theory true; and if a theory is true, then whatever exists according to the theory really *does* exist.'[7]

Second, because the theoretical terms in your description have been replaced by what we can imagine as indexed blanks, leaving only other, theoretically unproblematic vocabulary, these definitions pick out part of a pattern in other, already understood, and unproblematic parts or aspects of the world. You thereby have a philosophical or conceptual analysis of the subject matter of the theory, and one which is expected to dissolve your philosophical worries about that subject matter. And so where Quine treated the ability to paraphrase away a problematic vocabulary as showing that what was apparently being talked about didn't really exist, the Canberra Plan treats such paraphrases as showing that it *does*.[8]

Third, in much the way that Russell's Theory of Descriptions distinguishes the meaning of a term from its referent, the Canberra Plan distinguishes the folk-theoretical role picked out by a term (more or less, a slot in the structure described by the theory) from whatever occupies that slot. So it armors your meanings against contingency. Your folk theory might be false, but even if there are no beliefs, desires, and so on, you are nonetheless in a position to understand what those theoretical terms *mean*.

In the Canberra Plan, folk theory replaced what, in Quine's version of the recipe, was scientific theory, and in Davidson's, theory of meaning. A good index of how severe a departure from its predecessors it was might again be how it addressed the Question of Seriousness: Why take metaphysics done this way seriously? Here is one answer (not the only one, and I'll discuss a second reply below):

> It is far beyond our power to weave a brand new fabric of adequate theory *ex nihilo*, so we must perforce conserve the one we've got. A worthwhile theory must be credible, and a credible theory must be conservative. It cannot gain, and it cannot deserve, credence if it disagrees with too much of what we thought before. And much of what we thought before was just common sense. Common sense is a settled body of theory—unsystematic folk theory—which at any rate we *do* believe; and I presume we are reasonable to believe it. (*Most* of it.)[9]

Lewis often wrote as though you could defend a theory by showing that it agreed with and systematized your 'intuitions'—and this is still the methodological common currency of the present period. He may even to some extent have been to blame for that; in any case, he perfectly exemplified in this respect the practices of his philosophical subculture. But I don't suppose that appeal to intuitions was meant by Lewis to be a distinct method; rather, I take it that intuitions were being treated as expressions of the folk theory, and so as evidence for what the folk theory was.[10]

This response to the Question of Seriousness might seem to be very different from Quine's (and very different from Davidson's), in that it shifts philosophical practice still further away from the touchstone of empirical data. But there is a way in which Quine's answer to the Question of Seriousness is still in play in the Lewis Twist—or rather, in its Canberra Plan phase. An implementation or execution of the Plan is meant to assuage your worries about a problematic class of entities by showing them to be occupiers of slots in a pattern, where the pattern is characterized using exclusively physical concepts. But it was Quine's implicit answer to the Question of Seriousness (roughly, physics puts men on the moon) that privileged physical concepts in the first place. Canberra Planners are willing to take existence claims seriously only when they can be convinced that nothing in them outruns the ontology of a (present or perhaps future) physics textbook. So a certain class of empirical claims is still the touchstone.

Through the Canberra Plan, the Quinean Turn continues to set metaphysicians' agendas. As Exhibit D, take Frank Jackson's foray into metaethics, that is, the metaphysics of ethics.[11] He calls his metaethical position 'analytical descriptivism' (which is a tip of the hat to 'analytical functionalism'). Jackson proposes to take a theory he calls mature folk morality—'what folk morality will (would) turn into under critical reflection'—and ramsify it, deleting all the prescriptive vocabulary in the process. Then he proposes to go on to rearrange the uniquely-satisfied Ramsey sentence to define the moral (that is, the nondescriptive) terms one by one: 'Fairness is what fills the fairness role; rightness is what fills the rightness role; and so on.' Since the only terms remaining in the Ramsey sentence are descriptive, we are being given descriptive definitions of ethical terms: we have effected a reduction of the ethical to the physical, or at least displayed the way that the ethical supervenes on the physical. Jackson's solution to the problem of showing how ethical recommendations can be located in a solely physical world straightforwardly implements the Canberra Plan.[12]

10.3

It is now time to consider how the Canberra Plan runs aground on partial truth. The problem is that the folk-theoretical platitudes that are the inputs to ramsification have to be understood as including ceteris paribus clauses. But that faces Canberra Planners with a dilemma. If we construe the ceteris paribus clauses as making platitudes only partially true, ramsification fails at the conjunction step; if we construe the platitudes as fully true, ramsification fails at the term deletion step. Either way, the Canberra Plan can't be used on the sort of folk theories to which it is supposed to be applied.

Returning to our full-dress illustration of the Canberra Plan, recall the sort of platitudes about our mental lives from which our folk-psychological theory was to be reconstructed, for instance:

> When you desire a hat, and you believe that if you give the man behind the counter the money, you'll get the hat, you'll give him the money.

Platitudes like this one are true only ceteris paribus, or other things equal. For instance, you won't give him the money if, as it turns out, you have no money; or if there are other things you want to do with the money; or if you're too shy to ask *this* person for the hat; or… As always with such ceteris paribus clauses, there are indefinitely many of these sorts of further conditions; it is not, exactly, that there are *infinitely* many of them, but rather that it is always possible to think up more. So there is no point in trying to fill in the list of ceteris paribus clauses, and so to give a flatly correct rendition of the platitude. The defeasibility we're pointing out is obvious enough to the folk: that the platitudes come with this sort of qualification is part of the folk-psychological theory (again, to the extent that there is such a thing); it would misrepresent ordinary people's understanding of how, say, desires work to leave it out.[13] We accordingly have two alternatives: we might understand the platitudes to be held as fully true, with their ceteris paribus clauses serving as part of their content. Or we might understand the content of the platitudes not to include ceteris paribus clauses, but take the folk to advance their psychological opinions as only partially true: true other things equal, or true ceteris paribus.[14] Let's consider both options, starting with the latter.

The second stage of the Canberra Plan is to conjoin the folk's platitudes into a single long sentence; this step has a substantive presupposition, which is that if such opinions are true, more or less, they can be brought together to make up a single coherent and true (enough) theory. But the folk platitudes come with ceteris paribus clauses; for this branch of our dilemma, we are understanding that to mean they are held as partial truths; we have already observed that partial truth is not well-behaved under conjunction.[15] And that general observation carries over to the class of special cases in which the truths are partial because they include ceteris paribus clauses. For instance, on the one hand, if a student's dissertation is accepted, it is a significant and original contribution to the field. That's what the rulebook says, but it's true only ceteris paribus, and note that this is not a case in which exceptions are to be thought of as a small residue of low-probability outliers. On the other, if a student's dissertation is a significant and original contribution to the field, the advisor will intervene with an editor to get it published. That also is true only ceteris paribus. But now, if we put these two partial truths back to back, and try to draw the conclusion of the hypothetical syllogism, we get an almost-flat falsehood: that if a student's dissertation passes, the advisor will intervene with an editor to get it published.

Let's look at another representative instance of the problem we are after, this time one generated by the platitudes of folk psychology. Surely it must be a commonplace that people find ways of not drawing inconvenient conclusions; in Lewis-style folk-theory-speak, that if you believe that p, and you desire that not-q but rather r, then even if p entails q, you will not come to believe q but rather r. Of course, everyone accepts that this commonplace is only true ceteris paribus: not if your rigorous training in drawing correct conclusions overrides your wishful thinking; not if it's so obvious you can't *not* draw the conclusion; not if you are being pressed closely on it… Here, however, is another commonplace, frequently listed by philosophers in their enumerations of the platitudes of folk psychology: that people *do* draw the conclusions of their beliefs; again in Lewis-style folk-theory-speak, if you believe $p, q, r, \ldots$, and these entail s, you will come to believe that s. That commonplace is also true only ceteris paribus: not if you're being obtuse or self-deceived; not if you're distracted; not if it's too complicated for you to see that s follows…

Conjoin these two platitudes, and you get the claim that if someone believes premises with inconvenient conclusions, he will draw them and he won't, ceteris paribus. (It's hard to know what to make of *that*.) And there is also a hypothetical syllogism in the making, whose conclusion is that people draw the inferential consequences of their wishful thinking. But that is mostly (though not entirely) false—in any case, much more false than the initial platitudes from which it is derived. As we all know, wishful thinking tends to be protected by an unwillingness to think through its implications. Just for instance, people generally have good reasons to believe that cosmetics and cosmetic surgery don't make you look younger; rather, they make you look, respectively, made-up, and like you've had cosmetic surgery. Those who self-deceivingly believe that they make you look younger also know that many other people avail themselves of both options. So they ought to infer that many of those around them are older than they look. But they scarcely ever draw that conclusion; rather, they take themselves to be able to judge age from appearance.

Briefly, the platitudes of folk psychology may be true enough taken one by one, but if all they are is true-other-things-being-equal, then they cannot be conjoined to make a theory that is true enough to bother with. The Canberra Plan is predicated on the idea that the terms we find problematic are to be defined via their theoretical role—their role in a *whole* theory—and if we have no theory, we have no way of explicating problematic psychological terms. If the platitudes of folk psychology are partially true, the Canberra Plan cannot be implemented, and its defense of the Mind Over Matter thesis fails.

Let us consider the other branch of the dilemma, on which the platitudes are taken as fully true, with the ceteris paribus clauses taken to be strictly part of the content of the platitudes out of which we are going to assemble our folk psychology. Here the important point is that what are supposed to turn out to be the theoretical terms of folk psychology appear *within* the ceteris paribus clauses: e.g., you will do what it takes to satisfy your desire, unless (among many other things) there's something else you *desire* more.

That is, the *unless*-clause invokes further desires, and this is entirely typical of the folk theories to which the Canberra Plan has been applied. Take an ethical platitude: you should keep your promises. That's understood to be true only ceteris paribus: unless you have another and overriding *obligation* to some third party, unless you would be *cruel* to do so, unless the results of breaking it would be so much *better* as to make it excusable...[16]

At the third stage of the Canberra Plan, we are supposed to replace terms such as 'belief' and 'desire' with bound variables. But those terms, we saw, crop up in the platitudes' ceteris paribus clauses, and how are we supposed to quantify into such a clause? Remember, we cannot replace the clause with the list of qualifications it represents, because we do not know what is on the indefinitely long list. The formal way to put the point is that ceteris paribus clauses essentially contain an ellipsis, that one way to appropriate certain of Wittgenstein's *Remarks* is as the observation that the '...' is a little-noticed logical operator, and that we do not know how to construct a logic that deploys both this operator and the standard quantifiers: we don't know how to quantify into an ellipsis.[17] But the point is not just formal: ramsification is a way of exhibiting the relations in which the terms of the theory (or the items they represent) stand to one another; fully exhibiting those relations is what allows one to state that one has captured the functional role of the theoretical term. When indefinitely many of the relations between the terms (or entities) of the theory are concealed in, and masked by, ceteris paribus clauses, you are not in a position to identify a theoretical term via its role in the network of relations between such terms, because you have left indefinitely much of the structure or pattern of relations out of your description. Since the point of the Canberra Plan is to demystify problematic entities by identifying them with slots in patterns in an unproblematic, usually physical, subject matter, the enterprise has failed if you can't identify that pattern. Ceteris paribus clauses keep parts of the pattern (in principle quite large parts) out of sight, and that is what the formal problem about quantifying into ellipses amounts to substantively.[18]

10.4

Partial truth, we've been emphasizing, comes in many qualitatively different forms, and that means that we can't take the upshots of partial truth in any particular case for granted. Getting the informative diagnosis we are after is best managed, in this instance, by considering a handful of objections to the argument we've just finished; because they pull in different directions, I'll list them first, and then talk my way through them as a group.

First of all, you might be worried that the argument is directed against an inadequate characterization of the Canberra Plan. After all, there is visibly a gap in the train of thought I've attributed to the analytical functionalist. Why couldn't an occupier of a slot in a physically specified theory be itself nonphysical: qualia (i.e., looks and feels), or a state of your immaterial soul?[19]

Second, and allowing that I have made the point that theories assembled Canberra-style leave out of the final product indefinitely large parts of the pattern they are tracing, perhaps the materials we have will nonetheless be enough to identify the objects that occupy the slots in the pattern. That is, once we have identified them—once we have, in a phrase that is tied to a different thread of the history of analytic metaphysics, fixed the reference of those terms—perhaps we can, for the purposes of settling our ontology, ignore the ceteris paribus clauses as noise.

Third, if the argument I have given works, surely it proves too much. It is widely accepted by philosophers of science that special sciences (meaning sciences like geology or meteorology, but not basic physics) produce generalizations that are true only ceteris paribus. Are we to conclude as well that we can't read ontologies off the special sciences? But we believe, correctly, that cumulonimbus clouds exist, and we believe it because meteorologists say so.

Fourth and finally, the argument I have given rests simultaneously on our inability exhaustively to specify the content of ceteris paribus clauses, *and* on our inferential command of them. But, the objection will run, the only reasonable explanation for that inferential command is an implicitly held theory. If we share such a theory, even if it is not best described as held in the form of *platitudes*, specifying its content must be a legitimate and doable project.

The first of these objections highlights how the Canberra Planners' picture of what is going on does work that is not visible in the procedure. In this picture, what we find, when we look at a slot in a physical pattern, is a smaller piece of that pattern, not an item of a dramatically different kind.[20] But when we look at what Lewis and others have understood those smaller pieces of pattern to be, we have an answer to the second objection: those smaller pieces aren't independently identifiable *things* that you could pocket and walk away with, leaving the pattern behind. Lewis himself thought that you couldn't count on different beliefs—as ordinary people individuate them, that is, by their contents—pairing up one-to-one with individual physical objects, rather as though they were marbles (the ones it's so easy to lose). Instead, he took them to be different aspects of a single inner state. So if you were Lewis, there wouldn't be any 'Water is H_2O'-like identifications of the beliefs that p, q, r...with distinct physical objects; there would just be patterns in the multiply-accessed physical object that underwrites your psychology.[21] If you understand the item you are trying to characterize to be just a bit of pattern, it really does matter that you know what the pattern is.

Turning now to the third and fourth objections, let me remind you of an earlier disclaimer, that I am trying to be agnostic as to how far the view I am developing should be adopted within philosophy of science. That said, what would the argument be telling us about the special sciences, if it were indeed applicable to them?[22]

What the misbehavior of its platitudes under conjunction and quantification told us about folk psychology was that sticking those platitudes end to end does not give you a *theory*. So the concern is that if the argument stuck to the special sciences, it would also be telling us that the special sciences don't give us theories. And that is what would be proving too much.

But recasting the objection this way exhibits the dubious assumption that underwrites it. Evidently there are two distinct senses of 'theory' in play. In one sense, theories are whatever it is that scientists produce and work with; in this sense, *of course* the special sciences provide theories—but we ought not to be confident that we know what sorts of things these are.[23] In the second sense, a theory is the sort of item investigated by old-style logicians and philosophers of science: a set of jointly held sentences, closed under some list of operations (especially conjunction). We should not assume that to have a theory in the first sense is to have a theory in the second; Canberra Planners do (substituting folk theories for the scientists' theories), and that is why they attempt to proceduralize the production of such theories for their favorite philosophical topics. If my argument does work when it is applied to the special sciences, it shows only that we should not conflate these two senses of 'theory': that, even in the special sciences, the scientists' competences and results are not captured by anything as straightforward as a list of sentences they are said to believe. Accepting *this* conclusion would not be proving too much, not by any means.[24]

Once we have allowed that the we-know-not-whats that underwrite both everyday inferential competences and the accomplishments of scientists are not necessarily anything as straightforward as lists of sentences, we can meet the fourth objection as well. We have implicit theories that underwrite our command of ceteris paribus clauses...in the first sense, namely, there is something, we know not what, that supports the relevant competences. But we should not assume that it must be a theory in the second sense, i.e., a list of sentences, and that programs like the Canberra Plan, which proceed on that assumption, are thereby legitimized by the observation that we must have implicit theories.

If I am right, then, the most important lesson to learn from the failure of the Canberra Plan in the face of partial truth is that we should not be too quick to assume that domain-specific inferential competence and understanding is a matter of having a theory—in the 1950s–1960s philosopher-of-science conception of a theory. Instead, we should be looking for other ways of understanding what it is we are doing when we understand.

10.5

We've been looking at one of those bumps in a carpet. The folk are only going to accept the components of the theory proposed in their name as true-with-a-shrug, as broadly true. You can push the bump from the content to the assertion sign, or from the assertion sign to the content; maybe you can push it somewhere else, but it is not going to go away. Claims embedding ceteris paribus clauses have all of the markers we identified as typifying partial truth: inferences deploying them are defeasible; the claims themselves are inferentially restricted (and in fact that is exactly what a ceteris paribus clause specifies, restrictions on the inferential deployment of the claim); they exhibit slack with respect to direction of fit (we correct them when they don't match the way things are, but only if they are *too* far out of line).[25] Treating the ceteris paribus clause as part of the content of such a claim perhaps allows you to *say* that the claim itself is fully true; but (recalling once more the argument of Chapter 4) its inferential matching and more generally its intellectual role are anchored by the explicit content of the claim, and not by the never fully articulated hedge. The inferential management problems posed by ceteris paribus clauses drive the argument we have just given, and those remain no matter how you relabel the claims to which the clauses are attached. (If you like, we can reply that for inferential purposes it's *true enough* that the claim is partially true.) Once you have partial truth this much on board, the Canberra Plan fails fatally at one or another of its steps.

My own sense of how we should proceed past this conclusion (but this is trying to anticipate the results of detailed investigation of one or another attempted domain of application, and should not be treated as the conclusion of an argument) differs somewhat from the upshots of introducing partial truth into the Quinean and Davidsonian projects. Approximately true physical theories, and approximately true theories of meaning, are not straightforward guides to one's ontology, but they are worth thinking about carefully in that connection: as we saw in our discussion of Thompson, sometimes (not always) you can derive an approximately true ontology from an approximately true theory. But if I am right about how the Canberra Plan goes wrong, it is a mistake to think that attempting to execute it gives us a theory at all, as opposed to a heap of partial truths that we do not know how to assemble into a theory. (That is, bearing in mind the distinction drawn in the last section: in the 1950s–1960s philosophy-of-science sense of 'theory.') If we have no theory, we should not be expecting our theory to deliver even a partially true ontology.

Analytical functionalism ascribes a psychology of beliefs and desires to ordinary people. In Chapter 6, we saw an argument for adopting a more flexible psychology, one that allocates mental states to the roles that reasoning with partial truth requires. (To believe is to take to be true, and since we use what we take to be truths in our reasoning, we must be equipped with belief; once we have accepted partial truth, we must also be equipped with states that amount to taking to be partially true.) That might look like an approximation to belief psychology, and conversely, if we accept it, it might make belief psychology look like an idealization or approximately true psychological theory itself. But if it does, that is a result we arrive at by direct appeal to an improved theory of truth and rationality, and not by way of the Canberra Plan.[26]

I have suggested that we typically face the following choice: to work with one or another partial truth (an approximately true psychological theory would belong under this heading), or to reengineer a part of our world to make a description of it fully true. So we might consider under what circumstances it would pay to *implement* one or another theory that Canberra Planners have attributed to the folk. Sticking with belief-desire psychology as an example, we might attempt (and AI researchers have attempted) to build devices with a set of states that encode or represent goals, and another set of states that represent truths about the world. Or we might train people to conform to some variant of the theory in one or another restricted domain. In section 2.2, I used automobiles to pick out a domain in which we have engineered our way to a great many hard truths, and for the employees of an auto dealership I imagine there are well-defined goals that can be used to guide behavior; perhaps this is a domain for which training in the imagined folk theory would be a good idea.[27] The practical question is hardly ever posed, and so it is not one with which we have a great deal of experience, but it is in my view well worth exploring.

11

The Bare Necessities

When Lewis gave his final twist to the Quinean Turn—the one I have labelled the Reverse Twist—it was confined to a particular subject matter. His modal realism was the view that possible worlds exist in just the way the world we live in does. Possible worlds were supposed to be overall or global ways things might have been, each a complete cosmos unto itself, each causally and spatially isolated from all the rest, and all of them jointly represented as arranged in a fictitious super-space, in which the more similar possible worlds were nearer to one another, and less similar ones farther away. The actual world was supposed to be just one of these universes, distinguished from all the rest merely by being the possible world that we happen to inhabit. Lewis's intent was to provide a theory of modality, that is, of whatever is being talked about via the *coulds, musts, would've's, had tos,* and so on that mark out one of the most obscure parts of the subject matter of philosophy.

I'll first provide a bit more of an introduction both to the elements of Lewis's theory of modality and to their uptake in the discipline. I'll explain why Lewis's modal realism was an application of the recipe he had inherited from Quine, and provide a bit of compare-and-contrast vis-à-vis the other variants we've seen so far. Then I'll turn to the answer Lewis gave on this occasion to what we have been calling the Question of Seriousness, and explain how and why it differed from the one that had sufficed for the Canberra Plan. I'll argue that, given his reasons for taking his theory of modality seriously, he was committed to giving an account of the ordinary, garden-variety counterfactuals used by ordinary people on ordinary occasions (a counterfactual conditional being a sentence like, 'If so-and-so had happened, then such and such would have happened'). And I'll argue that he was committed to giving a *reductive* account of those counterfactuals: viz., a way of paraphrasing them away, without change in content.

With the setup completed, I'll go on to argue that Lewis's reduction of counterfactuals fails. The problem, it will turn out, is that if we take the ordinary counterfactuals as fully true, the paraphrases provided by Lewis's account turn out to be only partially true, and that short-circuits the Quinean move to the existence of possible worlds: once again, partial truth derails a variation on the Quinean program in metaphysics.

Lewis devoted a great deal of effort to the construction of a systematic metaphysics. This is not the place to engage all of it, and so I am going to divide up a more complicated argument between two separate treatments. Here I will focus on Lewis's modal realism, and defer the examination of the further and very interesting lessons of the failure of Lewis's reduction for our understanding of modality to a companion piece.[1] Because the present discussion is following the straightest line to its conclusion that it can, aficionados of his work are likely to have reactions of the form, 'But what about the many other resources that Lewis's system provides?' If that's you, please read the interlocking argument in that further discussion before deciding that I have overlooked some widget in Lewis's toolbox.

I will, however, consider one objection on Lewis's behalf here: that taking account of the similarities among possible worlds obviates the slippage between the ordinary counterfactuals and their Lewisian paraphrases. My reason for taking up the objection is that it will allow me to say what problem is really at the bottom of the failed reduction. That will in turn allow me to tie the reasons we cannot read an ontology off Lewis's theory of modality back to the arguments of Chapters 4 and 5.

I'll withdraw a claim I will have allowed for the sake of the argument, that the ordinary counterfactuals which Lewis was trying to reduce are fully true, this in order to remind the reader that the dilemma posed in Chapter 2 is still in force. Normally, I will suggest, we are forced to choose between, on the one hand, paying the price (often enough, the *financial* price) for bivalent counterfactuals, and, on the other hand, making do with counterfactuals that are only partially true. I'll conclude by reviewing the progress of the argument of Chapters 8–11, and assessing what partial truth means for analytic metaphysics.

11.1

The view I've just described, smacking as it did of parallel-universes science fiction, was considered so outrageous that the most common objection to it was, Lewis acknowledged, an incredulous stare: how could anyone talk himself into believing such a thing?[2]

Quite apparently, by applying the Quinean recipe that we've been considering over the previous three chapters.[3] I'm going to describe, a bit harshly, the way the application looks at first blush. I have three reasons for my uncharitable first pass over it: it will allow me to give the elements of the theory a quick once-over; it will put me in a position to explain how a view that was widely regarded as outrageous and incredible nonetheless served as a frame for much further work in metaphysics; last but not least, it will set the stage for asking what Lewis took the real motivations of the view to be.

When you looked around at the field, the modal realist's progress seemed to have two stages, the first of which consisted in elocution lessons. Lewis taught his students and followers to speak in what is probably best chararacterized as an unusual dialect. Instead, for instance, of saying, 'It might have rained,' one was trained to say, 'In some other possible world, it rained.' Instead of saying, 'It's necessarily the case that rubies are red,' one was trained to say, 'In all possible worlds, rubies are red.' In the odd accent that came to be spoken in analytic philosophy departments around the world, counterfactual conditionals like, 'If there had been more States, the flag would have had more stars,' were pronounced (roughly) like this: 'In nearby possible worlds'—i.e., near to us in the similarity space in which the possible worlds were imagined as embedded—'in which there are more States, the flag has more stars.' On occasion, the dialect required odd circumlocutions: one was, for instance, trained to replace the young Marlon Brando's line, 'I could have been a contender,' with, 'In some possible world, a counterpart of mine is a contender.' (If you're not quite sure what those counterparts are, that's all right; I'll get back to them.) Despite the dialect's awkwardness, graduate students and even undergraduates learned to speak it with remarkable fluency.[4]

At the second stage, the Quinean recipe was applied to the dialect. Speakers of the dialect were explicitly quantifying over possible worlds; whatever you quantify over, you are ontologically committed to; therefore possible worlds—other ways things might have been—really exist. Once again, we have a startling metaphysical conclusion arrived at by applying the Quinean formula. And once again, Lewis's application of the formula itself served—and as of the time of writing, still serves—as the framework for a great deal of further philosophical writing on a surprisingly diverse range of topics in metaphysics.

Some of this was framing of the direct sort that we have seen in previous chapters, and as Exhibit E I will use Gideon Rosen's 'Modal Fictionalism.' We have already gestured at an empiricist rebuttal to the Quinean Turn: that it's possible to use your scientific theories as tools for systematizing and predicting observable phenomena, without actually *believing* the theories; if you don't believe the theory, you need not believe what it says about what exists. Rosen adapted van Fraassen's anti-realist response into an objection to Lewis's modal realism: you could regard the ontology of possible worlds as a useful fiction, keeping the manner of speaking but disavowing belief, and so, the existence of all those possible worlds. (Why the shift from the empiricist to the fiction-alist way of putting the point? Presumably because you cannot observe what could have or would have happened, and so the purpose of the the-ory cannot be to predict observations.) This is a move that makes no sense unless Lewis's appropriation of the Quinean Turn is already the framework in which one's thinking—albeit in this case critical thinking—is taking place.[5]

As we will see, Lewis devoted a great deal of effort to finding ways to say one thing or another using the vocabulary of possible worlds. And so the most pervasive and most important manner in which the Lewis Twist came to frame further work in analytic metaphysics was the widespread adoption and entrenchment of the diaspora dialect I was describing a moment or two ago. Certainly philosophers had mentioned possible worlds before, but not with this frequency, not in connection with as many top-ics, and not nearly as casually. Even philosophers who did not accept Lewis's views about the full-fledged existence of other ways things might have been nonetheless signed onto the practice; that practice implicitly assumed that you could unproblematically paraphrase a great many modally loaded assertions into the vocabulary of possible worlds. Since modally loaded assertions are pervasive, that meant that the conceptual apparatus of possible worlds turned up throughout the metaphysical argumentation of an entire generation—not yet a previous generation—of philosophers. Now, to treat the paraphrases as unproblematic was to act as though the possible-worlds way of speaking really *was* no more than a dialect or accent; as though moving back and forth between the different forms of speech left the content of what one was asserting intact. To remind us again of where we're going, I'm going to argue that that assumption was a mistake.

11.2

As always, when we are determining what to make of a philosophical position, its answer to what we were calling the Question of Seriousness deserves our most serious attention. Why did Lewis think we should be taking his ontology seriously? I presented the ontology as having been extracted from something like a regional dialect, and I emphasized that the characterization has a certain amount of sociological truth to it. But of course the idea that you can read the metaphysical structure of the world off of a *funny accent*—especially one so artificially acquired—is just frivolous, and it certainly was not why Lewis thought that his hard-to-believe existence claims about possible worlds should nevertheless be believed. The main ingredient in his second variant of the Quinean recipe was no longer physics,[6] nor Davidson-style meaning theory, and since the quote I used to introduce the notion of folk theory in the last chapter was taken from Lewis's discussion of modality, you might suppose that Lewis was helping himself to a Canberra-Plan folk theory. In fact, although he seems never to have clearly discriminated his different responses, Lewis amended his former answer to the Question of Seriousness to meet the demands of a theory of modality, and here is some speculation as to how that happened.

First of all, metaphysical possibility and necessity are esoteric topics, there isn't all that much that ordinary people have to say about them, and when they do, their opinions seem not to be particularly strongly held: think of how many times you have heard someone say, shrugging, 'I guess *anything's* possible.' Second, recall that the philosophers had to be retrained to speak in a way that provided the theoretical terms that would serve as input to the Canberra Plan. It's not obvious how to apply the Canberra Plan to the previously available *woulds* and *weres*; but once you've substituted a more tractable way of speaking, you need an argument that you haven't inadvertently switched out the folk theory for something else. And third, even once you have laid out a folk theory, you still need to explain why you would want to take *that* seriously; some folk theories—e.g., of luck—are no better than superstition, and don't warrant commitment to their ontologies at all. Some other folk theories, and in particular folk psychology, have been said to have otherwise unobtainable predictive power to recommend them.[7] But again, prediction could not be the payoff of a folk theory of modality. All you ever see is what is actual, never what merely might have happened, so predictions about modal matters cannot be observationally confirmed or falsified.

Lewis inclined to the view that an appeal to a folk theory of modality, anyway on its own, wouldn't do the job. Instead, or as well, his theory of modality was to earn its keep by solving philosophical puzzles, and I will shortly consider which puzzles Lewis proposed to solve, and what would be required in order to solve them. If his solutions were successful, then, just as the usefulness of sets in mathematics gives mathematicians reason to believe that sets exist, so the usefulness of possible worlds in philosophy would give philosophers reason to believe possible worlds exist. Notice that the usefulness of mathematics in physical theory is no longer being appealed to; it is the fruitfulness of using sets in mathematics considered as an autonomous discipline. Taking the analogy as is means taking on possible worlds because of their usefulness in philosophy, considered as an autonomous discipline.[8]

This may be a better or worse answer to the Question of Seriousness than those given by Quine, Davidson—and by Lewis himself, when was wearing his Canberra Planner hat. One will want to think very carefully about this motivation for accepting an ontology; how *could* the ability to provide solutions to a repertoire of problems found only on the professional philosopher's bookshelf be a guide to the structure and contents of the universe? It is in any case different from those earlier answers.

11.3

Lewis's ontology of possible worlds was to be read off his theory of modality; his theory of modality was to be adopted perhaps because it was a folk theory, but in any case because it solved enough in the way of tough philosophical puzzles to warrant its ontological costs. What puzzles was the account of modality then responsible to; and if it was a folk theory, where was the folk theory to be found?

If the theory *is* meant to be a reconstruction of a folk theory, that folk theory must be something that ordinary people have a good many decently articulated opinions about. We have already mentioned that mere possibility and necessity are not like this.[9] However, ordinary people *do* advance, often with a good deal of confidence, a great many opinions about what *would* have happened, if… Such counterfactual conditionals do real work in our reasoning (even if it is hard to say what that work is), and we rest real weight on them (even if we as yet are not sure why). Our confidence and our control of the nuances of our counterfactuals rapidly dissipate when the objects about which we are framing them become exotic and unfamiliar.[10] So to the extent that Lewis is relying on his earlier answer to the Question of Seriousness, he is making his theory responsible to ordinary counterfactuals about ordinary, garden-variety objects.

Under the heading of philosophical puzzle-solving, the list of metaphysical payoffs included, to be sure, an account of possibility and necessity: something is possible if it's true in some possible world, necessary, if it's true in all of them. But, and more substantively, we've mentioned that counterfactuals were given a related analysis, as (roughly) truth of conditionals in 'nearby' possible worlds.[11] And, Lewis thought, '[i]f possible worlds help with counterfactuals, then, they help with many parts of our thought that we could scarcely imagine being without.'[12]

Just for instance, causation was analyzed in terms of counterfactuals; the direction of time was explained in terms of counterfactuals; colors were then explained using causation, as were, we saw in the previous chapter, psychological states. Causation was also used to analyze perception, action, and persistence over time, as well as to give decision theory a workaround for Newcomb's Problem.[13]

In addition, Lewis used possible worlds to explain propositions and the contents of propositional attitudes. These analyses do not at first glance deploy counterfactuals; just to give you their flavor, a proposition is thought of as a partition of the set of possible worlds, and so the content of a belief, for example, is (to a first approximation: the epicycles come thick and fast) the set of possible worlds in which the belief comes out true.[14] But here is a promissory note: it is going to turn out that those analyses of content succeed only if Lewis's analysis of counterfactuals also succeeds.

The important point to notice here is this. In the lengthiest and most important parts of the series of philosophical analyses that used Lewis's possible-worlds ontology, counterfactuals have the role of a bottleneck. If the account of modality is to be accepted on the basis of the puzzles it solves, Lewis's theory of modality is responsible to the counterfactuals, and not just any counterfactuals, but the ones that figure into the puzzles. Causation, perception, and so on are ordinary notions, and the philosophical theories Lewis constructed of them were held responsible to intuitions about ordinary objects. So again, the counterfactuals in question must be ordinary ones about ordinary things. So Lewis's amended answer to the Question of Seriousness requires his account successfully to analyze counterfactual claims about the ordinary sorts of things that ordinary people have occasion to talk about in their everyday lives.

11.4

Successful analysis, in this case, turned out to mean reduction, that is, eliminative paraphrase; thus, a successful analysis of counterfactual conditionals would be a formula for restating the content of a counterfactual conditional that used only the conceptual apparatus of possible worlds (and, of course, nonmodal vocabulary), and that emphatically did not itself contain counterfactual conditionals. That is perhaps a little bit of a surprise, and so we need to explain how it came to pass that Lewis accepted—and, I am going to suggest, not by mistake—a demand as unfashionable as this one.

Let me mention a possible red herring, both to get it out of the way, and to continue our comparison of the Reverse Twist with earlier versions of the Quinean technique. Per the Quinean formula, the move required showing that quantification over possible worlds could not be paraphrased or reduced away; the reduction of possible worlds to some other class of entity (such as world-descriptions, i.e., structures of symbols) would be to show, as in Quine, that they *didn't* exist. Accordingly, Lewis devoted a great deal of effort to arguing that you couldn't be reductionist about possible worlds; he dismissively labeled the threatened reductions 'ersatz' possible worlds, and allocated a lengthy chapter to blocking ersatzism.[15] As per usual, what matters for our purposes is not whether his arguments were successful, but what they tell us about what he was attempting to do. First, once again, the attempt to parry reductionist objections presupposed, and made sense only in terms of, the Quinean Turn. Second, we have reverted to the original Quinean recipe, as far as the role of reductions goes, and this is why I have been calling Lewis's treatment of modality the Reverse Twist. In the Canberra Plan, you will recall, a reduction served to show that a problematic class of entities *does* after all exist; Canberra Plan reductions are meant to assuage the worry that your ontology is outrunning the contents of current or plausibly future physics textbooks. But when it comes to possible worlds, it would be futile to try assuaging *this* worry.[16] The point to keep in mind just now is that we are not arguing about whether Lewis was a 'reductionist' or an 'antireductionist' (that's the red herring): he was committed to resisting reductions *of* possible worlds, and, I am about to argue, he was committed to the reduction of modality, including counterfactual conditionals, *to* possible worlds.

There are normally two distinct, albeit related, motivations for a reductionist program. One is the worry that you don't understand your own vocabulary, in this case, the *coulds, woulds, musts,* and so on; I will focus on this motivation in the companion piece I mentioned earlier. The second is metaphysical: *Coulds* and *woulds* and *musts* seem like spooky items, items that for one reason or another philosophers have found to be strictly incredible. In claiming that they were really just facts about the configuration of possible worlds, Lewis was getting rid of the spookiness: possible worlds were alleged to be places much like this world, so, not spooky at all.

Thus the Reverse Twist inherited some of the *spirit* of the Canberra Plan, which, we saw, meant to show that items like beliefs and desires were not spooky. Now, first, a thesis with the force of, 'There's nothing metaphysically spooky here, because the __s are really just __s' has to be given content, one way or another: without saying what the cash value of such a claim is, you don't know what's been said, or how to think about whether to believe it. (That's true no matter how newfangled one makes the idiom in which one states the thesis; for instance, if a metaphysician tells you that he's identifying the 'truthmakers' for modal statements, he owes you an explication of the content of that claim.) Over the earlier part of the twentieth century, it was traditional to couch claims of this form as reductions; for instance, the phenomenalist insistence that material objects were really patterns in the sense-data was redeemed as the claim that you could translate statements about material objects into statements about the sense-data. Later on, when reductions became less popular, the content was given by a supervenience claim. These were really the only two generally available options, and while Lewis usually preferred supervenience, he realized that, in this case, it was not after all a live option.

In Chapter 10, I introduced supervenience via Lewis's attempt to display items of one kind as features of patterns in items of another kind, but the official definition is given in modal terms: the psychological (for example) supervenes on the physical if (roughly) the psychological facts *could* not be different unless the physical facts *were* different, too.[17] A supervenience account of modality in terms of possible worlds would have to be committed to something on the order of: if the modal facts were different, the possible worlds would be different, too. Because the ontology of possible worlds is meant to eliminate spooky modal notions, and because the *woulds* of counterfactual conditionals belong to the category deemed spooky, there ought to be no sense given to the idea that the overall configuration of possible worlds might be (or would have been) different than it is. We do not have to worry that 'the geography of logical space is a contingent matter,' because contingency is one of the phenomena that the geography of logical space is to explain.[18] Because of the role of modal notions in supervenience accounts, supervenience is not available to cash out the content of Lewis's possible-worlds account of modality. And since the other available option was still old-style reduction, Lewis availed himself—for just this one subject matter—of that.[19]

Second, in a Quinean frame of mind, talking about spooky, strictly incredible items commits you to believing in them. A reduction avoids that outcome, by paraphrasing everything you need to say using the suspect vocabulary, without loss of content, into a vocabulary that does not commit you to the very spookiness you are trying to explain away. The parallel worry, which I discuss elsewhere, that you literally do not understand what you are talking about, equally requires that you do not explain what you are talking about in the vocabulary you suspect you do not understand.

On the two motivations we have identified for a reduction, the force of the demand turns out to be very much the same—regardless, that is, of whether you are making a metaphysical claim, or purporting to give a conceptual analysis. I'll introduce a bit of shorthand: vocabulary that does not carry along with it commitment to the existence of spooky modality I'll call *modality free*; vocabulary that does, I'll call *modality laden* or *modally loaded*. In the material mode, I'll call an object *modally extended* if it is found in more than one possible world, and *unextended* if it is found in only one.

There are already complaints about Lewis's reduction in the literature, to the effect that his paraphrase requires understanding what a possible world is, and in addition, that when you quantify over possible worlds, you must be taking for granted what possibilities there are. Because I don't think we will learn about partial truth by revisiting these arguments, I am instead about to construct a very different argument, one that turns on counterfactuals, and whose conclusion sticks even if the extant complaints are waived (in other words, *even* if you allow possibility, and what sorts of items count as possible, as acceptable and well-understood primitives). To help keep track of the distinctive problem that I mean to pose for Lewis's reduction, let's extend the vocabulary a bit further: vocabulary that commits you merely to possibility and necessity, but not to counterfactuals, I'll call *modally thin*. In the material mode, I'll similarly describe as *modally* or *counterfactually thick* the objects to which one is apparently committed by counterfactually loaded vocabulary: objects that have counterfactuals built into their metaphysical structure, and that cannot, without deploying counterfactuals, be distinguished from similar but unintended items.

Here's a comparison, to help you keep the requirement these terms outline in focus. Suppose that you thought that *lasting through time* was philosophically spooky (maybe because that sort of time, the sort that *goes on*, seemed metaphysically incredible to you), and that you proposed to do away with it by reconstructing enduring objects as stacks of temporal slices of those objects (as gets said these days, 'time slices'). If you did, you would require the time slices to have no duration themselves (to be 'temporally thin'); because temporally thick time slices would have the spooky lasting-through-time built into them, they would not serve to eliminate it. And so, in characterizing the time slices, you would need to avoid temporally thick descriptions that had the effect of imputing duration to them. Moreover, you would need to do so even if you were willing to allow temporal position—there being different times—as a metaphysical primitive. Analogously, if you want to do away with the spookiness of the *woulds* in your counterfactuals, by interpreting the subject matter of those counterfactuals really to be modally thin possible worlds, you will need to avoid counterfactually loaded descriptions that have the effect of imputing counterfactual breadth to those worlds.[20]

11.5

Since the test of Lewis's account is whether it can give reductions of ordinary counterfactuals, let's introduce a very low-key test case:

If I turned the key, the car would start.

In the diaspora dialect, the sentence is recast roughly as follows:

In the nearest possible worlds in which I turn the key, the car starts.

But in Lewis's recommended paraphrase, that is to say:

In the nearest possible worlds in which my counterpart turns a counterpart of the key, a counterpart of the car starts.

—which makes this a good occasion to introduce his notion of counterparts.

On Lewis's way of thinking, although counterfactuals seem to mention actual objects ('If I were to turn the key…' seems to be saying something about *me*), we should construe them as picking out corresponding but distinct objects in other possible worlds: your counterparts are not *you*, but items that are relevantly similar to you, both intrinsically and in terms of the roles or positions they occupy in their respective possible worlds.[21] Counterparts allowed Lewis to avoid the awkwardness of speaking as though *you* were an inhabitant of another world—as though you were both here and in some other place, one that's *so* very far away that it doesn't even count as far away.[22] More importantly for us, there is a reductionist motivation: modally thin worlds cannot contain objects that are not themselves modally thin. By decomposing counterfactually extended objects that won't fit into modally thin worlds, we obtain counterparts: their modally thin elements, which do fit.

The problem with paraphrasing our exemplary ordinary counterfactual, then, is going to be this: the ordinary objects it mentions—myself, my car key, the car—are not themselves modally thin. The paraphrase must produce counterfactually unextended counterparts of these items, in a way that preserves the content of the ordinary utterance. I am about to argue that this condition cannot be satisfied.

Once again, 'If I turned the key, the car would start' is being rendered as something along the lines of, 'In the nearest possible worlds in which my counterpart turns a counterpart of the key, a counterpart of the car starts.' Now, when I gesture at the person I might have been, sitting in the driver's seat, about to turn the key, I have in mind someone who is, inter alia, a *person*—and 'person' is a modally thick concept. (That's what's built into the ordinary understanding of ordinary counterfactuals that we are trying to paraphrase.) Suppose it were true of some lookalike of myself that, if you breathed on him, he'd vanish; then he wouldn't be a person, but (probably) a ghost. Or again, recall that most of a person's mental states are dispositional rather than occurrent.[23] If no such dispositional facts are true of my lookalike, then he doesn't have a mind; if he walks and talks anyway, then he isn't a person, and certainly isn't a possible version of *me*.

Being a person is in this respect typical of ordinary objects; to be an ordinary object is in most cases to possess indefinitely many modal properties. It's not a car, if, were someone to open the hood, it would try to devour him. (In that case, it's some kind of a monster.) It's not a car if, were you to shift into drive, it would suddenly disintegrate into a pile of dust. (Maybe, in that case, it's a dust sculpture.) It's not a key if, were you to divulge the plans, it would hurry back to the mother ship to tell the fleet commander. (In that case, it's an alien secret agent in disguise.) When I produce an ordinary counterfactual, I have in mind ordinary objects, and thus I am implicitly excluding such cases: I am committing myself to the car starting, when I turn the key, but I am not committing myself, one way or the other, to what would happen if something which looked a great deal like me, but was a ghost, turned an alien spy camouflaged as a key while sitting in an object that looked like a car, but, in virtue of its modal properties, was a monster or a dust sculpture.

If the reductive paraphrase is to preserve the content of the ordinary counterfactual that serves as its reference point, then it must exclude those cases. Because there are obviously indefinitely many of them, we must understand Lewis's rendering of my ordinary counterfactual to contain a ceteris paribus clause:

> In the nearest possible worlds in which my counterpart turns a key-counterpart, the car-counterpart starts...*unless*:
>
> were you to ask him a question, about anything at all, he'd draw a blank; or, were you to breathe on him, he'd vanish; or, were you to open the hood, the 'car' would try to devour you; or, were the secrets to be uttered, the 'key' would return to the mother ship; or, were the 'key' to be turned, the 'car' would disintegrate into a pile of dust...and so on.

But notice, now, that the ceteris paribus clause contains counterfactual conditionals, and these are the modally problematic items that the reduction was intended to eliminate. Of course, we can attempt to paraphrase the counterfactuals embedded in the ceteris paribus clause as well, but since they too mention modally thick objects (yourself, perhaps questions and breaths, hoods, mother ships, and so on), these paraphrases will come with further ceteris paribus clauses of their very own. If we leave the ceteris paribus clauses out, the paraphrase has different truth conditions, and evidently different content, than the ordinary sentence it is trying to render: in the example we have on the table, the Lewisian paraphrase commits you to a great deal about which the speaker of the ordinary sentence is agnostic. But if we include the ceteris paribus clauses, we are apparently launched on a vicious regress, at every stage of which the paraphrase contains yet more of the counterfactuals it was supposed to eliminate—in which case Lewis's reduction of ordinary counterfactuals fails.[24] And, once again, since Lewis's answer to the Question of Seriousness requires that what be effectively reduced is ordinary people's talk of ordinary, day-to-day objects—human beings, garden shears, and so on—Lewis's Quinean argument for modal realism fails as well.

In trying to reproduce the content of an ordinary counterfactual assertion in the possible-worlds vocabulary, it simplifies matters to think of its user as taking it to be fully true. If we do, then one way to put the slippage we're encountering is that, with respect to the fully true reference point, the paraphrase is only partially true, because true ceteris paribus. Recall the argument of Chapters 4–5: once we have invested in one set of inferentially interlocking intellectual tools, substituting an alternative for some of them will likely require forcing to get an inferential fit; here the ceteris paribus clauses mark the forcing between the older inferential tools and the modal realist's proposed replacement for them. We're now seeing an illustration of a related point as well: that novel inferential toolkits are not normally interconvertible with older ones. Attempting to substitute the alternative for *all* of the original tools will normally mean junking your original intellectual investment. In this case, because our interests, self-concepts, and concerns generally are given in counterfactually loaded terms, the price of doing so is especially high.

We can now redeem that promissory note. I claimed that Lewis's explications of the contents of mental states were unobviously dependent on the success of his analysis of counterfactuals. These analyses gloss my believing, say, that I have locked the keys in the car, as, again roughly, my taking the actual world to be among those possible worlds in which I have locked the keys in the car. But, as we have just seen, keys and cars are not modally thin objects. Picking out the worlds of my belief means getting right which modally thin worlds are excluded by the counterfactuals implicit in the unavoidable ceteris paribus clause. Generalizing: even though Lewis's possible-world analyses of content do not mention counterfactuals, they presuppose having on hand a successful reduction of counterfactuals to possible worlds. Counterfactuals really are the bottleneck in Lewis's answer to the Question of Seriousness.

11.6

We have one more longish lap before we are done with the argument proper. Recall that the analysis of counterfactuals drew on the relative proximity of possible worlds in a similarity space. Perhaps the relative similarity of possible worlds does the job of the ceteris paribus clauses, in which case the clauses can just be left off, and Lewis's proposed possible-worlds paraphrase of ordinary counterfactuals is fine as it stands. And there is something to be said in favor of supposing it to work that way: after all, possible worlds in which cars metamorphose into monsters when you open the hood are quite different from anything we're used to, and so such a world must be 'far away'; if the world in which I turn the key in the ignition is meant to be among the 'closest by' we can manage, it is going to be pretty close, and so, pretty 'far away' from cars-into-monsters worlds.

I think of similarity as a placeholder; in too many ways, it's another we-know-not-what, and merely a representative for whatever does the job of accounting for the truth values of counterfactuals, while satisfying the constraints imposed by Lewis's project. And I don't think this is all that far off from Lewis's own take on it.[25] In talking my way through this objection, I mean to stay as far as I can within the spirit of Lewis's proposal, but that is because I think that in doing so I can treat Lewis as a stalking horse for a more general target. The points I am making about similarity are intended to travel, and apply, suitably modified, to alternative or variant proposals.

There are two relevant constructions we might put on Lewis's conception of a similarity ordering over the space of possible worlds. On the first, similarity would be an objective or metaphysical relation, having to do with patterns of what Lewis called 'universals': the natural properties (or the features underlying them) picked out by our deepest theory of the world (which will be, if materialism is true, 'something not too different from present-day physics, though presumably somewhat improved').[26] Alternatively, possible worlds could count as more or less similar in virtue of whether the person uttering the counterfactual in question takes them to be; that is, the similarity relations over possible worlds could be a matter of the similarity judgments attributable to one or another ordinary speaker.[27]

Only the latter of these is suitable for capturing the content of ordinary counterfactuals: a world in which something that looks like a car is really a cleverly constructed piece of conceptual art, built to collapse into a pile of dust, might well be quite similar to ours at the level of basic physics. (Much Old Wave sci-fi is built around this presumption: it is *science* fiction because it sticks to the science, and it is science *fiction* because it describes goings-on that are dramatically different from what we see in the actual world.) It is true enough that a world in which one encounters dust sculptures and the like must be, intuitively, somewhat different from our own, and maybe even very different in ways that one or another science would recognize. But recall the task we are considering on Lewis's behalf: that of coming up with a counterfactual-free way of saying how to count those differences, in order to show that counting differences that way preempts the problem posed by ceteris paribus clauses for his proposed reduction. If the similarities and differences are made out at the level of special sciences like cultural anthropology—I mean that as an example of a science that might have something to say about how dust artists differ from sculptors who work in more familiar media—it is very hard to believe that they prove counterfactual-free. If, as Lewis perhaps anticipated, they are to be made out at the level of physics, then we need a way of rendering similarities and differences that appear in the descriptions of, say, cultural anthropology, into the vocabulary of physics. Philosophy of the twentieth century consisted in memorable part of a parade of philosophers attempting to produce such renderings; not one of them succeeded (and recall that in the last chapter, we saw why Lewis's own attempt at one such rendering failed); it is a fairly safe induction that those reductions are not going to be forthcoming.

Once again, Lewis was committed to capturing the content of ordinary counterfactuals: his first argument for the existence of other possible worlds was that the theory implicit in our use of ordinary counterfactuals, ordinary causal judgments, and so on quantifies over them (and conservatism, his reasoning continued, requires us to stick with that theory, for the time being anyhow). Second, since most of the philosophically important payoffs that he credited to his theory turned on analyses given in terms of counterfactuals, a successful treatment of counterfactuals proved to be, by Lewis's lights, a mandatory part of a theory of modality. What was being analyzed were the ordinary person's views of causation, of color, and so on, and so a treatment counted as successful only if it reconstructed pretty much the truth-conditions and entailments that ordinary speakers understand counterfactuals to have. This entails that we can confine our attention to the second reading of the similarity relation.[28]

11.7

Human beings have quite limited cognitive resources. This has consequences for what the raw materials used in constructing a similarity ordering over possible worlds must be, once we allow that they must be drawn from ordinary judgments of similarity. Notice first that possible worlds are supposed to be global or overall ways things might be (or might have been), and, except in trivial cases, no one has judgments about which of those global ways things might be are more or less similar to others: people don't pay enough attention to these sorts of objects of comparison, and, given their complexity, they really couldn't. Human cognitive limitations require that a global comparative similarity ordering be assembled from much more narrow responses to local features of those worlds.

Let me pause to address an objection to that observation. Lewis used to remark that we often are willing to answer questions along the lines of, 'Which city is more similar to Seattle, San Francisco or Portland?'—and that we do so even though cities are too complicated for us to really know what we're talking about.[29] But now, distinguish *thoughtless* from *thoughtful* judgments; although you might pop such a judgment out if asked, if anything important turned out to hang on it, you'd back off very fast indeed. If your answer *mattered*, you'd realize that you need to know in what respect you're being asked to compare those cities, and why; you'd put a lot more thought into the comparison; finally, you'd quickly turn to more local judgments of one or another aspect of similarity. The similarity judgments we're considering are being used to underwrite our assessments of counterfactuals, and counterfactuals are (this is a philosophical puzzle, but still an undeniable fact) among the practically most important categories of our thought. When we decide that such and such would or wouldn't have happened, that has practical consequences for our decisions, and it also makes a huge difference to our theoretical understanding of the world around us. This was the heart of Lewis's answer to the Question of Seriousness, and because you're not going to get thoughtful, dependable counterfactuals out of thoughtless, off-the-cuff similarity judgments, we are only interested in thoughtful rather than thoughtless judgments of comparative similarity. Now, *those* judgments are cognitively expensive.

The raw materials of a Lewis-style similarity ordering of possible worlds are cognitively expensive. Our own cognitive resources are limited. So, one way or another, explicitly or implicitly, we have to choose what to have opinions about. How must that choice have been made?

We are creatures that live lives that are throughly permeated with and interwoven with the modal and specifically counterfactual texture of our world. Here's a for-instance, just to give you a sense of how deep that fact goes. Recall the distinction between occurrent and dispositional mental states. It's obvious that most of your judgments as to what local features of a possible world make it more or less similar to another must be dispositional. (For just about any one I could mention, you weren't thinking about it a moment ago!) But that means that the raw materials for constructing a Lewis-style similarity metric aren't *actual* judgments, features of the possible world that we share. They're judgments you *would have had* if you'd been properly prompted, which is to say, those raw materials are judgments had by your counterparts, off in other possible worlds. That's entirely typical: in the Lewisian way of thinking about these things, *most of your mind* is off in *other* possible worlds[30]—which is an imagistic way of saying what I mean by: our lives are thoroughly permeated by modality, and by counterfactuals.

Because our lives are so thoroughly modality-permeated, almost everything we care about (or worry about, or strive for) has a usually elaborate counterfactual aspect. (We've just been reminded that being a person comes under this heading; likewise cars, keys, shoes, ships, sealing wax, cabbages, kings…) If we have to be selective in forming thoughtful judgments of comparative similarity, and if our interests are almost exclusively directed toward counterfactually permeated states of affairs, properties, and options, the judgments we make about the relative similarity of local ways things might be will largely—perhaps almost entirely—have to do with their modally and counterfactually laden properties. Briefly, the contents of our comparative similarity judgments are modality laden and counterfactually loaded; thus the raw materials available to construct a similarity ordering turning on modally thin features of various modally thin possible worlds will be negligible. But recall how we got here. We were considering how a Lewis-style reduction might cope with the counterfactual content or extension of ordinary objects and properties (like being a key, or a car, or a person). The strategy we were entertaining, generically characterized, was to offload that excess counterfactual content onto a special-purpose device, a 'similarity ordering.' The excess counterfactual content we were trying to cope with in the possible-worlds paraphrase of our counterfactuals has reappeared in the content of the judgments that constitute the raw materials for that ordering.

Here's the deep problem at the bottom of that argument. We care about understanding modality and counterfactuals in the first place because we live modally extended lives. But because our own interests are ineluctably modal, and our judgments of similarity follow our interests, they are ineluctably modal in content as well. That is enough to guarantee that we will be completely unequipped to provide the materials needed to assemble a counterfactual-free similarity relation over possible worlds (or, recalling that we are using Lewis's metaphysics as a stalking horse for more general lessons, to provide any functionally equivalent device). The sort of creatures who might actually have a philosophical use for a reduction of modality are precisely the ones who will be unable in principle to complete the reduction.

11.8

Let's return one last time to the Canberra Plan. The idea, recall, is to collect folk platitudes into a folk theory, and then to ramsify the theory; the slots in the ramsified theory are the types of entity to which the theory is committed. The occupiers of those slots can then be identified with metaphysically innocuous items, and the apparent spookiness of the entities of the folk theory discharged. We saw how analytical functionalism, for instance, picked out the metaphysically problematic psychological states as the roles or slots in folk-psychological theory; the Plan was to identify the occupiers of those roles with physical states, processes, and so on.

Perhaps the counterfactually loaded similarity judgments can be treated as jointly making up a folk theory of modality-relevant similarity. In that case, perhaps we can respond to the objection we have just been considering by teasing the structural roles out of that theory of similarity, and identifying the counterfactually unextended physical properties and objects that occupy those roles. These would then serve as the metaphysically innocuous respects in which one possible world would count as similar or dissimilar to another.

The nuts and bolts of this sort of proposal, once they are fully worked out, are bound to deviate in tricky ways from the canonical Canberra Plan. Nonetheless, this last resort of a possible-worlds reduction of modality is unworkable for reasons we have already encountered. I'll review them because they will contribute to our understanding both of modality and of the breakdown of the Quinean Turn.

We have pointed out that the raw materials for a similarity ordering over possible worlds are going to be local judgments, that is, judgments whose objects are one or another feature or aspect of a global way things might be. Now notice that these local judgments are advanced only other things equal. For example, the edgy competence of the baristas makes my two favorite coffeeshops count as more similar to one another than to other neighborhood cafés. But that judgment holds only ceteris paribus. If the baristas in one of the cafés were artists of the espresso machine in virtue of being controlled by radio signals beamed to the fillings in their teeth by space aliens…well, that would not just make the two coffeeshops *quite* unlike one another, but would cancel the contribution of the baristas' competence to their similarity.

The ceteris paribus clauses that aborted Lewis's possible-worlds reduction of modality have reappeared in the similarity judgments that were supposed to rescue the reduction, and this turn of events should not be mistaken for progress. The present application of the Canberra Plan meant to assemble local similarity judgments into a folk theory of similarity; but we have already seen that we do not know how to generate such a theory from components that contain ceteris paribus clauses, both because such components are not truth-functionally well-behaved, and because we do not know how to quantify into an ellipsis. Lewis's Reverse Twist fails as an analysis of modality in part for the reason the Canberra Plan failed as a treatment of mind and metaethics: our thinking in these areas is too fragmentary to be represented by a theory.

I suggested earlier that Lewis's reduction fails in the first place because of the kind of creatures that we are. The philosophical urgency of understanding modality derives from the way it is woven through our thought and speech. Lewis's reduction requires a great deal in the way of raw materials that are not counterfactually thick. The most important and irresolvable tension in the program is that the very pervasiveness of counterfactuals which motivated Lewis's reduction prevents it from succeeding. But Lewis's modal realism is also false to our ways of thinking about our modality-permeated world in a different respect. We navigate through that world using many rather small sketches that are, most of them, only partially true, but nonetheless true enough—and that do not fit together into a fully true Big Picture. I hope on another occasion to address the question of why creatures like ourselves would inevitably have an essentially fragmentary grasp of modality.

11.9

In Chapter 2, I suggested that we are repeatedly faced with a choice between using partial truths, such as approximations, and reengineering the objects of our thought. The choice persists even when when it comes to counterfactuals, and let's continue using the illustration on hand: If I were to turn the key, the car would start. It was a cause of great anxiety that, for a long time, I owned a car of which this was only partially true.

While sometimes we can manage full truth by changing only our concepts, language, and so on, I have been arguing that this is not in general a viable strategy. In the case of counterfactual conditionals, adopting this strategy normally means redrawing the conditional's antecedent. To redraw the antecedent is to replace the inadequate, because false, conditional, 'If I turned the key, my car would start' with the somewhat more cautious 'If the battery is not dead, and I were to turn the key, my car would start.' But if bivalence is the goal, the redrawing cannot stop there. If the battery is not dead, but has been stolen, the car will not start either; likewise if the fuel line is clogged, or the spark plugs are made out of cellophane, or the car is in a vacuum chamber, or if any one of indefinitely many other problems crops up. The antecedent, redescribed to include all of these, would allow us a conditional that was just flat true, and would describe circumstances in which the car would *have* to start, come what (else) may. (These circumstances have been called the 'total cause,' and, more traditionally, the 'sufficient reason' of the consequent.)

But sufficient reasons are, with occasional exceptions, inferentially useless. For one thing, the sufficient reason (or fully articulated antecedent) is almost never determinable. There are normally indefinitely many conditions cashing out the ceteris paribus clause, all of which have to be stuffed into the antecedent. I will never finish explaining what it would *really* take to start my car; a true conditional on the subject, made bivalent by this kind of narrowing, is not inferentially available to me. Even if it were, I could not check that the antecedent was satisfied, in which case the conditional whose antecedent it is cannot be inferentially deployed. It is all very well to insist that *real* causes are sufficient reasons, that everything has a sufficient reason, and so on. But if, in practice (and in principle), I can't know what they are, then there's nothing I can do with them.

For another, even allowing total causes or sufficient reasons to be determinable, the conditionals that deploy them are not inferentially useful, because not transferable. What I have in mind is this. The very special circumstances that jointly make my car start are rather different from those that make my neighbor's car start: I have spark plugs, while he has electronic ignition. So a narrowed-antecedent conditional that covers my car will not cover his, and when the time comes to borrow his car, the simple connection needed (turn the key and the car will start) will be lost in the welter of supplementary conditions making up the total cause. As the antecedent is made narrower, it becomes progressively more specific—or more disjunctively unwieldy. Useful conditionals are simple and reusable; conditionals with narrowed antecedents—sufficient reasons—are one-time-only disposables.

So the choice is either to live with partial truth (to decide that the conditional is true enough to be usable—or not), or to reengineer the world so as to make it fully true (or close enough to fully true), and here is what that looks like. My experience with my used car was very frustrating, and in the end, I bought a new car, thereby rendering the conditional for all practical purposes bivalent. I have emphasized that to engineer bivalence can be costly; here the cost of bivalence was about eleven thousand dollars.

11.10

The straightforward lesson of the failure of Lewis's reduction is that modal realism is an unsupported, and probably unsupportable, view. We were supposed to take the ontology seriously because ordinary counterfactuals could be paraphrased away into the vocabulary of possible worlds. They can't be, and so we had better surrender the ontological commitments.

But our real question is what we can learn about partial truth, and its consequences for the Quinean Turn. If we typically have to choose between reengineering the objects of our cognition to make our thoughts fully true, and treating those thoughts as partially true, and if we cannot expect to reengineer the universe to conform to Lewis's theory of modality, then perhaps an alternative to treating the theory as simply correct is to treat it as partially true: an approximation, maybe, or an idealization. (It certainly has the look and feel of extreme idealization!) Lewis would have regarded the suggestion as unfriendly, but I have, after all, been arguing in favor of using partial truths (of which idealizations are one form) on the grounds that we really cannot get by without them.[31]

In Chapter 5, we motivated partial truth by thinking about sunk cost. Once we have made heavy investments in one body of intellectual apparatus, we may quite reasonably be unwilling to junk it and start over, even if operating the apparatus involves forcing inferential and representational matches. Because we already have a lot of know-how when it comes to working with one set of concepts, names, and so on, it makes sense to use them in novel cases, cases where they do not quite fit. But we cannot justify deploying Lewis's modal metaphyics in this way; indeed, these very considerations give us strong reason *not* to.

Lewis's attempted reduction introduced a foundational ontology of very big, very thin (i.e., modally thin) items. Because we don't know how to slice everyday objects that thinly, and because we don't normally deal with objects that are nearly that big, we have, over the course of our history, invested almost nothing in this intellectual apparatus: neither in a suitable system of representations, nor in the inferential pathways that might connect them. Unsurprisingly, we have almost none of the inferential competences it would take to deploy the apparatus successfully; we don't know how to think productively in the terms into which we are being asked to clumsily reinterpret our ordinary modal claims. (Clumsily, recall, because the argument showed that the conversion from our present vocabulary to that one left a good deal of modal slop-over.)

It is one thing to accept forced fit in order to exploit investments we have made; it is another thing entirely to accept forced fit when there is nothing to exploit. The suggestion that we render concepts, names, etc., that we are good at using into a representational lexicon which we scarcely control, and with which we know how to do almost nothing, is perverse.

11.11

The four chapters we are now concluding haven't surveyed all of analytic metaphysics, not by any means. But we have looked at one important strand of it, and what we've found is that, once you drop the bivalence doctrine and allow for partial truth, you also have to drop the Quinean criterion for ontological commitment. You have to drop arguments that turn on Quine's criterion, like those in Field's *Science without Numbers*. You have to give up Davidsonian meaning theories, and you no longer have his arguments for an ontology of events. You no longer have Davidson's justification for the Principle of Charity. The arguments for the indeterminacy of radical translation can't be gotten off the ground, and so, it turns out, we have no good argument against the analytic/synthetic distinction. The original transition from logical positivism to analytic metaphysics requires a good reason for rejecting the analytic/synthetic distinction, and so it turns out to have been based on a mistake. The currently popular Canberra Plan is unworkable, and analytical functionalism—a solution to the mind-body problem, or anyway to the mind-physical world problem, which is still in play—has to be dropped. The arguments for modal realism do not go through, and the analyses of counterfactuals (and many other notions of philosophical interest) that Lewis gave, using the resources of modal realism, must be abandoned. Recall, moreover, that we saw in Chapter 6 that belief psychology, a metaphysical view about the contents of the mind, will have to be revised, as will exclusively knowledge-oriented epistemology. And if this is a fair sample of work in analytic metaphysics, we've just gotten started.

All this is by way of making the point that partial truth matters. 'Vagueness' isn't a tiny corner of the philosophy of language, a puzzle about how to defuse sorites paradoxes with no important consequences for anything else. We are going to have to rethink our metaphysics and epistemology, and rethink it from the ground up.

12

Conclusion: Metaphysics as Intellectual Ergonomics

If full-truth inference works primarily in artifactual domains which have been reengineered to make deductive reasoning feasible, then most of our theoretical reasoning must deploy partial truths. I have argued that accepting this conclusion about the logic of theoretical inference has consequences beyond logic: first, that belief psychology, while perhaps a satisfactory model for reasoning about the restricted artifactual domains I mentioned a moment ago, needs to be replaced with a more broadly applicable stretch of philosophy of mind, and second, that an important strand of analytic metaphysics is pervasively and fatally error-ridden. My own expectation is that those consequences are a fair sample of the sorts of correction we would find ourselves making were we further to investigate other projects within analytic metaphysics.

Even when the steps in an argument are only true enough, and even when the moves from step to step are defeasible, the conclusion may nevertheless be a flat-out truth. In addition to the two I have just mentioned, we have accumulated others as well: that the deflationist account of truth is misguided, because it overlooks the most important function of the intellectual apparatus of truth; that partial truth is necessary in order to have a unified intellect and opinions worth having, and for satisfactory theoretical reasoning; that transcendental arguments are an essential tool in philosophy of logic; that the objective of a general, unified and formal account of partial truth is a mirage. Much of our discussion has been argument for partial truth, but it has taken us to hard truths, both in our technical and in the more conversational sense.

A demolition job, on its own, is just a demolition job. The constructive task, which makes the ground clearing worth doing, is to replace the mistaken metaphysics with new and better projects, and with new and better theories. You might think that the enterprise is at any rate a familiar one: it will produce metaphysical theories that look a lot like the older, displaced theories, and which occupy the same marginalized role in our intellectual lives as those did. The difference will be that where previously bivalence functioned as a sometimes explicit (but usually tacit) premise, this premise's place will be taken by an acknowledgement of partial truth. In my view, that underestimates what is involved in reconfiguring metaphysics around partial truth. I want to conclude by suggesting that the consequences of the now-completed argument for metaphysics are deeper, more far-reaching, and much more promising than might have been anticipated.

12.1

Analytic metaphysics, I remarked at the outset of this treatise, has been to a large extent the projection of a picture of rationality. Having seen in some detail how the bivalence doctrine shaped the metaphysical projects of Quine, Davidson, and Lewis, we are now in a position to say a bit more about what that claim comes to.

The metaphysics that followed on the Quinean Turn proposed to answer questions by producing a *theory* (variously: a theory continuous with science, a theory of meaning, a reconstruction of folk commonsense, or a theory able to solve philosophers' puzzles). Theories have inferential structure, and the linking components of serious theories will be (if the philosopher can at all manage it) provided by the inferential machinery that he takes most seriously: in the case of the analytic metaphysician, by standard deductive logic.[1] In the strand of analytic metaphysics we followed out, the existential commitments of appropriate theories so articulated became the metaphysical theses: putative hard truths about what does and doesn't exist, such as numbers, or events, or beliefs, or possible worlds. To say that the metaphysics was a projection of a picture of rationality is, when we are speaking of this tradition, to say in part that philosophers' views of rationality, together with other available premises, determined both the way that metaphysical conclusions were arrived at, a characteristic look and feel that those conclusions ended up sharing, and a view as to the status of those conclusions: what analytic metaphysicians were finding out was what kinds of things exist—*really* exist, and exist *already*.

But the metaphor of projection (which I'm happy to have on board) is loose enough to unpack into more than one type of literal relation.

What metaphysics would be projected by a model of rationality that put partial-truth inference at its center? Presumably it would arise from the sort of theories (now in a suitably neutral sense: not necessarily the lists of sentences we saw being so labeled in previous chapters) that are articulated and connected using partial-truth inference, such as idealizations and approximations; more generally, from theories that involve partial truths of various sorts. So unlike the contrasting sort of metaphysics, there could be no presumption that what you were discovering was what things *really* exist. Idealizations and approximations are acknowledgedly *not* how things really are, and the relevant question is generally the practical one: under what conditions is such and such the right approximation to use? Sometimes that question is just one of convenience: there are different ways to frame your problems, and some of them are easier to work with than others. But when the choice is deep enough, and when it is forced enough—in the way that moves in a chess game are forced—then the investigation becomes metaphysical. Metaphysics which crystallizes around partial-truth inference will (or ought to) ask what partially true characterizations of the world we have to adopt, for it to be possible to think about it.

Nietzsche, if I am reading him correctly, took the view that it was approximations and idealizations all the way down. But however philosophically elegant a posture that is, it is overstated, because we can, I have argued, have hard truths when we are willing and able to do the work (and pay the price) to get them. What you are normally paying for, when you pay for hard truths, is modifying the objects you are thinking about, in order to make your thinking crisper and more routinized. Here the relevant question is also a practical one: when and how should one so redesign the objects of one's thoughts? Metaphysics which shapes itself around deductive inference made possible in this way will (or ought to) ask what changes we should make to the objects of our thought, in order to be able to think about them in ways that we need to. This second wing of metaphysics is a field closely related to architecture and product design.

I initially characterized metaphysics as historically addressed to the question: How must the world be, if we are to be able to think about it? On the reading I'm now giving that question, the force of the 'must' is *practical*: once partial truth is taken on board, metaphysics turns out to be an applied science, one which is naturally grouped with other engineering sciences. It asks what approximations or other partially true characterizations to adopt, if one is to think effectively about how the facts stand; it asks how you can redesign and rebuild parts of the world, to make it easier to think about.

When it's done right, metaphysics is intellectual ergonomics. Our ability to think effectively and clearly about the world around us is the precondition for our doing almost anything that matters right—and by 'our,' I don't now mean just metaphysicians or philosophers, but us human beings generally. This means that metaphysics so reconceived is not the irrelevant and unimportant professional subspecialty that its current practitioners take it to be, but rather a vitally important enterprise: if metaphysicians do their jobs, and do them well, we will all (all of us, including the least theoretically oriented members of the population) benefit, sooner or later; if they don't do their jobs, or do them badly, we will all (all of us) suffer, sooner or later.

I still owe an explanation for the current disciplinary self-understanding of metaphysics as an exotic and irrelevant area of inquiry; we are now in a position to discharge that debt. Metaphysics is, one way or another, a projection of one's theory of rationality. I have argued that the understanding of rationality that has been largely shared by analytic metaphysicians is unsuitable for creatures like ourselves, living in the sort of world where we have to live. Unsurprisingly, the metaphysical results that fall into place around it turn out to be almost entirely irrelevant to our intellectual activities. Equally unsurprisingly, that irrelevance is then rationalized by a conception of what metaphysicians are doing, on which it is *of course* irrelevant to any further concern.

Is that really all there is to metaphysics? After all, if a representation is an approximation, surely there's the way things really are, to which it approximates; if you're reshaping the world to make it easier to think about, surely there's the material you're reshaping, and surely there are metaphysical facts of the matter about it. I described metaphysics as the enterprise of figuring out what the world has to be like if we are going to be able to think about it. But there are more specific questions with which it has wrestled over the course of its history: just for instance, what is modality? It is fine to say that, for all we know, the machinery of possible worlds is a suitable approximation for thinking about modal matters under some circumstances, but not under others. But doesn't that leave the deeper question of what we are talking about, when we agree, say, that something *might* have happened, but didn't?

I do feel the pull of the objection that reconceiving metaphysics as intellectual ergonomics leaves a residue of problems and questions (what is modality? what is normativity? what is it to be a mental state?...), and that these are some of the deepest and most difficult questions of philosophy. Still, a disconcertingly large number of attempts to answer those questions turn out to be most charitably construed as ergonomic exercises of the sort I have been advocating, inadvertently executed. Perhaps the right view to take, at this stage, is that a response is premature. Only after we have seen how far the ergonomic reconception can take us will we be in a position to see what, if anything, is left over. Because metaphysicians have until this point seen themselves as concerned only with the completely impractical, the question of how far this new approach can take us is about as open as it gets.[2]

12.2

One part of seeing how far the ergonomic reconception of metaphysics will take us is to see how much of the history of metaphysics it can reclaim. With any luck, we will be able to improve somewhat the reputation of the metaphysics of the past.

On and off, but too persistently to ignore, 'metaphysics' has become a pejorative notion, dismissed not merely as of little relevance to other matters, but as deeply and ineluctably error-ridden: recall how Kant, Wittgenstein, and the logical positivists determined that metaphysics itself was the mistake, and did their level best to put an end to it once and for all. And, oddly enough, having rejected both the metaphysics of the past and metaphysics *tout court*, with the passage of time these philosophers for the most part have come to be regarded by their successors as metaphysicians themselves, whose views, even when counted among the milestones of philosophy, were as mistaken as before.[3] It is as though you can't do philosophy without doing metaphysics despite yourself, and that when you do, you inevitably lapse into error and illusion.

The ergonomic reconception of metaphysics has at hand an explanation for this aspect of the history. If what it is to do metaphysics is to produce intellectually useful idealizations, and if what metaphysicians were uniformly doing was mistaking them for out-and-out truths, it was inevitable both that useful and intellectually constructive philosophy amount to metaphysics, and that each metaphysician's successors came to realize that the last metaphysical system on the pile couldn't live up to the billing it had been given. It is not at all surprising that philosophers came to be sensitive to the look and feel of metaphysics, and correctly to anticipate that each new instance of it would fall to criticisms very like those that undercut its predecessors. After all, if I am right, the look and feel of metaphysics is, inter alia, the look and feel of approximations, idealizations, and partial truth, and approximations, idealizations, and partial truths are all subject to the criticism—if it *is* a criticism—that they are not (flat out, simply) *true*.

But if we think that idealizations and ergonomic designs are what metaphysicians *should* have been producing, that repeated disappointment was inappropriate. Of course idealizations are strictly speaking false; of course any successor idealization will be false, too. The real question to ask of an idealization is whether it is useful for one or another intellectual purpose (and when it isn't); the real question to ask of an engineering proposal is when it is a useful way of redesigning parts of one's environment. If the grand (and not-so-grand) metaphysical systems of the past are best regarded as having been idealizations, then we may yet be able to find uses for them, by finding domains for which they are useful idealizations.[4]

If metaphysics is about what the world has to be like, for us to be able to think about it, work in metaphysics should serve much more than idle curiosity. It can, if we give up our insistence on hard truths. Partial truth doesn't just matter for metaphysics; it makes metaphysics matter. Metaphysics is dead, long live metaphysics!

Appendix

Was There Anything Wrong with Psychologism?

The argument of Chapters 4–5 is psychologistic, by which I mean that it uses claims about human psychology to support a view about logic, i.e., about what the correct forms of inference are. For most of the twentieth century, psychologism played more or less the role in philosophy that communism played for McCarthyism: an accusation sufficient to place an opponent's position beyond the pale of respectability.[1] So I want to say something about why the long reign of antipsychologism—from which we seem to be emerging—was unwarranted.

Philosophy was given its antipsychologistic direction by the arguments of Frege and Husserl. This is not the place to review all of them (there are just too many—in fact, suspiciously many). But I will discuss a handful, those which will allow me better to explain the commitments of the view I am developing. I recommend to the interested reader a careful argument-by-argument examination of Frege's and Husserl's polemics. My own classroom experience is that even undergraduates are able to locate the fallacies in almost all of them; quality control was far worse than their reputations might lead you to think.

Both Frege and Husserl point out that psychologism entails relativism about logic: that different logics will be correct for different psychologies. They treat this as a reductio ad absurdum, but in doing so they beg the question; their psychologistic opponents had already endorsed that very conclusion, and one does not refute an opponent by pointing out that he is committed to a conclusion which he already accepts. Recent psychologistic work, e.g., in the bounded rationality tradition, explicitly endorses similar conclusions.[2] And here I have been arguing that reasoning with partial truth is mandatory for creatures with psychologies that are limited in roughly the ways our own are; I agree that the creatures who differ from us in that respect will have different logics, that is, I agree that creatures with suitably different psychologies will be logical aliens.

Husserl argues that relativism about logic entails relativism about truth, which he insists is self-refuting.[3] (If logic$_1$ labels p as true, and logic$_2$ labels p as false, then we have p labeled as both true and false; and even worse, Husserl worries, suppose that the users of logic$_2$ end up correctly labeling as false the claim 'logic$_1$ labels p as true'?) This is confused: different logics use different ways of marking inferential moves as successful, and the accounting systems need to be kept distinct. An analogous and equally bad argument would show that currency relativism is self-refuting: if what currency you used varied with where you lived, a commodity could be priced both at two dollars, and at one dollar—a contradiction! But of course when we subscript the dollars as US and Australian, the 'contradiction' disappears. A creature which reasons using a traditional bivalentist model of truth and inference may mark p as false, where a user of partial-truth inference will mark p as somewhat true, or true only in a particular respect. On the view I'm developing, that is as it should be.

Husserl complains that the relativist about logic, and so the psychologistic logician, is committed to the possibility of logics that may, for all we know, reject such basic rules as the Principle of Non-Contradiction and the Law of the Excluded Middle. That is entirely correct: as we have already seen, inference which deploys partial truth requires us to (depending on how you think of it) modify or reject both. That the most basic logical laws are up for grabs is in fact an important philosophical payoff of reconsidering truth and bivalence. It is question-begging, in this subject area, to take the logical laws belonging to one theoretical position as nonnegotiable, and to treat disagreement about them as refuting an opposing position.[4]

Husserl complains that there is no metaphysical bright line to prevent logical species relativism (different logics for different species) from sliding into a relativism that prescribes different logics to different individuals;[5] because he thinks that that means relativizing truth to individuals, he takes such an extreme form of relativism to be refuted in almost every introductory philosophy class. However, whatever we tell our students in order to get on with the lesson, I don't think that this extreme form of relativism *is* refuted in those introductory classes, and so I want to take a shot at quickly saying both what is really wrong with it, and why the position I am developing does not end up committed to it.

Logic, as I am using the notion, gives guidelines and constraints for rational inference. Guidelines and constraints are something like prescriptions, and one of the realizations of twentieth-century philosophy was that such things, if they are to be more than mere pretense, require correction and enforcement, normally on the part of others. Wittgensteinians have taken this to be the point of the so-called Private Language Argument, and have concluded that there could *never* be personal or private logics. I am less than entirely sure about that: the history of philosophy contains too many lone sages, such as Kant, and perhaps Wittgenstein himself, philosophers who developed and extensively deployed modes of argument which, at the time, no one but themselves was able to follow. But I agree that, perhaps modulo rare exceptions, your thinking is liable to slide off track if you do not have others to monitor and correct it. That normally means having others who understand your logic from the inside (that is, who share it). The overhead involved in being able effectively to deploy a method of inference involves not just immediate monitoring and correction, but initial education into the inference method for yourself and your monitors, as well as, for the more strenuous uses to be made of it, the presence of a community of experts who articulate the guidelines, figure out how to handle tricky cases, and so on.

Evidently, the costs of maintaining a logic are substantial. Now, it will simply not be financially feasible to pay that overhead for each and every person in a society. The tradeoffs resemble those that determine the extent to which niche marketing replaces standardization in the economy at large. The wealthier a society, the more (and narrower) niches it can afford to cater to: as we get richer, we can afford more diversity in our logics.[6] (Think of the proliferation of academic disciplines, with their strikingly different modes of argumentation.) But we will never be wealthy enough to afford a different logic for everyone. If logic had to be relativized to individuals, we would not be able to *maintain* the systems of inferential standards in which logics consist; that is why such relativism is a conclusion to be avoided (and not because it has been shown to be somehow self-contradictory). Husserl was right to think that there is no *metaphysical* bright line to stop the slide to a relativism of logic to individuals. There is instead an economic line: it moves as the economy changes, and so is not so bright; but it does stop the slide.

Notes

Chapter 1

1   Cf. a fairly recent *Mind* survey article about properties, which begins with a partial explanation for the lack of consensus about the problem: 'Although philosophy advertises itself as the reflective discipline *par excellence*, it is a familiar fact that philosophers lose themselves in projects for which they can provide no reflective description or justification' (Oliver, 1996). You can almost hear the sigh.

Something of this self-conception may have taken root at the very origin of the discipline: Aristotle seems to have thought of metaphysical contemplation as a self-contained activity, suitable to a god who would put it to no further use.

2   My claim now is not that this was what metaphysicians thought they were doing, but rather that this is the question you have to understand metaphysicians to have been answering, for the enterprise to make sense in retrospect. In particular, this question is not central to the disciplinary self-conception of today's philosophical professionals who put 'metaphysics' down as an area of specialization on their CVs. Since I am going to be discussing the metaphysics of the decades in which it was produced preponderantly by those philosophical professionals, I owe an explanation for how it is that they have, if I am right, come to be deeply confused about what it is they are doing. The armchair physics problem is one reason for thinking that they had *better* be confused: the idea that you could figure out what the basic building blocks of the world are by consulting your own 'intuitions' (standard practice, these days) either can't be taken at face value, or can't be taken seriously.

There is a second reason for overriding the current disciplinary self-conception: I have in conversation repeatedly found that such metaphysicians demarcate their field in ways that would exclude from it such figures as Plato, Leibniz, or Kant, and, in the twentieth century, Rudolph Carnap, Peter Strawson, and Robert Brandom. When this happens, a paradigm-case argument tells us that something has gone wrong.

3 Although formal logic has a richer recent history than philosophers tend to remember; for some discussion of its nineteenth-century non-Fregean roots, see Putnam, 1990, pp. 252–60.

4 Here are some entirely typical remarks expressing this view, from the first page of a mid-century volume whose avowed 'primary purpose [is] to record the first appearances of those ideas which seem to us most important in the logic of our own day': 'Logic is concerned with the principles of valid inference;…to prove a proposition is to infer it validly from true premises' (Kneale and Kneale, 1962, pp. v, 1). As Keefe, 2000, p. 46, remarks, however, 'the classical definition [of validity] can be expressed in a number of forms which, though classically equivalent, need not coincide in a non-classical framework'; she gives a short list.

5 While the usual label for this claim is 'bivalence,' there are others; for instance, Wright, 1999, p. 227, calls it 'absoluteness.' For one explanation of the doctrine's initial appearance, see Goldfarb, 2001, p. 30.

6 What is taught in the introductory logic class is usually truth-functional logic and the first-order predicate calculus. As Stanley Cavell has remarked, the text-books for such classes constitute the only part of the curriculum that one can be sure is shared by all analytic philosophers. So while there are deductive formal systems that use more than two truth values (Gottwald, 2006), these are not part of the common philosophical education, and have not made a noticeable difference to the standard picture of rationality. With the exception of continuum-valued logics, which will be taken up in ch. 7 under the heading of vagueness, I will leave them to one side here.

7 In the Kantian idiom, they have to be a priori and necessary, and so they turn out to be things like space, time, substance, causation, and so on: you encounter experience as spatially organized, as temporally ordered, as containing objects standing in causal relations, and all the rest of it.

   To say it's a Kantian thought is not to say that it's Kant's. John Rawls used to distinguish between '-ian' views and '-'s' views—e.g., between Rawlsian views and his own views—and something like that distinction is intended here. There are many reasons Kant would not allow himself the train of thought I am sketching here. For one, Kant's own argument does not permit him to occupy a position from which the things in themselves, and the cognitive processes that respond to them, are describable.

8 Kant, 1900–, vol. X, p. 130, English version from Kant, 1999, p. 133; I have slightly emended the translation. Entertaining a related thought, Hutcheson, 1726/2004, pp. 78ff., notices that 'irregular Objects distract the Mind with Variety,' and concludes that 'Beings of limited Understanding and Power, if they act rationally for their own Interest, must chuse to…study regular Objects.' The regularities that make the choice pay are a divine intervention: on our

behalf, 'the Deity...chuse[s] to...diffuse Uniformity, Proportion and Simili-
tude thro all the Parts of Nature which we can observe.' (I'm grateful to Beatrice
Longuenesse and Christoph Fehige for directing me to these passages.)

9 Nietzsche, 1873/1995; while this strikes me as an implausible origin for this
particular word, and incidentally also as a reminder that Nietzsche never got
fully free of many of the notions that we now think of as characteristically
Empiricist, there are surely words of which you could tell this story: someone
might say, for instance, that the current scandal is turning into a Watergate.

10 I am going to move back and forth between such pairs without a lot of formality
or ado, and I won't distinguish them typographically. It is a standard metaphysician's complaint about facts that they are shaped too much like sentences.
Likewise, particulars are shaped suspiciously like names, and properties—the
category at hand—like predicates. Not that I am complaining myself.

11 And of course there are many other such devices in the same family, some
actual, like the repeated application of names over time (that is, the invention
of temporally extended objects), and some possible (if we noticed more of the
proliferation of modalities, we would come up with representations that could
be used for ranges of them).

12 In practice, the qualification restricting the claim to reconstructions of reasoning is often forgotten; philosophers of mind write, frequently enough, as
though all there *is* in the mind are beliefs and desires. For further discussion,
see sec. 6.1.

13 The awkward but conventional term 'theoretical' should not be taken to invoke
the idea of a *theory*; reasoning is theoretical when it is directed toward finding out the facts, even when nothing as elaborate or sophisticated as theory
construction is taking place. See also ch. 6 n 2.

Chapter 2

1 Recall that there has been a recent wave of interest in vagueness, and the topic
has now become a self-contained specialization; I am going to discuss this literature in ch. 7. When I do, I will argue that the dilemma I'm about to pose for
the bivalence doctrine also sticks to logics of vagueness.

Two remarks. First, some philosophers have experimented with other ways
of dropping bivalence. For instance, Michael Dummett has used views about
bivalence to give content to traditional disputes about realism, and his work is
typical of one sort of attention given to the topic, which focuses on truth-value
gaps—cases where there's nothing to say to the question, true or false?—rather
than partial truth. (Again, for the policy I am following here, see ch. 1 n 6.)
There are other, narrower discussions in philosophy where bivalence comes

up as a live issue; a special case of the interest in gaps might be treatments of Aristotle's 'sea battle', i.e., discussion of future contingents.

Second, most philosophers tend to regard the sort of work I have just mentioned as exotic, and as not having much bearing on their own research. Thus consequences for central issues in philosophy of taking intuitionism, vagueness or partial truth seriously have not in my view been drawn, and it is in this sense that, despite the rapidly growing literature on vagueness, the bivalence doctrine is still being taken for granted. I hope on a further occasion to take up the question of why work on vagueness has been so very ghettoized.

That last generalization is of course true only for the most part: exceptions include Hyde, 2005, sec. 4, which floats a short list of philosophical lessons to be drawn from treatments of the sorites; Weatherson, 2005, sec. 7, which considers applying work on vagueness to the so-called Problem of the Many; Forbes, 1985, p. 186, which tries to assimilate the so-called Four Worlds Paradox to a sorites paradox, the idea being that a successful solution to the latter would handle the former; and—perhaps the most ambitious of the group—Sorensen, 2001.

2   Some terminological fine print: First, propositions might look like they belong in this list, but because I want to reserve the term for abstract objects that are bivalent by stipulation, I'll leave propositions to one side for now. They will come in for discussion in secs. 2.7 and 6.4.

Second, 'sentences' are nowadays often distinguished from 'statements' (as well as from 'propositions'). I would like to leave my own terminology as nontechnical as I can, and I am not going to use these words to mark the standard distinctions. There are a couple of reasons, one pragmatic, and one principled. Like a number of other, rather similar niceties (remember corner-quotes?), if you understand the distinction and what it's for, you don't need to have it drawn for you; if you don't understand it, having it drawn, occasion after occasion, is just clutter; either way, it's not needed, and better left out. More importantly, the argument we are about to embark on will put us in a position to reconsider whether we really do understand the distinctions that these terms are standardly meant to mark, and whether they really can be sustained. So you should treat the first two of these words as merely stylistic variants here; recall, however, that I'm reserving 'proposition' for the stipulatively bivalent abstract objects invoked by the theories I am arguing against.

Third and fourth, you should not take the word 'background' to be invoking what Searle has done with the term, and when I talk about holding up a sentence against a range of backgrounds, I of course don't mean that the background being invoked has to be located in the same place or time as the utterance or inscription of the sentence.

3   Describing sentences taken one by one as bivalent when they are flat-true-or-flat-false has precedent in, e.g., Hacking, 1982, p. 54. Hacking is also interested in a dispositional property of groups of sentences which he calls 'positivity',

and it is important to distinguish it from the dispositional property I have just introduced here. A category of sentence is 'positive' ('truth-apt,' in the analytic vocabulary) if it is assessable with respect to truth and falsity; positivity, however, does not require that the possible assessments be one of: true or false. Sentences assessable as, say, 'true for the most part' would be positive. That notion is appropriated from Foucault, and I'll touch on differences between the view I'm developing and the views of Foucault, Hacking, and Arnold Davidson in n 8, below.

4   Although, as we will see in ch. 7, 'vagueness' has recently become a technical term whose scope is much narrower than the contrast I am after here.

5   See Searle, 1979, p. 4; Searle, 1983, pp. 7f.; Anscombe, 1985, sec. 32. However, Vogler, 2001, p. 437, points out that Anscombe does not present her much-appropriated contrast as a way of distinguishing beliefs from desires. I will return to direction of fit in ch. 6.

6   'Like,' here, conveys something like enough to resemblance and similarity, and you may be worried that such notions are sufficiently elastic for the cloud to count as *like* a horse's head nonetheless—or perhaps that it will count as a horse's head in the context of a particular (stage of a) conversation. These notions *are* elastic, but please don't let that distract you. I will address the generic worry directly in sec. 2.3. The conversational-score variant of it invokes a popular theory of vagueness; I will discuss that variant in sec. 7.8. See also Lakoff, 1973, p. 485, for observations on the ways the hedges 'sort of' and 'similar' interact.

7   See Locke, 1690/1924, ch. 5. Locke provides his own explanation, not incompatible with the one given here, for the first conception falling into disuse.

8   The view I am developing is to be distinguished from that of Michel Foucault, Ian Hacking, and Arnold Davidson. I have already remarked that the Foucauldian interest in positivity (assessment along the dimension of truth and falsity) is not quite the same as my interest in bivalence (there being only two possible outcomes of such assessment). More to the present point, Foucauldians tend in the first place to look for the preconditions of positivity inside the mind and in language (or 'discourse')—in 'styles of reasoning' (Davidson, 1996). Hacking, for example, writes: 'Nothing's either true-or-false but thinking makes it so. It is [this] that preoccupies me' (1982, p. 49); I have been arguing that thinking on its own is not going to do a very good job of making it so.

When Foucauldians do look outside the mind and language, they see by and large only the social institutions that shape 'discourses' and the conflicts over how those institutions are going to work. Thus Foucault tries to distance himself from the naiveté of not looking outside language, but he does so by insisting that 'one's point of reference should not be to the great model of language and signs, but to that of war and battle' (1980, p. 114). That is, perhaps because of a focus on the social sciences, Foucauldians write as though the example I have just given, of bivalence produced by way of legal institutions, were typical in many more ways than it actually is. When one is preoccupied with social facts one can forget that not all engineering is *social* engineering.

9 To be sure, that bivalence involves real costs doesn't entail that the person whose thoughts or utterances are determinately true or false is the one who pays those costs. If I win my Honda Civic as a door prize, then as far as I'm concerned, the bivalence comes for free. Many of the costs of bivalence are invisible to us, because they were paid by others, often long ago.

10 Context of utterance is uncontroversially important when it comes to making out what someone is committed to by what he has said, and there is a tendency among some philosophers toward Procrustean contextualism, that is, trying to get context to do *all* the work, including the work I claim is done by partial truth. I will postpone the conversational-scorekeeping variant of this approach until later, and for now use a Wittgensteinian contextualist to make the point I need.

   Travis, 2000, observes that 'The ink is blue' may, on one occasion, come out true when it looks blue in the bottle, and on another, come out true when it dries to blue (even though it looks black in the bottle). He also notices that what you mean, on one occasion, by 'The table is six feet long' may not be refuted by showing, with very precise instruments, that it is 6.000002 feet. He then commits himself to bivalence, presumably because he assumes that partial truths of whatever kind can be forced into bivalent shape by the contextualist account. (See p. 212 for a gesture that comes very close to the standard score-keeping treatment.)

   But we have been given no reason to think that this sort of forcing has to take place. The occasion settles that whether 'The ink is blue' comes out true is determined by what it looks like when it dries, but *on* this understanding, the ink in question may be only *sort of* blue, and the sentence will come out only *sort of* true. On an occasion where a 6.000002-foot long table makes 'The table is six feet long' flatly true, a slightly longer table may require us to judge the sentence to be only *approximately* true. A British Airways advertisement once announced that 'sleeping fully flat is better than kinda sorta flat'; the context is one in which the relevant standards for flatness are those appropriate to first-class airplane seats (rather than, say, those appropriate to cutting boards), and with those standards in place, the advertisement implies that it is only 'kinda sorta' true of competitors' seats that they are flat.

   Travis invokes the principle of charity to insist on the best-fit bivalent inter-pretation; an item is properly placed in a category if it is 'better placed' there than in any other, which, he thinks, makes one of the competing 'understand-ings' always the flat-out winner (p. 152). But it begs the question to suppose that bivalence is what charity requires. First of all, good placement (like more familiar terms in the philosophical lexicon, such as 'fit' and 'coherence') is obviously a matter of degree, or something like degree. Why shouldn't that be reflected in our semantic assessments, by treating 'approximately,' 'basically,' and so on not as 'polite negations' (Travis's bivalentist spin on them, at p. 62), but as genuine alternatives to 'true' and 'false'? There is historical precedent: coherence theories of truth advanced by British Hegelians did this, and for more or less this reason. Second, although good placement—like 'fit' and 'coherence' in the philosophy literature generally—is left undefined, such notions are generally presumed to fold together many not-obviously-commensurable dimensions of assessment. Why shouldn't the presumption be that 'best placed' is often a vague or partially true ascription, and why shouldn't that be reflected in hedges applied to the statement being made? Third, Travis sees that what semantic assessments we provide on what occasions is a matter of what inferential policies we adopt (pp. 212f.); so if he thinks that bivalentist policies are the ones we ought to have, we should see some argument for inferential policies that require bivalent assessments. But there isn't any.

While Travis emphasizes the connections between introduction and elimination policies (e.g. at pp. 214f.), it is no accident that his examples (the color of ink, the grunting of pigs, and so on) do not have much inferential work to do. We imagine someone walking into a stationery shop, wanting some blue ink; if he decides that a particular bottle of off-blue ink counts as blue, that is good enough: there is no large body of costly inferential machinery waiting on this decision and requiring inputs that match *its* use of 'blue.' After I have explained (in chs. 4 and 5) how and why the inferential clients matter, we will be in a position to return to Procrustean contextualism, and show that such treatments of partial truth undermine inferential usability. Briefly, we will be able to show, *pace* Travis, that Procrustean contextualism is a bad policy.

11 There are, naturally, exceptions. Species, on one understanding of the notion, are reproductively isolated populations, but there may be, especially during speciation, no straightforward fact of the matter as to whether a given population is reproductively isolated. So statements about species membership, although pretty bivalent, are not 100 percent bivalent.

12 I owe this objection to Robert Nozick.

13 For instance, when chemical identifiers are used to ensure that mating takes place only between conspecifics, it's likely that the odors are also identifiable by predators. See Gould and Gould, 1989.

14 See Mayr, 1984, esp. p. 539. Natural selection works to produce bivalence on topics other than species membership; for a discussion of 'antithesis' in animal communication, see West-Eberhard, 2003, p. 454.

15 I will in due course explain why I'm being so concessive to the opposing view. Notice, however, that I needn't be, and to show how, I'll redescribe an

understanding of science advanced by Cartwright, 1983, so as to make it dove-tail with the position I'm developing here. Nature, she thinks, is genuinely messy. The aims of science, which require having laws that are easy enough to use, underwrite accepting laws that are, strictly speaking, false. They are partial truths, in a sense in which Mill might have meant the phrase: each law captures its share of the truth. But it is not that the laws are approximately true; rather, laws are chosen from which true conclusions about concrete cases can be derived. Sometimes real situations occur that match the laws (low-density helium as an ideal gas); sometimes carefully controlled experiments can be constructed (pp. 156, 160f.; in somewhat the same spirit, Ravetz, 1979, p. 112, points out that 'few "chemicals" can be found in the world of nature, outside the laboratory'). But such circumstances are unusual, and the business of scientific discovery is with 'the reality we have to hand' (Cartwright, 1983, p. 19). The normal choice, I have been suggesting, is between engineered bivalence and the unengineered failure of bivalence. Cartwright is accordingly giving a description of how science lives with the failure of bivalence. For closely related views, see Teller, 2001, 2004, and Wilson, 2006, on 'theory facades'.

16 I say 'for instance,' because most of science is not about confirming putative laws.

17 Think that's a naive view of what solutions to physics problems are like? So do I: remember, I'm being concessive to the opposing view.

Defeasibility will be a recurring motif of our discussion, and if the concept is new to you, inference is defeasible where the transition from premises to conclusion can be aborted by defeating conditions; see ch. 4 n 14, and sec. 5.8 for further examples.

18 For a surprising example of reengineering the objects on which experiments are being conducted, see the discussion of *drosophila* in Franchi, 2005, sec. 2. See also Ravetz, 1979, pp. 76–77, on the effort involved in bringing experimental apparatus under control.

19 Cf. Peter Galison's account of showing an experiment to be successful as an argument by exclusion (1987): the phenomenon can't be explained by this interfering factor, nor by this one, nor by the other one...and so the phenomenon is genuine. Arguments by exclusion only work when there are a (small) finite number of alternatives to be excluded, but this is atypical of unprepared circumstances. Successful experimental design is a matter of fabricating a situation in which there are only so many alternatives to be ruled out.

Not surprisingly, applying the exceptionless laws when the issue is not simply testing the law by and large goes much better when the application is constructed in much the way an experiment is: successful technology is managed by building artifacts of which the laws of one's science visibly hold.

On Cartwright's update of her view (1999), the laws are *only* true of the carefully structured artifacts and their accidental natural twins; she calls these 'nomological machines.' Ravetz, 1979, pp. 97ff., provides a nice description of the slowly accumulating experience, in mature sciences, of 'pitfalls' and how to avoid them; the practical skills are those I am going to argue are characteristically deployed in the presence of partial truth, and they are pervasive in the oldest and most muscular scientific disciplines. Once again, I am being more concessive than I need to be.

20 See Ravetz, 1979, pp. 78–79, 81, 83–84, 112n.

21 Lakoff, 1973, pp. 467f., 506, gives examples of what are plausibly mathematical approximate truths, and attributes to Zadeh the following instance: 'Three lines, each of which *approximately* bisects one side of a given triangle and goes through the opposite angle, form a triangle inside the given triangle and *much* smaller than it'—which is true, he observes, and even intuitively obvious, in a model of Euclid's axioms, but not deducible from them. Lakoff calls it 'an interesting curiosity,' and we have just explained why that assessment is about right.

22 These are meant here as generic illustrations of logical truths and falsehoods, not as restatements of controversial doctrines at issue (e.g., the bivalence doctrine) in formal notation.

   I'm going to ignore the finicky convention of corner-quoting expressions like those above, and will use ordinary quotation marks, with the effect of corner-quoting to be obtained from math-font italics. For atomic expressions, I'll leave off the quotation marks.

23 Once again, here and below we are restricting our attention to classical logic, and, with the exception of a discussion of supervaluationism in ch. 7, putting to one side nonstandard logics deploying truth-value gaps.

24 One alternative strategy might be to try to preserve the vagueness in the conclusion: if it's somewhat true that it's a path, it's somewhat true (not unlikely?) that I could follow it out of the forest. That will work sometimes, but often—especially when action is called for—we sooner or later have to arrive at definite answers. *Am* I going to proceed down the path?

25 We *do* have science*s* of artifacts: computer science, for example. But since artifacts are only sporadically engineered to make deduction feasible, deductive logic is not the science of artifacts in general; and in any case, artifacts differ too greatly from each other for there to be single science of artifacts in general.

26 We now have a meteorological vocabulary for classifying clouds, so notice that the descriptive repertoire it provides is not a means of asserting the sorts of daydreaming comparisons we were considering, only bivalently. To reiterate, it is no reply to the point that bivalence with respect to some subject matter is unavailable that it is available for some *other* subject matter.

27 I earlier remarked that we were concerned, not with the truth or falsity of sentences, taken one by one, but with the bivalence of categories of sentences. One reason, of course, is that the kind of engineering we are considering is

not cost-effective if there are no economies of scale; but we can now see that there is a further reason. The point of such engineering is to remove occasions for judgment, and that goal is generally not met if the reasoner has to use his judgment to determine whether he is facing one of the clear cases, or one of the tricky ones.

28 This kind of solution is very much in the spirit of Aristotelian moral philosophy, and of recent readings of Kant that emphasize the *Doctrine of Virtue* (1797/1994). See, e.g., Herman, 1993, McDowell, 1998, ch. 3.

29 There is a noteworthy phenomenon that the example highlights. In the early days of automobiles, who had the right of way on a narrow street or at an intersection could be a delicate social question (one depending on the relative social standing of the drivers, on how courteous they had previously been...). And it was, consequently, an ethical or moral question. Now that the relevant inferences are no longer defeasible, the solved problem does not look like an ethical or moral problem at all. Likewise, when a domain of inference has been so thoroughly reengineered that the conclusions can be drawn automatically, without any explicit thought at all, it too tends to be demoted: when the worker picks up a part, knowing that it just *will* fit into another standardized component, philosophers resist allowing that what he has performed is an *inference*.

30 Notice that the no-free-lunch hypothesis comes out pretty much true only when we're counting the many penumbral cases we've seen as contributing to the sway of the hypothesis (e.g., cases where costs accrue, but not quite on behalf of reengineering the external world in a way that changes off-truths into full-on truths). That is to say, the implicit accounting is in the spirit of the view I have been developing. When the accounting is bivalentist the no-free-lunch hypothesis comes out somewhat less true...but still, I think, true enough to be worth taking into account.

Chapter 3

1 I am using the terms interchangeably here. See O'Leary-Hawthorne and Oppy, 1997, for a taxonomy of various forms of minimalism. Views that I am classifying as deflationary sometimes abjure the title, or, alternatively, pointedly exclude other deflationary views from the group. McGinn, 2000, is an example of the former: he begins by announcing that 'disquotation is the essence of truth,' and claims that truth has 'no conceptual decomposition, and no empirical essence or nature,' all of which makes him, by my lights, a deflationist; but he calls his view 'thick disquotationalism,' and insists that characterizing it as 'deflationary' is 'wide of the mark' (pp. 87, 104, 106). An example of

the latter: Soames, 1999, which is in most respects an entirely middle-of-the-road synthesis of mainstream deflationist views, describes Grover, whom I will momentarily use as my representative of deflationism, along with others, as 'skeptics' and 'nihilists' about truth (e.g. at pp. 46, 48; one is reminded of the near-proverb that heresies loom largest inside the camp of the faithful). I mean to preempt the turn to deflationism, rather than participate in the infighting among those who have made it, and so I will be ignoring such differences among them.

It is worth noticing a tendency for the formal devices invoked by deflationist theories to increase in complexity over the years, as its proponents look for ways to avoid the semantic paradoxes. For instance, Yaqub, 1993, produces a theory complex enough to be described by its author as developing a deflationary conception of truth into a non-deflationary theory of truth—by which he means that the nonsemantic facts do not determine the assignment of truth values to puzzle sentences like the Liar ('This sentence is false') and the Truthteller ('This sentence is true'). I hope on another occasion to discuss the upshots of technical complexity for a view whose motivating thought is that truth is trivially simple. For now, we can observe that while Yaqub's distinction is probably overstated, it nonetheless suggests that the notion of a deflationary theory of truth is itself vague, and that we can expect there to be theories of which it is partly, but not entirely true, that they are deflationist.

2   MacIntyre, 1997, pp. 11–18. Canonical expositions of emotivism include Ayer, 1936, ch. 6, and Stevenson, 1959.

3   Adams, 1998, p. 51.

4   There is by now a quite substantial literature on minimalism or deflationism. Again, the strategy here is to bypass rather than engage it, but the reader should be aware of its existence. Useful entry points include Horwich, 1990, and Soames, 1999.

5   Grover, 1992; Joseph Camp and Nuel Belnap coauthored an early important paper in this collection. For complaints about prosententialism, see Wilson, 1990. For related recent work, see Azzouni, 2001.

6   The list we have given is not exhaustive. Brandom, for instance, mentions anaphoric prosortals, as in: 'Fido was a dog, and Rover was *one*, too' (1994, p. 438).

7   The expectation needs one qualification. Fully grammaticalized prosentences may be etiolated to the point where sentential structure has been abandoned. At one point in its history (though, *pace* Davidson, no longer), the 'that' in 'He knows that it is so' was a fully grammaticalized prosentential demonstrative. One now can say 'I believe *so*' or '*As* you know,' and there is always the one-word 'Indeed.'

8   Other English prosentences include 'that's a fact' and 'that's right.' If the realization that 'it's true' is a prosentence displaces metaphysical accounts of truth,

one would expect metaphysical accounts of facts to be similarly dislodged. And I am curious as to what a prosentential theory of right would look like; possibly there are anticipations of such a theory in Hare, 1972.

Grover and others model the prosentential account with substitutional quantification over sentences; that is, they treat sentences like 'Everything she says is true' as having the form '$(p)((\text{She says } p) \supset p)$', where the variable is thought of as representing a string that is to be plugged into the template '(She says...)$\supset$...'. This proposal has elicted two sorts of complaints, one of which is more interesting than the other. The less interesting complaint is that English sentences can't just be plugged into the slots in the template; they need all kinds of tweaking to get the right result. (Soames, 1999, pp. 43–46; this is uninteresting because it assumes that the substitutional approach is committed to non-tweaked substitutions, and because generating the right strings looks like a straightforward macro programming exercise.) The more interesting complaint is that the quantifications of which we need to make sense can outrun the expressive resources of a given language, as when we say, 'There are truths that can't be expressed in English.'

Notice that a proform can carry information over and above its simply picking out which previous grammatical element it is standing in for, as when a pronoun signals the gender of its referent; that information may be added to what was originally presented, as it is when the gender of the pronoun's referent is not given by the noun to which it points back. ('The Prime Minister returned yesterday from *her* trip to Washington.') Prosentences will be especially flexible in this regard; when they are grammatically sentences, they can carry additional information in the tense of the verb ('It was true'), in the mood ('Were it true...'), and so on. The grammatically available option of inserting adverbial modifiers allows an easy way of registering hedged reaffirmation of a previously uttered sentence, e.g., 'It's partially true,' or, in Austin's terse example of a partial-truth prosentence, 'True enough' (1950, p. 111). But—and this is characteristic of the spirit of deflationary views—I have never seen them developed in this way.

9 For a quite extended discussion of this sort, but one which takes landscapes as its topic, see Ruskin, 1906, vol. I; for an exemplary short stretch, see part II, sec. ii, ch. 1 ('Of Truth of Tone'). Ruskin does not use the vocabulary of partial truth that I am in the process of recommending, but notice the use of 'truth' and 'falsehood' as mass nouns, to much the same effect, as well as remarks such as those on the 'grammatical accuracy of the tones of Turner,' 'the facts of form and distance... [being] more important than any truths of tone,' etc.

10 Austin, 1950, sec. 5.

11 The example is from Bayley, 1999, p. 21.

12 For this last point, I'm grateful to Christoph Fehige.

13 Tarski, 1944, 1935/1986; for this sort of characterization of its historical role, see, e.g., Gupta, 1980, pp. 125f. In the *Genealogy*, Nietzsche suggests that some philosophers dislike the word 'truth' because it sounds too grandiloquent (1989, Essay 3, sec. 8); one way of describing Tarski's accomplishment might be that he made truth modest enough to be palatable to philosophers of that ilk.

14 The earliest is probably Ramsey (see Ramsey, 1991, which also contains foreshadowings of the prosententialist version of deflationism).

15 Not, to reiterate, the general culture: Grammatical behavior can indicate the uses of a lexeme, so notice that 'His answer seems true' is acceptable, as is 'That is true indeed.' 'Seems,' in this usage, requires a degree adjective, as does the postpositioned 'indeed.' (Bolinger, 1972, pp. 77, 97; see also Lakoff, 1973, p. 460.) So 'true' must be often used, by lay speakers of English, as a degree word.

The background against which truth seems to have next to no internal structure is also a background against which the concept will seem to have no history, a view to be found in Williams, 2002, p. 61. However, once we look past the degenerate cases, the concept of truth can be expected to have a history that is both rich and largely overlooked.

16 Dummett, 1978a, pp. 2–3; see p. 4 for his rendering of deflationism, and *passim* for criticism of the view.

17 See Fiell and Fiell, 1997, pp. 405, 529, and 587, for cases of this kind; p. 457 depicts an item of which it is partially true that it is a chair, and partially true that it is a chaise longue, but which satisfies the one-person rule. The idea that the content or force of a claim can be modified by restricting some of its consequences is not unprecedented; cf. Azzouni, 2004, pp. 34f., who uses 'quarantined implications' to pick out the merely instrumental adoption of a theory.

18 According to Brandom, 1994, the function of logical vocabulary is to let us make inferential commitments explicit; truth vocabulary is a special case of logical vocabulary. To say that everything so-and-so says is true is to make explicit your commitment to all the things that so-and-so said; this is important because once inferential commitments have been made explicit, they can be argued about. ('Everything she tells you is true.' 'Why do you think she's so very reliable?') Brandom endorses the prosententialist version of deflationism; part of our making-explicit is done using anaphoric devices such as prosentences. But Brandom's account is only half right. The function of our talk of partial truth is indeed to make our inferential commitments more explicit; but it is not usually to make them fully explicit.

19 That said, there's something that deflationism got right after all. An objection that we encountered in sec. 2.3, and which we will address in ch. 6, turned on the fact that, in most cases, the modifiers used to express the partial truth of a sentence can be moved into the sentence itself, and the mention of truth then

dropped. For instance, it is sort of true that Crescent Beach is crescent-shaped; but we could express the same opinion by saying that Crescent Beach is sort of crescent-shaped. In particular cases, then, it is more or less true that truth vocabulary is dispensable.

('More or less,' because these transformations don't always work entirely smoothly. For instance, moving a modifier into the sentence means moving it into a particular place in the sentence, and this often has the effect of assigning the qualification to one part of the sentence or another. In this example, we are choosing between qualifying our description of the shape of the beach, and qualifying our way of picking out the object to which we are ascribing a shape. The point might have been that a slightly different area, overlapping to a large extent with Crescent Beach, was fully crescent-shaped.)

Where it is not so easily dispensable—and this point is a close relative of a claim we saw made by deflationary accounts—is when we want to qualify a commitment to a group of sentences whose contents we cannot, or do not want to, enumerate one by one. I may warn you, as you descend into the archives to review press releases I myself have never seen, that the announcements of some government agency are only literally true, but unscrupulous otherwise. So even if it is not hard to get by without partial truth in any particular case, we need the vocabulary of partial truth, or some functional equivalent, both to produce such general qualifications for our assertions, and to theorize about them.

Azzouni, 2004, p. 24, points out that the deflationist's device is required by scientific uses of approximation. When you defend your approximation by arguing that it's close enough to what's actually true, and when what is true is not something you can derive or write down, you are in the business of endorsing sentences whose content you do not know and cannot state.

20 Timothy Williamson has recently argued that rejecting bivalence can be reduced to absurdity (1994, pp. 187–189), and here I want to walk through that argument, not in the first place to rebut it—other critics (Richard, 2000, Keefe, 2000, p. 215, Burgess, 1998, sec. 4) have already pointed out that it is question-begging—but to show how the analogies we are considering can make familiar logical theses seem optional rather than inescapable, and to show how, against the background of the view I am developing, they *read* differently.

Williamson formulates the principle of bivalence, for an utterance u, as

(B) If u says that P, then either u is true or u is false.

I've been suggesting that we think of the bivalence doctrine as analogous to a pass-fail grading scheme, and contrasting it with a more nuanced set of assessments: perhaps with straight As and straight Fs at the top and bottom, but with other letter grades as well, perhaps with paragraph-length written evaluations, and perhaps with grades that are announced to be neither passes nor fails.

(B) is then laid down by the pass-fail grading scheme: it is the stipulation that there are only two grades to give assertions. Williamson is attempting the analog of arguing that there *could* not be any other grading scheme. The analogy tells us that this is not promising: when faculty vote on whether to change what the grades can be, they are not voting on logical or metaphysical impossibilities.

Williamson then introduces variants of Tarski's T-sentences as 'central to our ordinary understanding of [truth and falsity]':

(T) If u says that P, then u is true if and only if P.
(F) If u says that P, then u is false if and only if not P.

Williamson is careful to allow that there may be more to truth than Tarski-like T-sentences, but he is nonetheless visibly allowing them the central sort of role that they occupy in the deflationist philosophical culture. He writes:

> The rationale for (T) and (F) is simple. Given that an utterance says that TW is thin, what it takes for it to be true is just for TW to be thin, and what it takes for it to be false is for TW not to be thin. No more and no less is required. To put the condition for truth or falsity any higher or lower would be to misconceive the nature of truth or falsity. (1994, p. 190)

That's true enough, but if we have it right, to think that you have locked in on truth when you have (something like) (T) and (F) in your sights is just to forget what truth and falsity are in the first place *for*. In our anti-bivalentist way of thinking, (T) and (F) are two clauses of a perhaps indefinitely long list of cases:

u is true if and only if P
u is false if and only if not P
u is kind of true if and only if P, kind of
u is barely true if and only if P, barely

$$\vdots$$

The proper use of the list is, simplifying somewhat, reading down to the trigger condition that is inferentially available to you, and then reading across to the correlated condition (not forgetting the further complication that the different cases are not all mutually exclusive). When you take the view of truth I have been suggesting, statements like (T) and (F) are leftovers, what you shrug and say when there is no need for the primary functionality of truth (namely, providing a subtle, nuanced and flexible system of grading and assessing one's claims).

Those of us who are academics have heard analogs of Tarski T-sentences in the world of grading—'An A is only for A-quality work!'—and we have heard our fellow faculty members insisting on them as though they were meta-physical bulwarks against lax standards. But even a desperate campaign against grade inflation is a campaign for one among many possible grading systems. Williamson's opponent will agree that the standard for p's being true is p; but the agreement is only verbal, because what he means by that will be *pickier* than what Williamson intends, because he is pickier both about when he will assert p ('Well, *kind of* ...') and about when he will assert that p is true; likewise, he is pickier about when he will assert $\sim p$ ('Well, there's *some* truth to it...'), and about when he will assert that p is false. And this is as it should be; after all, the standards built into the tokens of a grading or bookkeeping system should match the techniques for manipulating them, and changing the techniques will involve altering the standards.

Now, a counterexample to bivalence requires both that

(0) u says that P.

that is, it requires an utterance that is a potential truth-bearer, and

(1) Not: either u is true or u is false.

But here is how someone who rejects bivalence, in the way we have been recommending, will read (0) and (1): Because he is recommending a more elaborate grading scheme, he can agree that an assertion suitable for grading (the intent of (0)) might take not a pass (truth) or a fail (falsity) but some other grade. So (1) is read as:

(1′) Not: either u is true or u is false—because, in my preferred grading scheme, u might be kind of true, sort of true, true in a way, have a smidgen of truth to it...

—that is, while u should trigger one or more of the clauses on the indefinitely long list, it is going to trigger one or more of the *other* clauses.

From (0), (T) and (F) Williamson derives

(2a) u is true if and only if P.
(2b) u is false if and only if not P.

From (1) and (2) he derives

(3) Not: either P or not P.

And by de Morgan's Laws, the contradiction

(4) Not P and not not P.

However, again interpreting the branches of (2) as clauses on the list, someone who accepts partial truth can assent to (3) as well, but will gloss it roughly as follows:

(3′) Not: either P or not P: rather, as my preferred grading scheme sorts out the options, kind of P, sort of P,...

And finally, we arrive at the antibivalentist reading of (4):

(4′) Not P and not not P, but some other option picked out by the grading scheme: perhaps kind of P, or sort of P, or...

Williamson defends his use of the contradiction as a reductio by stating simply that, 'as for the absurdity of (4), no attempt will be made to argue with those who think it acceptable to contradict oneself' (1994, p. 189; cf. p. 136). However, we do not need dramatic Hegelian or Priestian disavowals of the Principle of Non-Contradiction to make sense of our innocuous conclusion. Since what we are transforming to obtain (4) is 'Not: either P or not P, but rather, R, or S, or T...,' what we get by distributing the negation is: 'not the first option (P), and not the second (not P), but rather R, or S, or T...' When you're working in a grading scheme in which there are more than two options, ruling out two options leaves the others, and so the nonbivalentist reading of Williamson's (4) is that, for a putative counterexample to bivalence of the sort Williamson wants us to consider, one of the *other* grading options must be the right one: which is no more and no less than we knew going into the argument.

Our analogy is a reminder that we can *read* the logical slogans differently, and of what sort of arguments we can and can't take seriously. You shouldn't believe that a six-line argument, one that moves around the tokens of one grading system to get the conclusion that no other grading system is acceptable, can really do what it purports.

21 In fact, even thinking about painting should correct that second presumption: hyperrealism is a *style*, and Rembrandt's portraits, which we admire for capturing the truth (the full truth, or very, very near to it) of their subjects' characters, are not hyperrealism, or failed hyperrealism either. Such portraits do not work in the way the correspondence theory would suggest: for instance, Nozick, 1989, p. 13, remarks that they typically compile bits and pieces of a sitter's facial expression at different times and from different angles, and thus

succeed as portraits just *because* there was no time at which the elements of the sitter's face were as the portrait depicts them.

22 There is a related and tricker point to bear in mind as well. In a money economy, and even in barter sitations where the commodities to be traded are suitably standardized, the two questions—what do you have? and, what could you get for it, if you had it?—are not just distinguishable in principle, but, normally, separately answerable. When it comes to one-of-a-kind trading goods, however, it is often not possible to arrive at a decent opinion about what you could get for such an item without having it on the premises and available for inspection— and perhaps not even without actually putting it up for auction. Or again, many of us have been asked by students what grade their paper will get if it satisfies one or another student-supplied description, and have had to reply that in order to say what grade the paper will get, we will have to see the paper. Partial truth can be a bit like that: often enough, you can't tell what is going to follow from a partial truth (you can't tell how true it is) without taking a close look at just *how* it is true. In such cases the ability to assess the correctness of a potential inference independently of having its premises available is in practice eroded.

23 See Wimsatt, 1987, pp. 30–32, for a preliminary list of uses to which oversim- plified models can be put, each of which would motivate a different type of partially true representation. (Wimsatt himself doesn't quite think of it this way: his title, 'False Models as a Means to Truer Theories,' describes the models as flat-out false—but then uses a comparative of 'true'!) For an incomplete but still lengthy list of hedges, and some discussion of the different ways a handful of them work, see Lakoff, 1973, pp. 472, 477f.

24 Hart, 1979, is a nice—almost lyrical—version of the observation, emphasizing the ways in which truth is something to be faced up to, how that often requires honesty with oneself, and how hard that is.

Chapter 4

1 There is, I think, intriguing linguistic support for the expectation. Our idiomatic vocabulary for registering partial truth is undergoing grammatical- ization. When a lexeme is grammaticalized, it tends to compress. ('I'm going to do it' becomes 'I'm gonna do it,' whereas 'I'm going to the store' does not become, 'I'm gonna the store.') 'Sort of' and 'kind of' have become, in spo- ken language, 'kinda' and 'sorta' when they are used as indicators of partial truth. (But not otherwise: 'It is one kind of the three kinds of tigers' does not get said as, 'It is one kinda the three kinds of tigers.') Grammemes are pro- duced pretty much only for high-traffic parts of a language. So the appearance

244 *Notes*

of 'kinda' and 'sorta' are evidence for the heavy use given to partial truth. See Heine *et al.*, 1991; for discussion of these modifiers, see Tabor, 1993.

It's also worth noting that hedging can be managed not only by standalone words but by choice of verb or syntactic construction (Lakoff, 1973, p. 490).

2   I don't here want to get into an argument with the community of Kant scholars over the use and ownership of the phrase, but I do need to say one thing. In the wake of Henrich, 1975, the distinction between a 'transcendental argument' and a 'transcendental deduction' has become almost a reflex. My own view is that Henrich's paper does not actually provide the means of making such a distinction, and so I will be treating the two phrases as interchangeable. Telegraphically, for those familiar with Henrich's exposition: to register the use of legal metaphors in Kant's work is as yet to have said nothing about what the literal content of those metaphors is; to the very limited extent that Henrich does extract such content, it is compatible with describing arguments of the kind I develop here as 'deductions.'

3   This complaint is made by, among others, Walker, 1978.

4   Transcendental arguments were invented as a response to skepticism, and we have just seen why they proved largely unsuccessful in that capacity: the original skepticism rearises with respect to whether the cognitive task that is the starting point of the argument has been successfully executed. There is a second, related reason as well: it is hard to construct interesting transcendental arguments without using empirical premises, and when the aim of the argument is to refute skepticism about the external world, empirical premises are usually regarded as off-limits. As a result, transcendental arguments have lost much of their popularity. But disenchantment with the argument form is so far unwarranted; we should rather take the lesson to be that transcendental arguments are to be used primarily for purposes other than refuting skepticism about the external world, and we should perhaps come to think of the transcendental deduction as (like Aristotle's practical syllogism) a *practical* argument form.

5   That one is in fact *thinking* belongs under this heading: if what one is doing is not, after all, thought, then efforts toward ascertaining a conclusion are a waste of time. Descartes famously said that the cogito—the *I think*—is beyond doubt, but this is not what I am getting at here; rather, doubt about whether one is actually thinking must, as a practical matter, be put to one side while one is trying to make headway on some concrete intellectual problem or another. Perhaps you are not *really* thinking; you can, after all, observe other people being psychologically active, but managing something less than full-fledged thought.

Sometimes this can happen to very bright people, and sometimes one can understand it as having happened to oneself. John Nash, of Nash equilibrium fame, went through a prolonged bout of mental illness during which he went in for pure (as opposed to applied) numerology, announced that Titan, Saturn's second moon, was the biblical Jacob, that Jack Bricker was Satan, that he himself was Emperor of Antarctica and the left foot of God on earth, and much else of the same ilk. Asked how he could believe such things, he is said to have answered that the ideas he had about supernatural beings came to him the same way that his mathematical ideas did. (See Nasar, 1998, pp. 258, 275, 326, 335.)

But if you are not thinking, then *this* is not a difficulty that you can think your way out of, and you might as well stop worrying about it for the duration. You must, in the course of trying to think your way to an opinion about whatever matter is in question, *take it for granted* that you are really thinking.

6 Cartesian arguments (the example of the previous note) are trickier, inasmuch as they turn on the point that you can't *just think* you're thinking. Because the neatness of the pragmatic contradiction overlays the point about what must, whether true or not, be presupposed, many philosophers have been misled as to the force of arguments of this kind.

7 I'm grateful to Sarah Buss for this example.

8 Notice that the requirement is quite unspecific: it is that you ought to buy property in general, not that you ought to buy any particular properties, or buy property on any given turn, or have any more narrowly framed acquisition strategy.

Because the content of evaluative claims is first and foremost practical, there may be room for similarly closing the gap when the conclusion of the argument is not merely directive, but evaluative. When you are playing chess, you had better treat the pieces (and probably the positions as well) as having values, values that differ from each other. (As before, the reach of this claim does not extend as far as their having any particular values; players can sensibly disagree, and the standard point system is too crude to insist upon. It does not commit one to precise values, or even to commensurable values; one may quite reasonably think it false that a knight is worth exactly a bishop, but also that it is false that knights are worth more, or that they are worth less.) A player who does not treat a captured queen as more of a loss than a captured pawn might as well not be playing chess, and there are probably deep reasons for this: even successful chess-playing programs work by assigning values internally to pieces and positions. But this is just to say that, within the context of a chess game, the pieces *do* have differing values. (However, it's not to say that the values directly dictate the moves: in a given situation, it may be much more important to hang onto the pawn than the queen. I take this kind of loose connection between evaluation and decision to be characteristic of value more broadly.)

9 That turn of phrase needs an anticipatory qualification: the argument I will shortly advance will show that the old-fashioned characterization of inference in terms of the Laws of Thought was conceived too narrowly; the project of working out guidelines for thinking should not generally be expected to eventuate in *laws*.

10   Representations generally have owners, or if not owners, default owners. (You may not want to ascribe the would-be psychological state to anyone, but if the grounds for your resistance were overcome, you usually wouldn't have any problem knowing to whom, of all those people out there, it would belong.) There's a deep question here that I want to duck, about how we even tentatively ascribe representations to people, or equivalently, how we group together representations into minds; but I will return to the uses one can make of this fact in ch. 5.

11   We do not need to assume that we are able to engage in inference with arbitrarily many components; realistically, there are only so many considerations we can juggle at once. One way we handle this difficulty is to reason in stages, representing progress in interim conclusions, and bringing new considerations to bear at most a few at a time. But it is likely that not all problems can be broken up in this way, and so there are very probably inferential problems that we are not in a position to solve. For discussion of related issues, see Millgram, 2005, ch. 9.

12   Brandom, 1994, argues for 'inferential expressivism,' according to which it is a mistake to think of an inference from p to q as involving a further premise, the conditional 'if p then q.' The reason for stating the conditional is to make explicit our commitment to the satisfactoriness of the inferential transition from p to q, but that transition is already perfectly in order as it stands. (The view is reminiscent of Mill's discussion of the importance of the syllogism.) If one takes Brandom's idea seriously, then it might appear that many of our inferences are much less complex than my argument requires.

First, however, the points I am about to make can be also made using Brandom's preferred mode of description. For instance, if we are committed to an inference that proceeds directly from p to q, we must have not just that commitment, but the assertion that p; that is, our assertion must match our inferential commitment if we are to move forward.

Second, notice that the reasons for reconceiving conditionals as merely expressing inferential commitments are equally reasons for conceiving beliefs or assertions that do not have the conditional form as also merely expressing inferential commitments, viz., commitments to the inferential consequences of the respective beliefs. That would give us the odd result that *no* inferences have *any* premises. Even if we were to accept this result, however, the inferential commitments, expressed or unexpressed, would still have to match one another.

13   This latter problem has in the past been put to use as a gear in ambitious philosophical argument, as in James Mill's insistence that 'Names, to be useful, cannot exceed a certain number. They could not otherwise be remembered' (1869, vol. 1, p. 136). I expect that a backup argument for my conclusion could be constructed around this consideration.

14 Using modus ponens as my example of matching might misleadingly suggest that interlocking premises are necessarily components of deductive inferences. However, inductive inferences also typically contain interlocking components: having examined many dogs, and determined that they all frolic, and having determined that Stiffy is a dog, I infer that Stiffy also frolics; but the inference is defeasible, and I retract its conclusion when it is brought to my attention that Stiffy is dead (McPhail, 1996). And we have already noticed that inferences deploying partial truths are defeasible as well.

15 Harte, 1985; the title is the punch line of a well-known joke, one version of which introduces the book. But lest you think that this is *just* a joke, or a merely toy example, here is a quote, plucked almost at random from an engineering report (Durney *et al.*, 1986, sec. 1.3):

> The rigorous analysis of a realistically shaped inhomogenous model for humans or experimental animals would be an enormous theoretical task. Because of the difficulty of solving Maxwell's equations, which form the basis of the analysis, a variety of special models and techniques have been used, each valid only in a limited range of frequency or other parameter. Early analyses were based on plane-layered, cylindrical, and spherical models. The calculated dosimetric data presented in this handbook are based primarily on a combination of cylindrical, ellipsoidal, spheroidal, and block models of people and experimental animals. Although these models are relatively crude representations of the size and shape of the human body, experimental results show that calculations of the average SAR [specific absorption rate] agree reasonably well with measured values.

Do not be tempted to fall back on the thought that the masses m_1 and m_2 are precise, and that we should just reason with those: recall that cows are vague objects; they do not have precise masses.

16 *Pace* Giere, 1990, p. 81, the issue is not *similarity*, but *usability*.

17 There is a secondary reason for treating the cow as a sphere, which I want to mention in order to put to one side: that one does not ordinarily know just what the spatial distribution of the mass of an actual cow is, and that information of this kind can be very hard to come by. (It is actually this kind of informational shortfall that the author of *Consider a Spherical Cow* is trying to teach students to handle.) The problems I want to address just now are not, in the first place, epistemological; they arise even when all the information is readily available. So by way of keeping distinct issues distinct, I am going to focus on examples where the difficulty of coming by a perfect match is not in the first place a matter of lack of information.

18 Not really true, even allowing for the elasticity of 'looks like'; as with our earlier example in sec. 2.2, once we have fixed the reach of the resemblance, we still have occasions to use it when it is half-true. Note also that I am varying the examples, so that some invoke resemblance and some do not; if you are inclined to disagree with my arguments against making too much of the flexibility of likeness (in ch. 2 n 10, and sec. 7.8), feel free to switch examples.

19 Cf. Mill's remark on the reasons for using what he calls 'approximate generalizations': 'We could replace the approximate generalizations by propositions universally true; but these would hardly ever be capable of being applied to practice. We should be sure of our majors, but we should not be able to get minors to fit; we are forced, therefore, to draw our conclusions from coarser and more fallible indications' (1967–1989, vol. VII, p. 594).

20 For his very interesting description of those problems, see Stella, 1986.

21 Since I have elsewhere presented a similarly shaped argument in which a claim about novelty occupied the role filled here by the Messiness Thesis (Millgram, 1997, chs. 3–5), notice that messiness and novelty are not quite the same thing. Very typically, novelty and messiness account for one another, because novel items don't fit available categories, and novelty often arises from a large pool of minor variations. But the world of Ecclesiastes, in which there is nothing new under the sun, might be a rather messy world.

22 I have on occasion had the view I am developing described to me as pragmatist. Pragmatism is a rich and multifaceted tradition, and this is not the place to ask how well the description fits. However, by way of suggesting that it should not be obvious how pragmatist the present argument is, recall that one well-known pragmatist slogan tells us that it's true if it works. We have been examining cases where it works precisely because it's not true. Notice further that pragmatists— with recent exceptions such as Rorty—aspire to approach ever more closely to the ideal limit that is truth; on the view being developed here, it's often perfectly reasonable to stick with an approximation, and not to attempt or even desire to get closer to the truth. And finally, notice that the claims about what does and doesn't work that pragmatists need will preponderantly come out being, by present lights, only partially true.

23 Paul Teller (personal communication) has come up with a nice argument to the effect that trying to stick to central as opposed to borderline cases of a predicate will not get you out of having to use partial truth. The reason is that partial truths, and idealizations in particular, are normally embedded in the models presupposed by application of many of our predicates. For example, if the predicate is 'under six feet tall,' I clearly belong in the extension of the predicate; I am not a borderline case, and so I am a case in which inferential matches come easy. But the background idealization is that I have a height, one that is precise enough to be represented as a real number. And *that* is some sort of partial truth: does my hair count as part of my height? does my scalp have

a precise border? what do we make of the fact that I compress slightly over the course of a day?

24 Smart, 1987. Anthropic arguments as I have just characterized them are some-times called 'weak anthropic arguments,' to distinguish them from their less intellectually respectable 'strong' relatives. For other anthropic arguments, see Barrow and Tipler, 1986, and for a parody, Stewart, 1995; for related discussion, see Dennett, 1995, pp. 164–181. Roush, 1999, has described arguments of this form as naturalized transcendental arguments; see also Roush, 2003. I'm very grateful to Sherri Roush for discussion on this topic.

25 You might wonder if this last claim can be counted on to stick in a much less messy world. (If there are only two brightness states, 'day' and 'night,' a brightness sensor can be built much more simply.) But notice that, in our own world, two-state sensors (such as smoke and carbon monoxide detectors) have been gradually evolving toward increased functionality, in a way that evidently requires just this rich type of option space. And notice also that we have exam-ples of the phenomenon in artificially simplified worlds. Softbots are treated as robotics testbeds, because they can live in the very clean world of (e.g.) a Unix directory structure; they are implemented, not in messy, uncooperative *mat-ter*, but in one or another higher-level programming language (Etzioni, 1993). Nonetheless, softbots evolve incrementally, and have to be debugged; if you were not able to tinker with softbots, there wouldn't be any softbots. (And it's telling that there's a programmers' word for making the sort of small changes I'm talking about: to *twiddle*.)

26 Williamson, 1994.

27 Two remarks. First, even here there is residual imprecision at, say, the picosec-ond level: it's true for all practical purposes that it's 9:00, but *already* no longer absolutely true. Second, inferences on just this topic were very important to the development of the technology. Acrimonious disputes about when the work-day began were once an ongoing source of friction, and during the early stages of the social transition to working by the clock, employers tried to control the clocks in order to lengthen the working day. See Dohrn-van Rossum, 1996.

28 That said, notice that even here we do not restrict ourselves to inferences that deploy full truths. We retain the vague vocabulary to which 'morning' belongs, and we use more precise vocabulary in inferences that help themselves to forced matches. An old joke illustrates the point nicely: the difference between the American professoriat and its German counterpart is that, in American uni-versities, a meeting scheduled for 2:00 will begin at about 2:15, whereas in Germany, a meeting scheduled for 2:00 will begin at *exactly*…2:15.

29 I am occasionally asked how the account I am developing differs from Wittgen-stein's, and here is one of the differences. In the *Philosophical Investigations*, Wittgenstein asks when it is 5:00 on the sun (1998, sec. 350); the point of his question is that utterances apparently very similar to plainly sensible utterances

may be quite simply nonsense, if the preconditions for making sense of them have not been put in place. We determine time of day on the earth using the position of the sun in the sky; so no sense has been given to determining the time of day on the sun.

Wittgenstein fails to consider what it would really take to give this sentence a sense, but we can do so ourselves. There would have to be, first of all, people living and working on the sun in order for there to be economic reason to introduce a solar time zone. There would have to be economic reasons for there to be a *single* solar time zone. And of course there would have to be clocks that could be used on the sun, a technological advance we can take for granted if we are already imagining people able to live on the sun. The important point here is that the 'forms of life' in which particular forms of words can be sensibly used have *technological* preconditions, which is why bivalence is normally an *engineering* achievement. That Wittgenstein does not usually pursue this kind of inquiry is mildly surprising, both in view of his own engineering background and of his historical proximity to the engineering achievement that produced time zones; time of day as we know it was the late-nineteenth-century response to the need to coordinate railway schedules.

30　And recall that we would not really want it any other way. To adapt the relevant claim of sec. 2.8 to an example from this chapter, ruthless censorship could put us in the position of having only works of art that fell cleanly into some small number of categories (paintings or sculptures, but perhaps more likely, portraits of Stalin and heroic depictions of proletarians in the approved Socialist Realist style), and the jobs of museum curators would be greatly simplified thereby. This is not, however, a case in which the benefits of cleanly interlocking premises are worth their price.

Chapter 5

1　As per usual, I'm putting paraconsistent logics and such to one side; the point I am making sticks, whatever logic you happen to endorse, and whatever platitudes it substitutes.

2　See, e.g., Cooper, 1990, which demonstrates that the intractability persists even once one adopts a now quite popular simplifying device, Bayesian or Pearl Networks.

3　You might be worried that there's so much freedom in drawing lines around types of persons that I've just introduced a philosophical wild card. I'll say a little more about how I intend these types to be circumscribed in the Appendix; in the meantime, you are invited to scrutinize the argument as it develops, to verify that the clause is not being abused.

4 Frege, 1977, esp. pp. 1–3, 14–17; 1967, pp. 16ff.; 1978, pp. 34–38; Husserl, 2001, vol. i, pp. 13–133. For a sociology-of-knowledge reconstruction of one branch of the psychologism debate in philosophy, see Kusch, 1995. Philosophers are for the most part unaware of the role played by accusations of psychologism in the larger German academic culture; for an overview of the history, see Ringer, 1990, esp. pp. 295–298.

There has been some erosion of the antipsychologistic dogma over the last few decades: philosophical work on the border of cognitive science (e.g., Bach, 1984), the tradition in economics started off by Herbert Simon, and work on practical reasoning have taken psychology as input to the theory of correct inference. However, the movement away from antipsychologism seems to have been inadvertent: those bodies of work have included almost no explicit reconsideration of whether psychologism is in fact methodologically legitimate.

5 See Stich, 1990; Dummett, 1978a, pp. 2–4; Fodor, 2000.

6 In other words, to the objection that it's a *fact* that, say, $(p \land (p \supset q)) \supset q$, regardless of what people's psychologies are like, we can respond that what picks out a mathematical truth as a truth of *logic* is that it is a guide to rational inference. A putatively logical fact for which no such explanation could in principle be given would not count as part of logic.

7 For instance, Mill, whom it is most charitable to suppose Frege never actually read, was quite clear that the Laws of Thought in which he was interested were to be understood on the analogy of laws of the state, not laws of nature: as concerned with how thought *should* proceed, and not with how it actually *does*:

> I conceive it to be true that Logic is not the theory of Thought as Thought, but of valid Thought; not of thinking, but of correct thinking. It is not a Science distinct from, and coordinate with, Psychology. So far as it is a science at all, it is a part, or branch, of Psychology; differing from it, on the one hand as a part differs from the whole, and on the other, as an Art differs from a Science. Its theoretic grounds are wholly borrowed from Psychology, and include as much of that science as is required to justify the rules of the art. (1967–1989, vol. IX, p. 359)

See the note on the previous page for the distinction between descriptive and prescriptive laws, or again, p. 361. Here is Mill once more, in an editorial footnote to his father's *Analysis of the Phenomena of the Human Mind* (Mill, 1869, vol. I, pp. 435f.):

> The problem of Evidence divides itself into two distinguishable enquiries: what effect evidence ought to produce, and what determines the effect that it does produce: how our belief ought to be regulated, and how, in point of fact, it is regulated. The first enquiry—that into the nature and

probative force of evidence: the discussion of what proves what, and of the precautions needed in admitting one thing as proof of another—are the province of Logic, understood in its widest sense...

Cf. Mill's description of 'evidence [a]s not that which the mind does or must yield to, but that which it ought to yield to, namely, that, by yielding to which, its belief is kept conformable to fact' (1967–1989, vol. VII, p. 564); or again, vol. IX, p. 300, where Mill contrasts Psychology ('the analysis and laws of the mental operations') with Logic ('the theory of the ascertainment of objective truth'); or yet again, vol. VII, pp. 12–13.

8   This is, to be sure, to take what is in historical perspective a controversial position on the correct reading of the *Critique of Pure Reason*; during the reign of antipsychologism, antipsychologistic readings were preferred. For background, see Anderson, 2005; Kitcher, 1990, marks a return to readings of Kant's theoretical philosophy that do not attempt to expunge its attention to the mind.

9   For some discussion of the way different types of requirement jockey for position, see Kelly, 2003; for pointers to the older 'ethics of belief' literature, see his note 16. MacFarlane, 2000, pp. 7–30, is a very clear statement of the observation that a distinction between the logical and the nonlogical requires a philosophical motivation.

10 To be sure, if Kant was right, that last is not really an option. His Transcendental Analytic is an attempt to show that his version of unity of consciousness— the so-called transcendental unity of apperception—involves a great deal of specifically intellectual integration as well. For discussion, see Anderson, 2001; for a recent overview of various things that might be meant by 'unity of consciousness,' see Bayne and Chalmers, 2003.

11 For versions of these complaints, see Rorty, 1979, Williams, 1996, van Fraassen, 2002, pp. 5–10, 18–25.

12 I will not here attempt to improve the explanation of why it does. Still, it is important that our appeals to consistency be motivated, rather than merely the expression of a kind of philosophical habit. When we are working on the foundations of logic, non-contradiction is one of the pieces in play, and cannot be taken for granted.

As indicated a moment ago, I am foregoing other, more pragmatically oriented ways of motivating the consistency requirement. (For instance, that consistency in belief is essential for effective action: if one phase of your action is governed by the belief that *A* is a way of accomplishing your end, while another phase of that action is governed by the belief that *A* will preclude accomplishing your end, and if this pattern is typical of your activities, you will not be a particularly successful agent.) I also do not want to overstate the decisiveness of the interest; we may have reason to tolerate inconsistency in a system of beliefs, if, for instance, we anticipate that resolving the inconsistency at too early a stage would turn out to have been a tactical error.

13   See, for instance, Williams, 1978, ch. 2.

14   Russell asked, of the set of all sets that are not members of themselves, whether it was a member of itself. For the way the statement is standardly adjusted, see Suppes, 1972, pp. 5ff. Another example in a nearby territory: Moore, 1978, recounts some of the stages in sorting out what had once seemed to be the obvious observation that any set can be well-ordered.

15   Usually, that you know you have a hand; that for all you know, you might be a brain in a vat, in which case you wouldn't have a hand; and that, if, for all you know, you might not have a hand, then you do not know that you have a hand. See, e.g., Neta, 2003.

16   I'm grateful to Bob Goodin for reminding me of this example.

17   The example is David Finkelstein's.

18   See, e.g., Schlick, 1959. It is no accident that these vocabularies have not worked out as their originators expected. The fantasy of a language for reporting 'sense-data' is just that: the image or picture of starting points that are already completely hedged in advance, and that, because the hedging is complete, do not require knowing what they are being hedged against. But it is only a picture, because, before you run into one or another concrete problem, you can't know *how* you will have to hedge—in just the way that there is no such thing as developing a 'problem-proof process' in advance of knowing what problems you might run into. So there is nothing that would actually do the job that the sense-datum theorists' imaginary vocabulary was for. (For a humorous but quite convincing version of the general observation, see Dikkers and Kolb, 2006, pp. 171, 174. The narrower point is nicely made by Austin, 1962, pp. 112f.)

19   This is the Voters Paradox from the point of view of a social scientist, not a philosopher, who will have a rather different take on what is worrisome here.

20   For further background, and an attempted solution to the problem, see Bendor *et al.*, 2003.

21   Here's an example of how it *is* a simplification. If you are informed that 20 percent of microfleems are subradiante (Adams, 1999, p. 17), there is no real inferential use to which you can put this bit of information, since you don't know anything else about microfleems or about the property being ascribed to them. But this is not to say that you cannot go ahead with, roughly, junk inferences: to the proposition that 80 percent of microfleems are not subradiante, to the conjunction of the original proposition with anything else you happen to believe, to the disjunction of the original proposition with anything, and so on. So junk inferences can be used to produce (junk) inferential connections between any sets of beliefs, however disparate in subject matter. This means that in thinking of the mind as a collection of boxes we have to ignore the junk inferences.

22 There may be compensating effects, and these should not be underestimated. For instance, Gigerenzer *et al.*, 1999, presents a 'recognition heuristic,' which is only successful when one is not too well-informed; more knowledge is likely to degrade performance on some tasks.

23 The example is by no means unique, and here's one more for good measure. McMullin, 1985, pp. 258, 260, mentions an idealization used both by Newton and Bohr, that of taking, respectively, the sun and the nucleus of an atom to be at rest; he points out that in both cases this is tantamount to assuming, again respectively, the sun and nucleus to have infinite mass. Notice that if the sun *did* have infinite mass, the Newtonian model tells you that the planets would fall into it; and even though gravity can normally be ignored at the atomic scale, if a nucleus *did* have infinite mass, Bohr's electrons would fall into it. That is, this idealization, used in every introductory physics class, works *in virtue of* being an incoherent description. (There are of course more sophisticated versions of the idealization, e.g., involving limits, but these are *not* used in introductory physics classes.)

24 For illustrations, see Fiell and Fiell, 1997, pp. 246, 273, 275, 410, 474, 482.

25 That's a big idealization: a human being would be unable to store in memory such a vast and heterogeneous collection of representations, or if he were, would be unable to index them for timely retrieval, and would end up like the well-known Borges character who remembered everything, lost in the clutter of his own mind (1999). For some discussion of this sort of problem, see Cherniak, 1986.

26 For background, see Nozick, 1981, pp. 33ff., or Forbes, 1985, p. 189n.

27 The protagonist of Witold Gombrowicz's *Cosmos* (1985) is someone who does think that there must be significance to any such detail, and Gombrowicz's novel has attained cult status as a convincing rendition, from the inside, of a particular sort of insanity.

28 Goodman, 1979; though, as Davidson, 1980, pp. 225–227, pointed out, it's tricky to put the problem cleanly, because grue-like predicates can seem to pan out into (bogus) inference licenses, such as 'Emeroses are gred.' But see sec. 5.11, below.

29 See Stalker, 1994, for an overview. In fact, these efforts were misguided for more reasons than one, because some grue-like predicates are obviously satisfactory starting points for inductive inference. 'Fashionable,' for example, is a predicate with a grue-like structure: x is fashionable if x is a green pleated Prada blouse and worn in spring 2007, or if x is a blue quilted Armani jacket and worn in fall 2008…but there are few more inductively sound conclusions than that certain people will always be wearing something fashionable.

30 I owe this point to Laura Schroeter; her idea cuts deeply against much recent philosophy of language, where the argument has been about what the semantics of words *are*, as though what was at issue were a psychological or linguistic

matter of fact. Whereas the question (for H. Procrustes and for all of us) is really what the right semantic *strategy* is: it's not a question of what the meanings brutely are, but of what *to* mean. And it would be a bad strategy to mean your words in the essence-seeking way, before you had any reason to think that that was an inferentially useful way to mean them.

31 There is a nice example of Putnam's that can be used to make the same point (1990, pp. 60, 282). *Sometimes*, by 'water,' I intend 'to refer to whatever ha[s] the "deep structure" of [my]…paradigms,' and then anything that is mostly H_2O counts as water: I am using 'water' as a natural kind term. But *sometimes* I will refuse to count as water H_2O containing certain impurities; when I insist that what I have in front of me is not water but coffee or tea, I am not using 'water' as a natural kind term. Now, why should I pin myself down to one or the other of these semantic commitments for the word 'water' before I know what is at stake in the discussion?

32 This egregious simplification is very widespread, and not usually regarded as egregious, or even as a simplification. For thoughtful discussion of the ways that concepts are patched together out of very differently functioning components, of techniques for extending them to accommodate novel applications, and of the ways concepts or special-purpose components of them may be implemented that do not conform to the crude extensional model, see Wilson, 2006. It should be emphasized that the typically patchwork nature of concepts does not obviate the need for partial truth (for the reasons given at ch. 2 n.10), and in fact Wilson provides rich and well-worked-out historical examples of a general claim I will make below, that partial-truth applications of an already-patchwork concept can be an indispensable preliminary to adding or reconfiguring patches (i.e., to adjusting the shape of the concept), and so permitting further full-truth applications of the revised concept.

33 That we do just this is substantiated by Holland *et al.*, 1986, pp. 230–249.

34 Laqueur, 1990, chronicles the surprisingly recent demise of the Aristotelian notion, with its consequence that there can really be only one biological sex, and that women must therefore be defective men. There are many subtler ways in which the Aristotelian version of the species concept is off-base, but this one is eye-openingly blunt.

35 For defences of epistemicism, see Williamson, 1994, Sorensen, 2001, and Graff, 2003.

36 The standard complaint about epistemicism is that it floats free of our inventory of philosophical explainers. Arguments go back and forth over whether the benefits of keeping logic classical are worth the costs of insisting that we have dispositions which account for those crisply delineated boundaries—or alternatively, worth surrendering the idea that a concept's having boundaries in a particular place has to be explained at all. Although I want to bypass that debate, it is important that the debate is going on, and is conducted on these terms.

Complaints in this ballpark include Ray, 2004, p. 185, Burgess, 1998, pp. 234f., Keefe, 2000, pp. 75–83, Horgan, 1998, sec. 5, and Unger, 1979, p. 126. A typical reply appeals to companions in blame: 'Since no one knows what…an account [of the connection between meaning and use] would be like, the epistemic view of vagueness should not be singled out for its failure to provide one' (Williamson, 1992/1996, p. 275). Those who make the point that the primary motivation for epistemicism is retaining classical logic include Williamson, 1994, p. 186, 1997, p. 921, Horgan, 1998, sec. 5, Shapiro, 2006, p. 61, and Sorensen, 2001, p. 11.

37 Epistemicists are normally antipsychologistic, and so they are not likely to try arguing for epistemicism in the way that I have been arguing for partial truth. But we can imagine what such an argument would look like: sharp boundaries are a presupposition one has to endorse while one is in the course of one's theoretical reasoning, so we accept that they are there. However, that move would only be nonoptional if theoretical reasoning had to consist in applications of classical logic.

38 Nozick, 1981, p. 4.

39 Again, this argument will not go through as is, if theoretical inference cannot be treated as a relatively self-contained activity—in the older language of faculty psychology, if the distinction between theoretical and practical reason cannot be maintained. We are here taking the workability of that distinction as at any rate a temporary framing hypothesis.

40 For a reproduction, see Hodgkin, 1995, p. 116, or the present volume's dust jacket.

Chapter 6

1 The other half is that practical reasoning—reasoning about what to do—requires only the addition of desires.

Although belief psychology is the default, it's not quite the consensus. Bratman, 1992, dissents in a way congenial to the position being developed here. Other complaints include Stich, 1983, Churchland, 1981, and de Sousa, 1990.

There are also authors who introduce distinctions between types of mental states that may sound close to the one I am working up, but which prove to be quite different in spirit. For a short survey of some of these, see Velleman, 2000, p. 250 n.12. Notice that while belief psychology must in any case be adjusted to accommodate the assumptions used in hypothetical reasoning, the objection I am about to work up remains even when that adjustment has been made.

2 That is, belief-desire psychology is in error even when only reasoning about how things stand, and not about what to do (that is, theoretical rather than practical

reasoning), is on the table. Theoretical reasoning is very often introduced (and I have myself in the past introduced it) as reasoning about what to believe, but this characterization would beg the question we are now considering. The characterization's pervasiveness is worth remark because it indicates how entrenched the view I'm about to contest really is. Velleman, 2000, esp. chs. 1, 8, 11, is a good example. He insists that truth is the aim of belief, and takes himself to be introducing a standard to which theoretical reasoning is responsible. But he has only done so if theoretical reasoning is correctly characterized as reasoning about what to believe, and Velleman evidently takes this assumption to be too obvious to need defense—although it does get explicit mention, at p. 180. As we will be seeing, this is a live and *practical* question: *should* theoretical reasoning aim at belief, or rather, often, at attitudes which advance partial truths?

In my alternative locutions—thinking about how things stand, about what the facts are, and so on—no great emphasis is being placed on words like 'fact' or 'thing,' and no ontological commitments made by using such terms. See also ch. 1 n 13.

3   Following a wave of counterexamples, justified-true-belief accounts were supplemented with additional conditions, while continuing to treat knowledge as especially successful belief; see Shope, 1983, for a summary. Alternatives to justified-true-belief views tend to retain the central role of belief; for example, Nozick's account makes knowledge out to be belief that 'tracks' the truth (1981, pp. 172ff.). However, there is interesting work in epistemology that does not make belief central to its account of knowledge (Craig, 1990; Williams, 1973, pp. 145–147).

4   Anscombe, 1985, sec. 32.

5   For further references, see ch. 2 n 5. Notice that our characterization of direction of fit—and the same point will hold for our upcoming introduction to inferential role—was deliberately neutral as to whether it tells us what you in fact *do*, or whether it amounts to directives that specify what *to do*. On the first way of spelling out direction of fit, a belief is something like a disposition: you are disposed to change your representation when you see that it doesn't match the world (in the inferential-role variation, it will be something from which you are disposed, e.g., to draw the appropriate conclusions). On the second way, the world is something like a standard for belief (in the inferential-role variation, a belief will be something like a standard to which downstream inferences are held): its role is prescriptive rather than causal. Smith, 1987, is a well-known exposition of the dispositional version of direction of fit; Quinn, 1993, Essay 12, criticizes the dispositional account, as does Collins, 1987, chs. 1–2, which also provides a nondispositional alternative: on Collins's view, to believe that *p* is to run the epistemic risk of being wrong about *p*. Fodor, 1975 and 1987 are paradigm-case renderings of the functional-role approach: inferential structure is reflected as causal structure, and prescriptions, commitments, and so on

remain offstage. By contrast, Brandom, 1994, renders belief ascription as the ascription of inferential commitments; if you believe that p, you may be held to the consequences of p, and causal structure remains offstage. I am going to construct the upcoming argument to accommodate both sorts of view.

6   The phrase is borrowed from Forbes, 1985, p. 174.

7   The metaphorical contrast in the *directions* of beliefs and desires seems to be still in place, and I want to acknowledge that; but now recall from ch. 2 that the way we normally guarantee full-truth-or-falsity in a given domain is to reengineer it.

8   Cf. Azzouni, 2004, p. 46, which suggests that we use what he calls the quarantined implications—in my vocabulary, the inferential restrictions—'to determine *to what degree* the tabletop fails to be Euclidean.' That is, a judgment that the fit of a representation is loose is often coordinated with, and made out in terms of, restrictions on its inferential deployment. But I won't take a stand on whether that is necessarily and always the case.

9   These do not have to be short qualifiers (such as 'somewhat true,' 'roughly true,' etc.). Even when there is a summarizing phrase, that may indicate a hedge that takes some spelling out; for instance, Pietroski and Rey, 1995, esp. p. 89, provides a definition of ceteris paribus laws that, by the lights of the account I am developing, makes them out to be an example of partial truth understood via relaxed direction of fit: the law does not have to be corrected as long as its defeaters can be explained by factors that are in a suitable sense independent of the law.

Such summarizing phrases may also be misleading in that they can stand for more than one substantive hedge. Against the literature to which the treatment I just mentioned belongs, Woodward, 2002, p. 306, objects to the 'presumption…that some single analysis will apply to all or most [examples of ceteris paribus laws]…the various proposed analyses of [ceteris paribus] laws… attempt to capture generalizations with very different content by means of a single analysis.' Especially if we are working with the idea that partial truth comes in indefinitely many qualitatively different varieties, we should not just assume that ceteris paribus clauses are all one kind of thing.

10   Ordinary citizens may not have had occasion to introduce a generic name for such attitudes, but I am not the first philosopher to consider doing so. Elgin, 2004, endorses the move from what I am calling partial truth to states that are not belief, on the grounds that 'a belief fulfills its goal in life only if it is true,' and endorses partial truth on the basis of observation: it is widely used in, for example, scientific contexts or political theory. Her label for the alternative attitude is 'cognitive acceptance': '*To cognitively accept* that p, is to take it that p's divergence from truth, if any, does not matter cognitively.'

11   Another but less interesting worry is the circular appearance of the definition as I have just phrased it. Recall the comparison of semantic values like true

and false to grades. Just as the object of writing a pass-fail exam is a pass, so the object—the 'formal object'—of belief is truth. Back in the days when the middle of the letter-grade scale was called a 'gentleman's C,' that might have been the object of an exam written by an unambitious student; likewise, the object—the 'formal object'—of the relaxed sorts of attitude we have seen deployed in inferences allowing certain sorts of defeasibility, and subject to certain restrictions on their application, is partial truth. It is not empty and uninformative to say that partial truth is the object of the attitudes deployed in partial-truth inference, because the content is supplied by what we *do* (or *are to do*) with the attitudes—by our methods, our dispositions, and the like—in roughly the way the content of our grades is fixed by the procedures for assigning them, and the further administrative uses that are made of them.

12 For a recent attempt to reconstruct the Aristotelian view that species forms underwrite defeasible inferences, see Thompson, 2008, chs. 1–4.

13 But see ch. 3 n 19 for a qualification. Recall a further objection, which needs to be disentangled from this one: that 'like' or 'resembles' forms a context-sensitive predicate, one which makes the claim about the cloud fully true. The views at work in this latter objection are taken up in sec. 2.3, ch. 2 n 6, sec. 7.3 and sec. 7.7.

14 See sec. 2.3; ch. 3 n 19.

15 There's a Wittgensteinian argument out there to the effect that such guiding devices can't do all the work: you still need judgment, even to follow rules like 'add two' (e.g., McDowell, 1998, pp. 58ff.). It's important not to let this point get in the way of our argument. Even if you still need that sort of judgment, there's a reason you rely on yardsticks, calculators, and so on. The Wittgensteinian point is not to be understood in a way that makes such aids incomprehensible.

16 In a manuscript that is, as far as I know, destined to remain unpublished.

17 There have been some initial forays in this direction. Elgin, 1996, calls what's provided by an element of a successful reflective equilibrium 'understanding.' These elements, she repeatedly emphasizes, can include approximations and idealizations (pp. 123–125, 171). However, hers is not a success concept tailored specifically to approximations or partial truths; it also indiscriminately covers putative truths, metaphors, emotions, artworks, and perhaps much else. Kvanvig, 2003, ch. 8, advances a related success concept, which he also calls 'understanding'; this 'requires the grasping of explanatory and other coherence-making relationships in a large and comprehensive body of information.' Kvanvig's success concept is, however, unsuited to the assessment of partial truths, because '[t]o say that a person understands that *p*…requires that *p* is true'; 'to understand [something] is to have beliefs about it, and… understanding…requires that these beliefs are true.' Finally, Alston, 2005, advocates turning away from the analysis of justification to study other 'epistemic desiderata' for beliefs. However, he restricts the discussion to beliefs; he identifies the

'epistemic point of view' via its 'aim at [*sic*] maximizing true belief and minimizing false belief' (p. 23); no attention is paid to partial truth; and indeed,
his list of desiderata is quite traditional, and not at all suited to evaluating
approximations, idealizations, and other partial truths.

18 The history of epistemology suggests that the concept of knowledge is a forced fit
even for many of the applications in which philosophers have been interested; if
it weren't, there wouldn't have been so much twiddling. However, in suggesting
that we supplement this success concept with others, I don't mean to imply
that we should give this one up; one of the lessons of our argument is that an
intellectual apparatus in which substantial resources have been invested may
be worth using even if it often produces forced matches and partial truths.

19 In the previous chapter, I used the notion of 'opinions worth having' as a
placeholder for such a success concept, or for several of them. Thus our program
for extending epistemology already has some results on the table: e.g., to have
opinions worth having, you have to have a unified intellect; to have opinions
worth having, you need to work with partial truth.

Chapter 7

1 For surveys of the vagueness literature, see Williamson, 1994, Tye, 1995, Keefe
and Smith, 1996, Keefe, 2000, Graff and Williamson, 2002.

2 Cf. the final sentence of Hyde, 2005, sec. 2.

3 Cf. Williamson, 1994, p. 71, Keefe, 2000, p. 10, Williamson, 1997, p. 921,
Sorensen, 2003, Hyde, 2005, Graff, 2003, p. 197. For reservations, however,
see Shapiro, 2006, p. 4, and while Soames, 1999, ch. 7, devotes his treatment
of vagueness to the sorites, he insists that vagueness is a broader phenomenon
(p. 217).

4 See, e.g., Tye, 1995, pp. 10f., Zadeh, 1965, Lakoff, 1973, Priest, 2001, ch. 11,
Edgington, 1996. For complaints, some of which also take issue with views I've
been developing, see Haack, 1996, pp. 229–258. Surprisingly many phenomena
can be construed as having the structure of a spectrum; for an amusing illustration, see Priest, 2003, p. 9. For an overview of nonnumerical degree accounts,
see Williamson, 1994, pp. 131–135.

5 Then why isn't 'verity' just probability? I'm in full agreement with Edgington's
own answers to this objection (1996, pp. 312f.). First, formal calculi aren't self-
interpreting, so the fact that it looks like the probability calculus doesn't mean
it can't be given some other use. (Auyang, 1998, observes that the probability
calculus *has* already been given various uses.) Second, verities do not interact
with utilities in the way that probabilities do; recall that utilities have been used
to define probabilities. Expected utility theory requires that if you prefer X to Y,

then if you're offered a lottery ticket (a probability mixture) that gives you p chance of getting X, and $1 - p$ chance of getting Y, you have to prefer X to the lottery ticket, and prefer the lottery ticket to Y. But it's obviously perfectly acceptable to prefer extremes over a 'verity mixture' (or conversely, the mixture over the extremes). For instance, one might prefer something that's definitely coffee over something that's definitely tea over Pohl and Kornbluth's 'coftea'.

6 The solution is a relative of the proposal at Goguen, 1968–1969, sec. 3 and p. 357.

7 Fine, 1975/1996 is the *locus classicus*; the quote is at p. 136. Views in this family include Dummett, 1978b, pp. 255–257, Evans, 1978/1996, Lewis, 1986, pp. 212f., 244n., Lewis, 1999, ch. 9, Keefe, 2000, ch. 7. For reservations about the slogan, see Keefe, 2000, p. 157.

8 Although epistemicism, which we encountered in sec. 5.10, is not a logic of vagueness, there's an obvious way of reinterpreting precisificationist treatments to suit this position. When you produce a vague thought or utterance, there are a range of things it could mean, for all you know. It is definitely true if, on all the epistemic possibilities, it comes out true; the epistemic possibilities—the contents that, for all you know, you've expressed—map onto the precisifications of a vague utterance. Williamson, 1994, p. 164, briefly endorses this appropriation of precisificationism; Sorensen, 2001, pp. 49f., objects that the fit is unobviously bad.

9 At, variously, Thomason, 1982, Mehlberg, 1958/1996, Forbes, 1985, p. 20 (where 'refinement' is, however, being used in a supervaluationist treatment not focused on vagueness), Fine, 1975/1996, e.g., p. 125, Shapiro, 2006, p. 66. The term 'specification' is shared with work in practical reasoning, on which figuring out what to do often partly consists in finding a more fully specified version of a vaguely described goal or rule or standard; in my view it is worth thinking about this theory of deliberation together with the precisificationist approach to vagueness.

10 Supervaluationism is the *ur*-form of the view which I have been calling 'precisificationism'; I'm using the latter term to emphasize that supervaluationism is one of many ways of tightening up the generic idea. See Fine, 1975/1996, pp. 126f., 130–133, 139f.; Keefe, 2000, chs. 7–8. Fine gestures at a range of theoretical choices available to the precisificationist theorist, and much of his argument is taken up with providing reasons to prefer the 'super-truth' precisification of precisificationism over what he calls the 'bastard intuitionistic' precisification.

11 See Williamson, 1994, pp. 147f. A further set of options for precisifying precisificationism: Evans, 1978/1996, expected that the correct formal representation of vagueness would take after S5 (a modal logic whose model theory has every possible world 'see' every other possible world), but clearly you could construct alternatives that assume more restrictive accessibility relations

Notes

(and it's an interesting exercise to find attractive interpretations for them). Williamson, 1994, pp. 156–161, argues that higher-order vagueness requires dropping S5.

12 Our present flag of convenience is 'logics of vagueness,' but you should be aware that this one is widely thought of as a model of the *pragmatics* of vagueness, rather than its *logic*. We've been accumulating reasons for rethinking this distinction from scratch, and in the meantime I'm going to stick with the label we've got.

13 Lewis, 1983–1986, vol. 1, ch. 13; for the treatment of vagueness, see pp. 244–246. Oddly, Shapiro, 2006, p. 16, insists that Lewis 'does not invoke conversational score to deal with sorites.' Soames, 1999, ch. 7, appropriated Lewis's proposal, adding the idea that the scorekeeping account is best restricted to 'a realm of discretion' between the regions in which a predicate determinately applies or determinately doesn't (p. 210).

14 Shapiro, 2006.

15 Formally, a tree is a connected, cycle-free graph; for an introduction, see Tutte, 1984.

16 Raffman, 1994.

17 For gaps, see Tye, 1994/1996, Soames, 1999, ch. 7. For extra values, Tye, 1994/1996, p. 281, Keefe, 2000, p. 90. These options are sometimes only artificially distinguishable from one another, since a gap can look a lot like an additional truth value.

18 For overviews, see Oddie, 1981, Niiniluoto, 1998, Oddie, 2001.

19 For an initial characterization of idealizations, see McMullin, 1985, p. 248. But the territory of idealization is itself heterogenous; for three contrasting varieties, see Rueger and Sharp, 1998.

20 The point I'm making isn't tied to the particular illustrations we have on the table. Consider metrics discussed in the verisimilitude literature; the standard complaints about them notwithstanding, each is an attempt to capture a notion of partial truth that is appropriate to *some* problems about *some* subject areas. (For a view of verisimilitude that I take to be in this spirit, see Psillos, 1999, ch. 11.) Notice, for instance, that these measures of how off-target one is all require consistent and coherent approximations; for now—and for as far into the philosophical future as we can see—inconsistent descriptions resist integration into a metric. Recall that we've already encountered idealizations that work *by* being inconsistent descriptions (in sec. 5.3, and we will see another in sec. 8.3). So while these techniques are probably suitable for some problems, they are not suitable for others, and in particular, not for problems that involve internally inconsistent approximations.

21 Eiseman and Herbert, 1990, p. 7.

22 For this approach, see Edgington, 1996, p. 297; cf. Lakoff, 1973, p. 462, on an older spectrum model: 'there is far more right than wrong about it, which is

what makes it an interesting approximation.' The idea that a theory of vague-ness is an idealization, and that not all of the idealization's features represent features of the phenomenon it describes, is obviously congenial to our way of thinking about partial truth; it sometimes gets discussed, in this litera-ture, under the rubric of 'modeling.' There is, however, disagreement as to whether we need a metatheory of which features represent and which don't. (The metatheory usually seems to be conceived as a list, but we shouldn't expect that plausible such metatheories will be that simple.) Keefe, 2000, pp. 49–59, insists that unless you can provide such a metatheory—unless you can state the respects in which the model is both realistic and unrealistic—the approach is unsatisfactory. Cook, 2002, attempts to discriminate artifacts from repre-sentors on Edgington's behalf. Shapiro, 2006, pp. vi, 49f., is an example of a self-declared model builder who accepts Keefe's demand, but modulates it by suggesting that the 'boundary between [representors and artefacts] is not sharp.'

23 Latour, 1996, p. 28.

24 Interestingly, Latour pins Aramis's ultimate failure on the unwillingness of those involved to violate a condition that Fine, 1975/1996, pp. 127, 129, takes to be a *sine qua non* of the precisificationist approach: that truth values remain stable under further precisification. It was the engineers' and project managers' insistence on sticking with the defining features of their vague ideal ('nominal Aramis') that made the political compromises necessary for Aramis's survival impossible. The lesson Latour draws from Aramis's failure is that the workabil-ity of any realistically large project involving precisification of this kind depends on one's ability to give up the truths fixed by one's initial, still-very-vague description. (See pp. 48, 99–101, 108f., 119f., 281, 295.)

25 Though for some second thoughts, see Wilson, 2006, p. 604; color turns out to be messier than most philosophers think.

26 Fine, 1975/1996, p. 135 (cf. also p. 150n.) registers a problem in this general area, but dismisses it as constructivist (i.e., mathematical intuitionist) bias: 'One can quantify over a domain without being able to specify an object from it. Surely,' he tells us, 'one can understand what a precise shade is without being able to specify one.'

27 A special case of the problem: One of the precise ways an interestingly and ambitiously vague situation can be is: inexpressible in any precisification of *that* language. As the engineers on the Aramis project developed new parts, new procedures, and new design features, they also developed new vocabulary to describe them: vocabulary that was not part of the language in which Aramis had been originally and vaguely described. Without the new vocabulary, one is not in a position to distinguish substantively different precisifications of 'Aramis' from each other.

28 Sec. 2.8 and sec. 4.6 n 30.

29	The jacket art for Shapiro's book shows Tenniel's illustration of Alice talk-ing to Humpty Dumpty, and the epigraph of the book is Humpty Dumpty telling Alice that words mean what you want them to mean: it all depends on who's the master. Both epigraph and illustration are more appropriate than Shapiro intends. Humpty Dumpty has just used the word 'glory' to mean some-thing it normally does not (Carroll, 1976, p. 214). That is, he has rudely and inappropriately changed the meaning of his words, mid-conversation, without bothering to inform his interlocutor. (He explains himself only when challenged by Alice.) The conversational scorekeeping treatment of vagueness turns out to represent—and *invite*—just such behavior.

30	I'm grateful to Maneesh Modi for discussion of techniques used in the business world.

31	For contrast, recall that in ch. 2 n 10 we considered an appeal to context that stumbles at this point: Travis, 2000, discusses sorts of context-sensitivity that do not seem to have much to do with vagueness, and takes it that when sentences are evaluated with suitable sensitivity to context, they will come out fully true or fully false. However, he provides no argument for that latter claim, and lo and behold, in arguments about vagueness, a standard first move is to put to one side the sorts of sensitivity to context that Travis actually discusses. For instance, Shapiro, 2006, pp. 33ff., begins by bracketing ' "external" factors—comparison class, paradigm cases, contrasting cases, etc.,' the idea being to treat those as fixed or determinate, and then proceed to consider what turn out, in the context so fixed, to be the borderline cases and gray areas.

32	For an especially direct pronouncement of this kind, see Sorensen, 2001, p. 10.

33	But for a philosopher's discussion of some of these, see, once again, Wilson, 2006.

Chapter 8

1	The founders of logical positivism were mostly native German speakers, and German is full of words—particles like 'doch,' 'ja,' 'eigentlich,' and so on—that add flavor to a sentence but would be left out of a translation into English; so the positivists' position was entirely natural for a German speaker: the notion that there are many more such flavor-only words than you might have thought…in fact, *all* of the proprietary vocabulary of metaphysics.

2	For a terse and elegant example, see Austin's attempt to defuse the traditional philosophical preoccupation with the nature of reality by giving an account of the correct usage of 'real' (1962, pp. 70f.).

3	The technical-sounding obscurity of these phrases to the layman is one of the markers that the debates belong to an unabashed professional subspecialty, and if these phrases are new to you, their highly professionalized sound is more important right now than actually knowing what they mean. I'll introduce both topics a little later on, in secs. 9.1 and 11.5.

4   For my first witness, I would like to call Hilary Putnam:

> If we ask *when* Ontology became a respectable subject for an analytic philosopher to pursue, the mystery disappears. It became respectable in 1948, when Quine published a famous paper titled, 'On What There Is'...
>
> I can tell you just how bowled over I was when I read it as a first-year graduate student in 1948–49; and I think my reaction was not untypical.

(From Putnam, 2004, pp. 78f., to which my discussion here is much indebted; Quine's papers are reprinted as the opening chapters of Quine, 1963.)

5   See, for instance, Ayer, 1936; for a more three-dimensional portrait of the movement, see Friedman, 1999.

Formally, this isn't such a convincing argument: Suppose that listing the ingredients in the dish isn't criticizing it. And suppose that explaining what it takes to be a quality ingredient isn't criticizing it. It doesn't follow that doing *both* wouldn't be criticizing it.

The logical positivists seem to have been of two minds as to the status of the claim that all sentences are either analytic or synthetic but not both. In one mood, that was simply the way things were (when you analyzed the sentences correctly); in another mood, that languages should be regimented in this way was good advice, and so the claim was true of what they said because they were taking their own advice. On either rendition of the claim, however, the explanation I've just given, for why the positivists thought they weren't doing metaphysics, stands. (I'm grateful to Hilary Putnam for pressing me to clarify this point.)

6   A *bound* (as opposed to a free) variable is one inside the scope of a quantifier, that is, one that functions as a pronoun referring back to its governing quantifier, rather than a free-standing name. Some fine print: First, since Quine didn't want ontological commitments hidden inside proper names, he also required, as part of the canonical rewriting, the unusual step of replacing names, like 'Socrates,' with peculiar-looking predicates, like 'Socratizes.' Second, it was common at the time to construe scientific theories as couched entirely in conditional form, e.g., as asserting claims like 'Electrons are such that...,' where this was interpreted to mean, '(x)If x is an electron, then...' So universal quantifiers came to be treated as guides to the ontological commitments of such theories also. Lastly, it's worth registering that Quine's own view subsequently evolved, becoming at once more subtle, more modest, and more radical. Because the later view had much less

uptake in the broader culture of analytic philosophy—possibly because Quine only worked his way around to 'ontological relativity' and the 'inscrutability of reference' after the program I am describing had taken root and spread—I'm not going to reconstruct these further developments of his position.

7 It was characteristic of early analytic philosophy to be ostentatiously ignorant of history, and to adopt a pose of ignorance when it was too late for innocence. The distinction to which Quine professed not to be able to give any clear sense had in fact been introduced with admirable rigor; for a lucid account of Kant's original distinction and its philosophical point, see Anderson, 2004.

Let me allow that saying no one had thought to ask is—just slightly—an overstatement; Quine later cataloged anticipations of his point (1960, pp. 67–68n7). Perhaps it would be better to say that it was as though no one had ever asked.

8 I will explain the Theory of Descriptions in ch. 10, but actually, this much had been clear long before Russell. Lewis Carroll, for instance, in *Through the Looking-Glass* (1976, pp. 223–225), had used the point about logical form to amuse young readers:

> 'I see nobody on the road,' said Alice.
> 'I only wish *I* had such eyes,' the King remarked in a fretful tone. 'To be able to see Nobody! And at that distance, too!'

Notice, returning now to a point we made in ch. 6, that rejecting the bivalence doctrine has put us in a position to ask why we should suppose that there is such a thing as *the* logical form of a sentence. Sentences that we characterize as partially true have inferential potentials that depart, in hard-to-characterize ways, from the inferential potentials that are, let us suppose, captured by the logical form of the sentence when it is regarded as fully true. That is, the representation of the sentence as having a logical form is, in these cases, an *approximation*: and we already know that there is no such thing as the right approximation *tout court*, as opposed to the right approximation for one purpose, and one occasion, as opposed to another. (For remarks in roughly the spirit of this observation, see Shapiro, 1998, p. 137.)

9 Quine's third move, incidentally, is a supporting reason for taking the objection to the analytic/synthetic distinction, in 'Two Dogmas,' to have the force of a rhetorical question rather than attempted argumentation. What *looks* like argumentation there seems to be directed at showing that you can't give a clean and non-circular definition of the distinction. But in the Quinean recipe, showing that you can't define—that is, reduce away—an element of your theoretical apparatus is how you show that the element *does* exist, and not how you show that it *doesn't*. I'll explain below how Quine finally did try to argue against the distinction.

10 Field, 1980; it did allow itself *other* archetypally mathematical entities, such as points and lines, which Field however insisted were physical and spatial rather than abstract. Keep in mind that our interest here is not in whether the argument succeeded, but merely in how it was motivated. For some criticism of Field's program, see Maddy, 1992, and Azzouni, 1998; for related discussion, see Bueno, 2005, and Gross, 2006.

11 See, first and foremost, Quine, 1960, ch. 2, but also Quine, 1969, chs. 1–2, 4.

12 Quine actually says: 'the forces that he sees impinging on the native's surfaces'—as though forces were something one *sees*!

13 So the behaviorist jargon turned out, in practice, to be window dressing for ordinary descriptions of situations and utterances. You can't describe the way light falls on subjects' retinas when they see rabbits, so you end up saying things like 'rabbit-like ocular stimulations'; you can't characterize the subjects' vocalizations except by appealing to their content, to what they say, so you end up saying things like '"rabbit"-utterances.'

For a somewhat different complaint about the scientific credentials of Quine's treatment, see Armstrong, 1980, p. 8.

14 And Quine seems to know it: he reminds himself that 'Turks' [gestures of assent and dissent] are nearly the reverse of our own' (1960, pp. 29f.). Massey, 1992, argues that if we don't allow the fudge, Quine's indeterminacy thesis comes out trivially true.

15 Some fifteen years later, Hilary Putnam did him the favor of filling it in—albeit not in a way Quine himself was willing to take on board. See Putnam, 1983; cf. Putnam, 1981, pp. 32–38, 217–218. For Quine's demurral, see Quine, 1969, pp. 60–61. For a recent and recommended discussion of the argument, see Bays, 2001.

16 Even when we restrict our attention to two-valued assent and dissent, this is quite a reach. According to Dave Barry, Japan has a culture in which it is extremely impolite to say 'No,' and he amusingly recounts his wife's inability to communicate with a travel agent who just won't say straight out that there *is* no plane to a particular destination (1993, pp. 35–37). I have no idea if Japanese culture really is like that, but certainly many cultures, including our own, are like that to one or another degree. Think of the many ways of turning down a date politely: saying 'no' is not one of them. Often you need a great deal of linguistic and cultural sophistication just to know when someone *is* assenting to or dissenting from some proposition.

17 Quine's own remarks on the uses of 'Yes and no' (1960, p. 59) don't do justice to cases like this one.

18 A related point is made by Hampshire, 1953, p. 231, that a good way to explain the use of an expression is to contrast 'favourable conditions of its application…with specimens of dubious and borderline cases.'

19   And, as we've already mentioned, who don't have codes of etiquette that require polite circumlocution instead of straightforward yes-or-no answers, and for that matter who don't play practical jokes. For documentation that this last is also a real problem, see Freeman, 1999.

20   Recall that the argument of chs. 4–5 allows me to remain agnostic about the extent to which the hard sciences are pervaded by partial truth. My examples are in the style of the so-called Stanford School in philosophy of science (now dispersed to the four corners of the earth), but with this difference: perhaps with exceptions such as Teller, 2001 and Giere, 1999, they have tended to concentrate on laws rather than ontology.

21   Azzouni, 1997 provides another example in much the same spirit; see also Azzouni, 2007. In addition, it's worth thinking about an illustration in Auyang, 1998, pp. 155–160; she describes phonons (classical vibrations in a crystalline lattice, represented as particles to simplify one's calculations) as part of a theory that you don't think of as flat-out true, but rather a usable approximation; for a dated but very readable introduction, see Reissland, 1973. Condensed matter physicists whom I've asked about this case resist both the instrumentalist and realist interpretations of it.

22   I'm grateful to Paul Fendley for talking through the example; for the backstory, see Schweber, 1994.

23   Plutynski and Evans, 2005, pp. 579–580; they discuss the interest of 'a mathematical derivation starting from assumptions…known to be false'; the Hardy-Weinberg Theorem provides a 'neutral or equilibrium model…for the purposes of evaluating the baseline state of a Mendelian system absent perturbing forces.'

24   Winston, 1999, pp. 337–338. Similarly, Hamilton and Haber, 2006, p. 389, remark that, unlike clades, 'higher Linnaean ranks do not correspond to any real biological objects—i.e.,…to biologically cohesive individuals.' (Clades are, roughly, subtrees of the tree of life.) Quine himself would have presumably insisted on seeing higher taxa as mere sets of organisms.

25   Benton, 2000. For an advocate of reform, see Mishler, 1999; for complaints about stability, see Nixon and Carpenter, 2000, p. 314. For a journalistic overview, see also Pennisi, 2001.

26   The best-known instance is probably van Fraassen, 1980, but much of the treatment in Azzouni, 2004, with which the present discussion has several points of contact, takes this approach. For instance, the point that scientists' quantifications are explicitly only sometimes commital is made at pp. 189f., and Azzouni interestingly suggests that physical theories are often as useful as they are only because they govern a great deal more than is real, namely, idealized entities that we take to be nonexistent but find mathematically tractable (pp. 194f.).

     Notice that we now have available an account of van Fraassen's theory which resolves the many problems in its ontology of observations. That theory is all-too-obviously itself an idealization: it is only approximately true, and its ontology of observations is not one to which we ought to be ontologically over-committed.

27   van Valen, 1976, p. 235.

28   See Dawkins, 1989, ch. 11. Not all meme theorists like the word; on the contrary, perhaps for the reasons we are about to take up, Boyd and Richerson, 2005, 1985, and Sperber, 1985, avoid it.

   Notice that meme theorists take copying to be from mind to mind; they don't discuss memes copying themselves within a mind, presumably because only mind-to-mind transmission counts as copying (rather than refreshing). That is to say, even meme theorists presuppose the assignments of psychological states to persons that we discussed in ch. 5.

29   An illustration of this point, due (I think) to Carl Hewitt: most computers nowadays are networked, and there is no upper bound on the time it takes for the network to deliver a message. Recursive functions are functions, and so their inputs determine their outputs uniquely. A networked computer can send a message to another computer requesting a reply, and start counting; when the reply appears, it returns the number to which it has counted. So a networked computer can return different outputs on the same input.

Chapter 9

1   Davidson, 1980, pp. 107, 136, 138, 156; for Davidson's views on logical form, see, e.g., pp. 138ff. Following in Quine's footsteps, Davidson never gave anything like a tight argument that only his rendering could reproduce these entailments; his modus operandi was rather to review a number of available proposals, explain why they were unsatisfactory, and then produce his own.

2   Yablo, 1987.

3   In assessing Davidson's intentions, we have to take account not just of proclamation but of practice. Davidson proclaimed that '[t]he ultimate evidence…for the correctness of a theory of truth must lie in available facts about how speakers use the language' (1990, p. 301). Indeed, he also said that 'there's something to test the theory against besides just speech behavior, and that's the rest of behavior' (1974, p. 346). But it is not as though Davidson had come up with the linguistic data used to argue for his ontology of events by, for instance, conducting a survey. That is, although the pronouncements might have suggested otherwise, it was not as though physical science were being replaced by *social* science.

4   Carnap, 1939, pp. 5ff.

5   Actually, it matters where in the sentence you add the 'nicht,' so this isn't quite enough, but I won't dot the *i*s and cross the *t*s. Carnap put the 'nicht' up

front, thus giving preference to his habits as a logician over his habits as a native German speaker; in addition, probably because he thought they would have invoked the Theory of Descriptions, he left out the definite articles, which I'm adding back in.

6 Davidson, 1990, p. 314; at Davidson, 1996, p. 265, he calls it 'an indefinable concept.'

7 Davidson had a plausible motivation for turning theories of the Tarskian form to a use incompatible with their original purpose. It was an old complaint that because Tarskian theories were theories of truth for particular languages, they were unsatisfactory as an account of truth-in-general, because they had nothing to say about what it was that the true sentences in different languages had in common. But, Davidson realized, if what you have are theories of *meaning* for particular languages, then it's not a problem—after all, what else would you *want*? See, e.g., Davidson, 1996, pp. 269f.

8 Davidson, 1984, pp. 199–201, 2001, pp. 150–151.

9 Here we have the Davidsonian descendent of the idea that the meaning is the method of verification; see, e.g., Davidson, 1984, p. 8. I should perhaps put on the record that I am not myself endorsing the notion that meaning is just a shorthand for truth-conditions.

10 Davidson acknowledged the requirement, writing: 'The concepts used to express the evidence must not beg the question…Such a theory must be based on some simple attitude that an interpreter can recognize in an agent before the interpreter has detailed knowledge of any of the agent's propositional attitudes' (1990, pp. 315, 322). He thought that he could adapt treatments of Bayesian decision theory to solve the problem (pp. 316f., 326–328), but it's quite clear that nothing along these lines will solve the problem I am posing for him: the probability calculus has no way of assimilating the indefinite qualitative multiplicity of partial truth.

11 Davidson's own inclination was to exhibit the workings of assertion-to-a-degree by embedding it in an axiomatized theory; he thought of Ramsey's treatment of probability as a fairly straightforward model (1996, pp. 276ff.).

12 Davidson would have objected to my claim that there are indefinitely many qualitatively different ways of modulating the truth of an assertion. On his view, if you can't 'specify, in a way that depends effectively and solely on formal considerations, what every sentence [in a language] means,' then that language isn't learnable (1984, p. 8). It's unfair, however, to think that the choice is between 'effective' (i.e., algorithmic) formal specifications and 'at some point suddenly acquir[ing] an ability to intuit the meanings of sentences on no rule at all' (p. 9). The non-mechanical but thoughtful ways of reasoning out what it would be for a particular sentence to be kind of true in such-and-such a situation may not lend themselves to what Davidson called a 'coherent semantical account' (p. 32), but that's because Davidson had an unreasonable

bias for the algorithmic. One of the lessons of the last half-century of computer science has been that we have (in Davidson's intended sense) very little in the way of effective procedures for doing what we do—and indeed, for doing what we do with computers!

13 Thompson, 2008, chs. 5–8.

14 Or, alternatively, variants such as 'Why are you doing that?' or 'Why are you going to do that?' An agent may 'refuse' an answer by saying something along the lines of, 'I didn't mean to do that'; however, saying, 'For no reason,' or 'I just felt like it,' does not count as refusing an answer.

15 For a terse overview of aspect, see Appelbaum, 1996.

16 Thompson endorses 'the intuition that, where instantaneous "actions" can be said to exist, it is as a secondary or dependent phenomenon' (p. 106) which might sound like willingness to accommodate the claim I just made; but he instances winnings and findings as possible examples, which shows that he thinks of them not as cases in which the control systems that govern action are giving out, but rather as an action-theoretic variation of 'Cambridge properties.'

I want to distinguish the upshots of partial truth from older and more familiar ways of resisting commitment to the apparent ontologies of theories. In sec. 8.4, I discussed perhaps the most familiar of these, the idea that one can treat theories merely as devices for, e.g., systematizing and predicting observations. I'll say something about a recent variation on it in sec. 11.1. Right now I want to illustrate further a point I made earlier, that understanding theories to be partially true typically has a very different look and feel than regarding them as simply false but useful.

That contrast in look and feel turns up not just when the theories are those of physical science, but when they are Davidson-style theories of meaning. Go back for a moment to Davidson's argument for events, and let's take airline flights—I mean, items like Delta 1529—as apparently a type of event. You might think that if Davidson's argument works at all, it works for flights: that Delta 1529 departed on time, carrying a full load, with a good tailwind, and so on, entails that Delta 1529 departed on time, that Delta 1529 was carrying a full load, etc. Still, we saw that Davidson and his followers recognized an obligation to give criteria of identity for events, and that demand is visibly out of place for airline flights. Don't invoke the equipment, which can be changed out; nor the origin and destination of the flight, which can be and are changed all too frequently; nor the carrier ('Delta 1529 will be operated by Midwest Express tonight'); nor the pilot, crew, and passengers. And don't look to Davidson's own candidate, the flight's location in the matrix of causes and effects, because the flight isn't a part of that matrix. It's not that airline flights are merely bookkeeping artifacts; money is also a bookkeeping artifact, and monetary transactions are causes if anything is. It's that they're *casual* rather than *causal*. I can't simply say of a five-dollar bill that it's now three euros, and have that be thereby true. But low-level flunkies can and do declare that Delta 1529 has just been cancelled, that its first leg is now a Lufthansa codeshare, and its second leg is now Delta 321. When we say that Delta 1529 crashed, and that the crash killed the passengers, notice that 'Delta 1529' is, in such a causal usage, a name for the *aircraft*, and not for the event.

A very natural way to talk through this is to say that, regardless of apparent quantification over airline flights, utterances about them properly take something analogous to an instrumentalist construction: no one really believes the flights exist. ('Instrumentalist,' once again, in the philosophy-of-science, not the practical-reasoning sense.) What happens (we think) is that we load up an aircraft and send it out; it's easier, for bookkeeping purposes, to talk as though there were these odd entities, flights—but we don't bother doing the work of giving them identity conditions. What we say about airline flights isn't true or false. It's just a *device*: a way of getting the right customers onto the right planes. But because talk of flights is merely a fast-and-cheap device, the suggestion that we were happy to countenance when we examined Thompson's treatment of action—that the ontology is approximately but not entirely accurate—is out of place.

Thompson remarks on the incoherence of antirealism about practical explanation, when the antirealist goes on to account for our use of it 'pragmatically,' i.e., by giving a practical explanation for doing so (p. 86). The contrast between the antirealism appropriate to airline flights and the way I am treating Thompson's own account as partially true shows why his complaint does not stick to the view I am advancing.

17 I expect that Thompson would not accept my treatment as a friendly amendment. In the reading of Frege which he is using as a model, you are to start with the inference patterns; these allow you to segment the propositions, that is, to elicit their logical form. Those inference patterns are rock-bottom: they are where your explanation starts.

I have been suggesting that the logical forms Thompson has identified will figure into, not the true *Begriffsschrift*, but an approximately true *Begriffsschrift*. But approximate truth is not the rock-bottom: it is not where your explanation starts. While the notion of an approximately true *Begriffsschrift* would have given Frege conniption fits, I have already characterized the approach I am taking here as psychologistic (in ch. 5), and I am providing some argument against Frege's rejection of psychologism (in the Appendix). So I am in a position to describe a logic as a decent fit for creatures like ourselves (but not a perfect fit, and perhaps a much worse fit for quite imaginable other creatures).

One further bit of anecdotal evidence to support my partial-truth construal of the logic of aspect: On my view of it, we have a logic of aspect because it works... *enough*. But if that is right, there ought to be many minor variations on it, all of which would work *enough*. And that expectation is borne out. For instance, ancient Hebrew has the so-called prophetic perfect: a prophet may speak, in God's name, of a future action of God's in the past perfective, since, after all, if God intends to do it, it is as good as done. (See, e.g., the contrasting temporal markers at Hosea 2:25.)

18 Harman, 1986. Enough time has passed to make his view self-refuting. Harman deployed computational-complexity considerations in the service of an argument that procedures of belief revision that are too hard must be given up for easier procedures that are thereby rational. The work has not gotten a lot of uptake over the past two decades, and it is clear enough why: the theory of computational complexity is too hard for most of the philosophers. On Harman's own view, we should abandon appeals to computational complexity, such as his own, in favor of easier styles of argument.

Chapter 10

1 There's an ambiguity in the usage: the term means, on the one hand, a cluster of positions characteristic of a group of philosophers formerly or currently at the Australian National University in Canberra, and, on the other, the methodological core of that cluster. O'Leary-Hawthorne and Price, 1996, where the term was introduced, meant to invoke the stultifying and artificial urban environment of Australia's capital city, but the label has not kept the pejorative connotation. Here I'm going to use 'Canberra Plan' to mean just the methodology.

2 I'll discuss supervenience further in sec. 11.4.

3 Russell, 1905/1973.

4 Lewis, 1983–1986, esp. vol. 1, ch. 6, Lewis, 1999, ch. 16; he was drawing on work by Frank Ramsey (1990) and Rudolph Carnap (1963, pp. 962ff.). See also Hempel, 1958, pp. 80–81.

5 In ch. 6, above; Millgram, 2005, pp. 47f.; 1997, Introduction and sec. 2.8. Lewis, 1999, p. 320, provides samples of what he took to be platitudes.

6 Here I'm ignoring issues having to do with the opacity of the propositional objects of the beliefs and desires, and adopting, for the moment, Lewis's notion that beliefs and desires are to be thought of as freestanding items related to the freestanding propositions that are their objects. There are also complications introduced by second-order quantifiers which I'm not going to talk through now.

7 Lewis, 1999, p. 256.

8 See especially Lewis, 1983–1986, vol. 1, pp. 78f., 1999, p. 256.

9 Lewis, 1986, p. 134. A complication: At one point, Lewis seemed to have adopted much of Davidson's view (Lewis, 1983–1986, vol. 1, ch. 8); perhaps that would

allow folk theories to be underwritten, Davidson style, by the Principle of Charity, in which case the shift would not be nearly as big as it looks.

10 Jackson, 1998, pp. 30ff., suggests that the role of articulated folk theory and of intuitions is simply to ensure that your metaphysical theory is not changing the subject on you.

11 Jackson, 1998, ch. 6. Interestingly, he does not take the Canberra Plan to establish *that* the ethical supervenes on the physical (that claim he takes to be already a fixed point), but rather, to show *how* it does. Very late in his career, Lewis himself adopted this apriorist stance as well (1999, p. 292).

12 For a further example, see Peter Menzie's program for producing a philosophical account of causation (1996, secs. 3–4): first we are to collect folk platitudes about causation (he identifies the three he thinks are the most important); we are to conjoin them into a single longish sentence; then we are to define the causal relation as the occupier of the role specified by his three preferred platitudes. After a lengthy and direct comparison of his account with Lewis's treatment of the mind, Menzies considers how to give a physics-textbook characterization of the occupant of that role, with energy-momentum transfer serving as his illustration of what kind of thing it might turn out to be. See also Armstrong, 2004, pp. 453ff., which volunteers a handful of additional platitudes about causation, and Lewis, 2004, for criticism.

13 Recall that, on my own view, these pronouncements are expressions of a philosophical theory of rationality. However, everyone who traffics in this theory, the folk included, correctly understands the inference patterns it lays down to operate only other things equal.

Three exegetical points. First, Lewis originally required the 'definitive causal role of [a psychological state to be] expressible by a finite set of conditions,' but agreed that the condition could be relaxed to 'allow the set of conditions to be infinite, so long as it is recursive' (1983–1986, vol. 1, pp. 102 and 102n.7). Ceteris paribus clauses, however, can be cashed out neither by finite sets of conditions nor by infinite-but-recursive ones.

Second, at various points in his philosophical career, Lewis seemed attracted by the idea that the underlying folk psychology was in fact captured by the formalism of decision theory, in which a probability function replaces beliefs, and a utility function replaces desires. Now that Daniel Kahneman has been awarded his Nobel Prize, it ought to be platitudinous that decision theory is a highly idealized model of human cognition; in our vocabulary, it is (and the folk recognize it to be) only approximately true. So it will not be an alternative to making room for partial truth in the Canberra Plan. Lewis himself toyed with a notion of verisimilitude, and you might wonder whether he was in a position to agree that folk psychology was not quite true, but only true enough. (He seems to have thought he was; see, e.g., Lewis, 1983–1986, vol. 1, p. 95, Lewis, 1986, pp. 30, 223f.) As we will shortly see, the answer is No.

Third, Lewis allowed that the platitudes might 'identify [a psychological state] as that state which is *typically* caused in thus-and-such ways and *typically* causes thus-and-such effects, saying nothing about its causes and effects in a (small) residue of exceptional cases' (1983–1986, vol. 1, p. 104). In a similar vein, Alan Hájek has suggested to me replacing the ceteris paribus clauses with a clause like 'with high probability.' But this is not how other-things-equal qualifications work in these folk theories; it misconstrues the logical function of ceteris paribus clauses. Just for instance, the ceteris paribus clause of our sample platitude must be understood as including or as expandable to include the condition, 'unless there's something else you want more.' But this is not something we find only in a small residue of exceptional cases, or only with low probability: my desires are *mostly* such that there's a competing object of desire which I want more. Again for instance, military platitudes are normally true ceteris paribus, but the exceptions are not low probability, because one's military opponents will do their very best to identify and exploit them. I will give another example of this kind in the coming paragraph; for a further but related point, see Hempel, 1988, p. 153.

14 Earman and Roberts, 1999, pp. 465f., suggest a view of ceteris paribus clauses that, although intended dismissively, could be taken as a precedent for this way of construing them.

15 See p. 171, above.

16 Again, leaving to one side the worry about whether they really *are* folk theories; I'm pretty sure that moral philosophers take these to be platitudes, but I'm much less sure about the folk.

17 See, e.g., Wittgenstein, 1975, secs. 141f., 177, 181, and his Appendix, 'The Concept of Infinity in Mathematics.' Wittgenstein was worried about the 'and so on' or '...' alternatively expressed by phrases like 'etc. ad infinitum'; we may need to distinguish that from the 'and so on' or '...' appropriate to the open-endedness or indefinite expandability of a ceteris paribus clause. Either way, the point is the same. (I'm grateful to Hilary Putnam for discussion.)

18 The extremely brief gesture in Hempel, 1988, p. 155, may be intended to point toward the considerations we have just discussed.

19 Jackson, one of the prominent Canberra Planners, is known for having formerly entertained an antiphysicalist position about qualia; Putnam, 1975b, p. 412, mentions the latter possibility in laying out his own form of functionalism.

20 Cf. Lewis, 1999, pp. 302f.: 'if materialist supervenience is true, and every feature of the world supervenes on fundamental physics, then the occupant of the role is some physical state or other—because there's nothing else for it to be.'

21 If you weren't Lewis, there'd be a much more direct way to make this point. Davidson, computational functionalists, and others were motivated by the recognition that you were not going to get type-type identifications between the mental and the physical; at best, they thought, you would be able to identify

token mental states with token physical states. The Canberra Plan picks out *types* of mental states as the occupiers of the slots in the pattern; pulling free of the pattern, in a way that would let you write down its incompleteness as irrelevant, would be to fix the reference of the underlying types using the pattern. Since other theorists conceded that you couldn't do that, they were conceding that there was nothing to pocket and walk away with. (There were exceptions; these tried to identify the fine-grained types with items like inscriptions in 'mentalese.' I won't recount the ensuing discussions.) Lewis was willing to split the difference: to identify *subtypes* of mental states with physical types, as e.g. beliefs-in-*humans* with neurophysiological states, beliefs-in-*Martians* with...(1999, pp. 305f.).

22	The argument of the previous section turns on a feature common to analytical functionalism and the other subject areas which we have seen Canberra Planners propose to treat: namely, that the vocabulary which the procedure proposes to explicate appears in the ceteris paribus clauses that come with the platitudes. In many discussions of the special sciences, the focus is on ceteris paribus clauses (or those stretches of them) which contain vocabulary owned by other, usually lower-level sciences. For instance, there are some very nice geological generalizations about the development of bends in a river; these do not cover cases in which engineers build dams, rechannel the river, and so on; the barriers, channels, etc. are thought of as described in physical but not geological vocabulary (Fodor, 1994, p. 157n.10).

23	Familiar proposals include Kuhn's paradigms (1970), Ravetz's 'lattices of facts' (1979, ch. 6),...Evidently, scientific practice and its objects do not make up a well-understood subject.

24	Are there topics on the standard philosophical menu that *are* simple enough to take a Canberra Plan treatment? I have had the folk understanding of color suggested to me as a candidate; Lewis, 1999, ch. 20, treats it as Canberra-Plannable; one is inclined to think that this is where the Plan will work, if it is going to work anywhere.

I am myself of two minds as to whether it could work, even here; color is more complicated than most philosophers, even recently, think. The history of the visual arts is a history of the accumulation of technique; a substantial, constant, and ongoing portion of that accumulation consists of novel devices for assigning color to objects in paintings, without using paint of that color; these devices are, typically, exceptions to folk generalizations about color; they typically exploit surrounding colors, and so have to be described using color vocabulary; they don't seem to be running out. That is, the history of art strongly suggests folk generalizations about color to be qualifiable by ceteris paribus clauses, themselves invoking the vocabulary of color, that are just as inexhaustible as any of those on our plate.

On the other hand, these devices have to be *invented*, which suggests that the exceptions to the generalizations of folk chromatics are not themselves part of the folk understanding of color.

25 Schiffer, 1991, p. 2, complains of sentences containing ceteris paribus clauses that such a sentence 'expresses no complete proposition, nothing that could even be believed'—both of which, if such sentences express partial truths, are correct, but no cause for complaint. He also complains that such a sentence 'is good for nothing…let alone play[ing] some explanatory role,' but as we've seen, that doesn't follow: approximations, for instance, aren't believed, but explain nonetheless. For another sort of rejoinder, see the remarks on Pasteur in Fodor, 1994, pp. 152f.

26 Canberra Planners sometimes make allowances of the following sort: we identify as the physical objects picked out by the theory those that satisfy the Ramsey sentence *or most of its clauses*. (See Bedard, 1993, for related formal experimentation.) That gives us a notion of approximate truth to apply in the context of Canberra Planning, but notice that it is not one that makes the psychological theory ascribed to the folk come out approximately satisfied. *Most* of the clauses of the would-be theory have a ceteris paribus clause tagging along, and so—taken in the stripped-down form that allows them to be assembled into a Canberra-style theory—are at best partially true. By the lights of bivalentist theory construction, that makes them not true at all. So, in this sense of approximate satisfaction, nothing approximately satisfies a Canberra Planner's Ramsey sentence.

More generally, and returning to the analogy with academic grading: Call someone who thinks that partial truth must amount to something like full truth of a high enough percentage of a long conjunction a *Tractarian bivalentist*. That is like a grader who takes the letter grade merely to summarize how many exam questions the student has answered (fully) correctly. But even when one has a grading template, intelligent grading involves judging a student's response to be qualifiedly correct in one or another of indefinitely many ways—e.g., correct, ceteris paribus. Tractarian bivalence is a philosophical view suitable for teachers who think that multiple-choice exams are always a fully adequate method of assessment, and not for anyone else.

But what's wrong with teachers like that? Notice that the grasp of the more nuanced assessments is what allows us to construct the grading checklist in the first place, when we do use one. How *else* would you decide what questions belong on the exam, and how they ought to figure into the overall grade? Tractarian bivalence is an illusion because control of partial truth is the *prior* competence. (I'm grateful to Chris Martin for this last point.)

27 If I am right, this is the best way to think about the recently popular variant of belief psychology (which we noticed Lewis occasionally attributing to the folk, and Davidson leaning toward as well) on which beliefs are replaced by

probability functions, and responsiveness to evidence is understood as Bayesian updating. That is, we might ask *when* we would want to implement states that encode (fully endorsed) probability assignments. That's a trickier question than you'd think: Bayesian updating is often computationally intractable (see ch. 5 n.2), and presumably you'd want to implement, e.g., a Bayesian epistemology only when it would do you some practical good.

Chapter 11

1 Millgram, 2008.
2 Though Lewis, 1986, pp. 80–81, 125, made a point of distinguishing his possible worlds from those of science fiction. For the 'incredulous stare,' see Lewis, 1973, p. 86, 1986, p. 133.
3 For an especially explicit appeal, see Lewis, 1973, p. 84.
4 The locutions in the dialect were adapted from what had by then become standard model-theoretic semantics for modal logics; talk of the variously sized spheres of nearby possible worlds was Lewis subsequently attempting to extend the standard semantics to handle counterfactuals. For an overview of semantics for modal logics, see Hughes and Cresswell, 1996, Forbes, 1985, chs. 1–2, or Priest, 2001, chs. 2–4; for Lewis's extension, see Lewis, 1973.
5 Rosen, 1990; see ch. 8 n.26, for further references. Divers, 2006, is a related response to Lewis; Divers, 2002, compiles a great deal of direct follow-on to Lewis's work, and surveys at length a family of constructions in a spirit rather similar to Rosen's. Lewis had briefly entertained fictionalism about possible worlds himself, and thought that it had at least this to be said for it: 'We know better what it is to be inspired by a muse for knowing the myth of the muses, even though we reject the mythical analysis that says that someone is inspired by a muse if and only if there exists a muse who inspires him' (1973, p. 70).
6 It is not as though physics textbooks do or are one day likely to contain chapters on possible worlds—at any rate, in the philosopher's sense. There are so called many-worlds interpretations of quantum mechanics—for an overview, see Albert, 1992—and there were attempts to identify the possible worlds of interest to philosophers of modality with those described by scientific theory, as in Skyrms, 1976. However, Lewis seems not to have regarded the suggestion as a way of filling in his own view, and in a while we will be in a position to see why it would not be one.
7 Occasionally by Lewis as well, e.g., at Lewis, 1999, p. 298.
8 Lewis, 1986, pp. 3f., 23. The idea that a philosophical position is warranted when it gives one the means to solve a collection of puzzles is not unprecedented: Russell says of puzzles that they 'serve the same purpose [in logic] as is served

by experiments in physical science' (1905/1973, p. 110). But it's important that Russell thinks the topic is *logic*, and even then, it's important to ask (and have a real answer to): on what conception of logic could puzzles play the role of experiments?

9 Subsequent surveys of the literature on possible worlds too often confine themselves to possible-worlds treatments of thin modal notions such as possibility and necessity, and do so even when they announce themselves to be following in Lewis's footsteps. (See, e.g. and once again, Divers, 2002; for an alternative recent answer to the Question of Seriousness, one that is also much less demanding regarding what it takes to sign onto a modal ontology, see Melia, 2003, pp. 36, 59, 62.) They are implicitly assuming that this narrow region of the subject matter is enough of an anchor for an answer to the Question of Seriousness. It isn't, and the problem is not just that opinions are sparse and underconfident; Nozick, 2001, pp. 120–125, 133–155, provides arguments that the track record of our opinions about this part of the modal subject matter, and the likeliest explanations for our having them, are very good reasons for not taking 'intuitions' about possibility and necessity seriously at all—whether they are the intuitions of ordinary people, of scientists, or of philosophers.

10 The point is acknowledged at Lewis, 1983–1986, vol. 2, p. 173.

11 Lewis, 1983–1986, vol. 2, ch. 16; 'roughly,' to sidestep complexities introduced when the ordering of possibilities by 'nearness' does not have maximal elements; see pp. 6–10.

12 Lewis, 1986, p. 23.

13 Respectively: Lewis, 1983–1986, vol. 2, ch. 21, Lewis, 2000; Lewis, 1983–1986, vol. 2, ch. 17; Lewis, 1999, ch. 20; Lewis, 1983–1986, vol. 2, p. 165 (and see n8), Lewis, 1983–1986, vol. 2, pp. xiii; Lewis, 1983–1986, vol. 2, ch. 27. For an overview of the payoffs, see Lewis, 1986, pp. 23, 27–69. For an example of a philosopher deploying the apparatus to solve further puzzles, see Nozick, 1981, ch. 3, which uses the Lewisian rendering of possible worlds in laying out and solving problems in the 'tracking' account of knowledge.

14 Lewis, 1999, p. 374.

15 Lewis, 1986, ch. 3.

16 There did remain a vestige of physicalism. Since the other possible worlds are just more worlds, Lewis could be physicalist about *them*, or anyway about the 'nearby' or 'similar' ones (1983–1986, vol. 2, pp. x–xi).

17 Lewis, 1986, p. 15.

18 The quote is from Lewis, 1986, p. 224n.17; see p. 80 for a decision against scaling up the possible-worlds apparatus to allow for this sort of variation; see p. 221 for argument against a different sort of supervenience thesis.

   One of Lewis's followers has offered a recipe for paraphrasing modal claims about the possible-worlds machinery: on the redundancy interpretation in Divers, 1999, statements like 'It is possible that there are many worlds' are allowed, but they are flattened down to 'There are many worlds.' So notice that using this device to state supervenience claims about modality disbars them from doing any of the work that we needed supervenience for: we can no longer capture the thought that, were the modal facts to vary, the configuration of the totality of worlds would have to vary as well. (Cf. Divers, 2002, pp. 55–57, and see pp. 208f. for a reminder that some types of reductionism about possible worlds can accommodate supervenience claims naturally.)

19 It's worth note that Lewis came to use the term 'reduction' differently than I am using it here, and not to mark the distinction I am now making; see Lewis, 1999, pp. 294f.

Reductions are so unpopular, nowadays, that it may seem uncharitable to attribute the approach to Lewis, even after I have recapitulated the reasons that made it inevitable. In the companion piece I will produce the paper trail, documenting both that Lewis accepted the constraint, and that he has been widely read as having done so.

20 This way of identifying the target removes the modal analog of the Davidsonian Swerve from the crosshairs: the enterprise of reconstructing patterns of modal inference, identifying implicit quantifications, and deriving small-scale ontological commitments, without signing onto a metaphysics of global ways things might be that has been halfway or entirely purged of modality. That is a somewhat more modest project than Lewis's. A garage mechanic, staring at my burned-out engine, tells me that I shouldn't blame myself, because it *had* to happen. When I ask him what he means, he replies that, *whatever* happened, my engine was going to burn out: i.e., it was necessary that my engine burned out means that, in every possible way things might have gone, my engine burned out. Ordinary people talk this way, but when my mechanic partitions the space of possibility into discrete possibilities, he doesn't slice them so thinly as to make them modally dimensionless: he is talking about my *engine* in those other possibilities, and an engine is a functionally identified object, therefore, one which is to be understood by way of a great many counterfactuals.

21 Just in case you're jumping the gun, my complaint about Lewis's reduction is not that in our counterfactuals we mean to be talking about actual objects rather than counterparts; whatever its merits, that objection is by now old hat. They *are* about actual objects, but indirectly: 'by trafficking in mere possibilities we describe actuality' (Lewis, 1999, p. 375; cf. 1973, p. 69).

22 Lewis also gave an argument turning on what he called the 'problem of accidental intrinsics' (1986, pp. 198ff.); because I find both the argument and the subsequent literature it generated overly image-driven, I won't now recapitulate it.

23 Here's the quick refresher course in the contrast between occurrent and dispositional beliefs. You weren't, a moment ago, thinking that the President of the United States once ate rhubarb, but you believe it. We normally attribute

the belief to you in virtue of the fact that, if anyone ever asked, you *would* say, of course he once ate rhubarb. So your belief was dispositional, and, now that you're actually thinking about it, occurrent.

24 The argument is modeled on a technique successfully used against reductions over the course of the twentieth century. For examples, see Chisholm, 1948 (which deployed it against phenomenalist reductionism), and Putnam, 1975a (against logical behaviorism).

25 For remarks pointed in this direction, see Lewis, 1986, p. 21, and 1983–1986, vol. 2, pp. 181f. (on 'tailoring'). When he entertained the notion of similarity orderings, Lewis was ambivalent about the idea of writing down such things: he took the similarities in question to be vague, incomplete, and context-sensitive, and even suggested that any way of making them completely precise might thereby misrepresent them (Lewis, 1986, p. 254). 'Imprecise [comparative similarity] may be; but that is all to the good. Counterfactuals are imprecise, too. Two imprecise concepts may be rigidly fastened to one another, swaying together rather than separately, and we can hope to be precise about their connection' (1983–1986, vol. 2, p. 6). See also a remark on 'the questionable assumption that similarity of worlds admits somehow of numerical measurement' (p. 12), and related discussion at p. 163, as well as at Lewis, 1973, pp. 50–52, 67.

26 Lewis, 1999, ch. 1; the quote is at p. 37.

27 Divers, 2002, p. 123, is an example of a philosopher taking it for granted that appeal to ordinary judgments is the only alternative that is appropriate for the job similarity is to do. Lewis, 1983–1986, vol. 2, p. 146, talks about 'balancing off respects of similarity and difference against each other according to the importance we attach to them,' suggesting that Lewis thought so too.

28 There may be convergence between the two prongs of the fork; recall that, on occasion, Lewis appropriated Davidson's uses of the Principle of Charity (see ch. 10 n.9), and in particular held that the naturalness of an interpretation (of someone's psychology or utterances) constrained its eligibility. E.g., we interpret someone as meaning *green* by 'green,' rather than grue (see sec. 5.5, if you've forgotten what that is), because green is a more natural property than grue.

29 Lewis, 1973, p. 92.

30 This fact, together with the extreme context-sensitivity of the counterpart relation, as Lewis understood it, make up the ingredients for an additional, very elegant refutation of Lewis's reduction. I leave assembly of the argument as an exercise for the interested reader.

31 I don't think it's helpful to stay in character while considering the option, however. Very tersely, Lewis had two ways of thinking about partial truth: On one of these, vagueness was understood via precisification; on the other, it was verisimilitude or truthlikeness, analyzed as closeness of idealization to actual world, in a possible-world similarity space. The suggestion that Lewis's theory

of modality was partly true can't be cashed out as: in some relatively nearby possible world, modal realism is true. And treating vagueness as 'semantic indecision' (Lewis, 1986, pp. 212, 244n.32) requires that there be precise options (in this case, complete, precise similarity orderings over possible worlds) between which one remains undecided; I've just indicated why that's a misguided way to think about the cognitive resources we bring to bear in our counterfactual judgments. So Lewis's own ways of construing the suggestion at hand seem unlikely to be the most promising ways to explore it.

Chapter 12

1 Recall the so-called D-N (Deductive-Nomological) model of explanation in philosophy of science. The appeal it exercised for so long is best accounted for in terms of the desire to make deductive entailments of the structural connectors of the most respected theories.

2 We should take this response guardedly, however: maybe it will turn out that there is a descendent of Quine's complaint against the analytic/synthetic distinction, namely, that the distinction between approximation or ergonomic decision and residue isn't clean or firm enough to use, perhaps in part because of the underdetermination of choice of approximation by data, and of design decisions by the constraints normally imposed on them. In that case, there won't be a border up to which the ergonomic reconception takes us, and beyond which we will find, left over, the pure or purified problems of metaphysics.

3 This reappropriation-as-metaphysician is fully in place for Kant and the logical positivists, but not (yet) for Wittgenstein, Rorty, and perhaps others. If I am right, however, it is only a matter of time before even these most antimetaphysical of philosophers are widely and uncontroversially regarded as having been metaphysicians as well.

4 In this vein, I suggested at the end of ch. 10 that belief-desire psychology might be something we would want to implement, on suitable occasions. Here is a further example of the kind of thing I have in mind: the classificatory hierarchies of the Leibnizians are reproduced by the inheritance mechanisms of object-oriented programming. This means, for instance, that the problems that Kant ingeniously pinned on Wolff reappear as practical problems for software engineers working in object-oriented programming languages. (See Anderson, 2004, for the Leibnizian conception and its problems.) And so Kant's criticisms of his predecessors are worth thinking about while sorting out what kinds of domains object hierarchies can be used to represent, and what kinds of domains they can't.

Appendix

1 Antipsychologism has been directly brought to bear on the positions we've been considering. For instance, Sorensen argues: 'Logic is about the consequence relation. It is about what follows from what. Consequently, pure logic cannot have any contingent implications. Therefore, logic cannot be refuted or confirmed by a discovery that reality, as it happens, is continuous. Or chaotic. Or what have you' (2001, p. 10). For the present, we need only mark the presuppositions of his argument: that logic is a science about a matter of fact (what the consequence relation is like), rather than, e.g., a set of guidelines that we might change for practical purposes; therefore, that features of the world cannot be relevant to logic by making a difference to how you would do better to reason; and that it is not an option to find out empirically what the reliable mental transitions are, and let *that* stand as the consequence relation. In other words, it is taking antipsychologism for granted that makes Sorensen think that he can, in only four lines, dismiss the relevance of the messiness of the world to our logic.

2 See, for instance, Simon, 1957, pp. 262ff., considering what practical rationality would be for 'a simplified (perhaps "simple-minded") organism.'

3 Husserl, 2001, ch. 7.

4 Recall that we have seen one example of such question-begging argument in ch. 3, n. 20.

5 I sympathize: I produced a version of this complaint myself at one point, in Millgram, 1991, secs. 3–4.

6 There are other related considerations to take into account as well; the fewer people who share my logic, the fewer people I have to talk to, and the fewer people with whom I can share, e.g., a research program. (I'm grateful to Bob Goodin for suggesting this tradeoff.)

References

Adams, S., 1998. *I'm Not Anti-Business, I'm Anti-Idiot*. Andrews McMeel, Kansas City.

Adams, S., 1999. *Dilbert Gives You the Business*. Andrews McMeel, Kansas City.

Albert, D., 1992. *Quantum Mechanics and Experience*. Harvard University Press, Cambridge.

Alston, W., 2005. *Beyond 'Justification'*. Cornell University Press, Ithaca.

Anderson, R. L., 2001. Synthesis, cognitive normativity, and the meaning of Kant's question, 'How are synthetic cognitions a priori possible?' *European Journal of Philosophy*, *9(3)*, 275–305.

Anderson, R. L., 2004. It adds up after all: Kant's philosophy of arithmetic in light of the traditional logic. *Philosophy and Phenomenological Research*, *(69)*, 501–40.

Anderson, R. L., 2005. Neo-Kantianism and the roots of anti-psychologism. *British Journal for the History of Philosophy*, *13(2)*, 287–323.

Anscombe, G. E. M., 1985. *Intention* (2nd ed). Cornell University Press, Ithaca.

Appelbaum, I., 1996. Aspect in Fox. *Contemporary Linguistics*, *2*, 23–46.

Armstrong, D. M., 1980. *Nominalism and Realism*. Cambridge University Press, Cambridge.

Armstrong, D. M., 2004. Going through the open door again. In Collins, J., Hall, N., and Paul, L., eds., *Causation and Counterfactuals*, pp. 445–457, MIT Press, Cambridge.

Austin, J. L., 1950. Truth. *Proceedings of the Aristotelian Society, Supplement*, *24*, 111–128.

Austin, J. L., 1962. *Sense and Sensibilia*. Oxford University Press, Oxford. Ed. G. J. Warnock.

Auyang, S., 1998. *Foundations of Complex-System Theories*. Cambridge University Press, Cambridge.

Ayer, A. J., 1936. *Language, Truth and Logic*. Gollancz, London.

Azzouni, J., 1997. Applied mathematics, existential commitment and the Quine-Putnam indispensability thesis. *Philosophia Mathematica*, *5(3)*, 193–209.

Azzouni, J., 1998. On 'On what there is.' *Pacific Philosophical Quarterly*, *79(1)*, 1–18.

Azzouni, J., 2001. Truth via anaphorically unrestricted quantifiers. *Journal of Philosophical Logic, 30,* 329–354.

Azzouni, J., 2004. *Deflating Existential Consequence.* Oxford University Press, Oxford.

Azzouni, J., 2007. Ontological commitment in the vernacular. *Nous, 41(2),* 204–226.

Bach, K., 1984. Default reasoning: Jumping to conclusions and knowing when to think twice. *Pacific Philosophical Quarterly, 65,* 37–58.

Barrow, J. D. and Tipler, F. L., 1986. *The Anthropic Cosmological Principle.* Clarendon Press, Oxford.

Barry, D., 1993. *Dave Barry Does Japan.* Random House, New York.

Bayley, J., 1999. *Elegy for Iris.* St. Martin's Press, New York.

Bayne, T. and Chalmers, D. J., 2003. What is the unity of consciousness? In Cleeremans, A., ed., *The Unity of Consciousness,* pp. 23–58, Oxford University Press, Oxford.

Bays, T., 2001. On Putnam and his models. *Journal of Philosophy, 98(7),* 331–350.

Bedard, K., 1993. Partial denotations of theoretical terms. *Nous, 27(4),* 499–511.

Bendor, J., Diermeier, D., and Ting, M., 2003. A behavioral model of turnout. *American Political Science Review, 97(2),* 261–280.

Benton, M., 2000. Stems, nodes, crown clades, and rank-free lists: Is Linnaeus dead? *Biological Reviews, 75(4),* 633–648.

Bolinger, D., 1972. *Degree Words.* Mouton, The Hague.

Borges, J. L., 1999. Funes, his memory. In *Collected Fictions,* pp. 131–137, Penguin, New York. Trans. A. Hurley.

Boyd, R. and Richerson, P., 1985. *Culture and the Evolutionary Process.* Chicago University Press, Chicago.

Boyd, R. and Richerson, P., 2005. *Not By Genes Alone: How Culture Transformed Human Evolution.* Chicago University Press, Chicago.

Brandom, R., 1994. *Making It Explicit.* Harvard University Press, Cambridge.

Bratman, M., 1992. Practical reasoning and acceptance in a context. *Mind, 101(401),* 1–15.

Bueno, O., 2005. Dirac and the dispensibility of mathematics. *Studies in the History and Philosophy of Modern Physics, 36,* 465–490.

Burgess, J. A., 1998. In defence of an indeterminist theory of vagueness. *Monist, 81(2),* 233–252.

Carnap, R., 1939. *Foundations of Logic and Mathematics.* University of Chicago Press, Chicago.

Carnap, R., 1963. Replies and systematic expositions. In Schilpp, P. A., ed., *The Philosophy of Rudolf Carnap,* pp. 859–1013, Open Court, La Salle.

Carroll, L., 1976. *Complete Works.* Vintage/Random House, New York.

Cartwright, N., 1983. *How the Laws of Physics Lie.* Clarendon Press, Oxford.

Cartwright, N., 1999. *The Dappled World.* Cambridge University Press, Cambridge.

Cherniak, C., 1986. *Minimal Rationality.* MIT Press, Cambridge.

68424

286

References

Chisholm, R., 1948. The problem of empiricism. *Journal of Philosophy, 45(19)*, 512–517.

Churchland, P., 1981. Eliminative materialism and the propositional attitudes. *Journal of Philosophy, 78(2)*, 67–90.

Collins, A. W., 1987. *The Nature of Mental Things*. University of Notre Dame Press, Notre Dame.

Cook, R., 2002. Vagueness and mathematical precision. *Mind, 111(442)*, 225–247.

Cooper, G., 1990. The computational complexity of probabilistic inference using Bayesian belief networks. *Artificial Intelligence, 42*, 393–405.

Craig, E., 1990. *Knowledge and the State of Nature*. Clarendon Press, Oxford.

Davidson, A., 1996. Styles of reasoning, conceptual history, and the emergence of psychiatry. In Galison, P. and Stump, D., eds., *The Disunity of Science*, pp. 75–100, Stanford University Press, Stanford.

Davidson, D., 1974. Replies to David Lewis and W. V. Quine. *Synthese, 27*, 345–349.

Davidson, D., 1980. *Essays on Actions and Events*. Clarendon Press, Oxford.

Davidson, D., 1984. *Inquiries into Truth and Interpretation*. Clarendon Press, Oxford.

Davidson, D., 1990. The structure and content of truth. *Journal of Philosophy, 87(6)*, 279–328.

Davidson, D., 1996. The folly of trying to define truth. *Journal of Philosophy, 93(6)*, 263–278.

Davidson, D., 2001. *Subjective, Intersubjective, Objective*. Clarendon Press, Oxford.

Dawkins, R., 1989. *The Selfish Gene*. Oxford University Press, Oxford.

Dennett, D., 1995. *Darwin's Dangerous Idea*. Simon & Schuster, New York.

de Sousa, R., 1990. *The Rationality of Emotion*. MIT Press, Cambridge.

Dikkers, S. and Kolb, C., 2006. *Homeland Insecurity*. Three Rivers Press, New York.

Divers, J., 1999. A genuine realist theory of advanced modalizing. *Mind, 108(430)*, 217–239.

Divers, J., 2002. *Possible Worlds*. Routledge, London.

Divers, J., 2006. Possible-world semantics without possible worlds: The agnostic approach. *Mind, 115(458)*, 187–225.

Dohrn-van Rossum, G., 1996. *History of the Hour: Clocks and Modern Temporal Orders*. University of Chicago Press, Chicago. Trans. T. Dunlap.

Dummett, M., 1978a. Truth. In *Truth and Other Enigmas*, pp. 1–24, Harvard University Press, Cambridge.

Dummett, M., 1978b. Wang's paradox. In *Truth and Other Enigmas*, pp. 248–268, Harvard University Press, Cambridge.

Durney, C., Massoudi, H., and Iskander, M. 1986. Radiofrequency radiation dosimetry handbook (4th ed.). Prepared for USAF School of Aerospace Medicine; USAFSAM-TR-85-73.

Earman, J. and Roberts, J., 1999. *Ceteris paribus*, there is no problem of provisos. *Synthese, 118*, 439–478.

Edgington, D., 1996. Vagueness by degrees. In Keefe, R. and Smith, P., eds., *Vagueness: A Reader*, pp. 294–316, MIT Press, Cambridge.

Eiseman, B. and Herbert, L., 1990. *The Pantone Book of Color: Over 1000 Color Standards*. Harry N. Abrams, New York.

Elgin, C., 1996. *Considered Judgment*. Princeton University Press, Princeton.

Elgin, C., 2004. True enough. *Philosophical Issues, 14*, 113–131.

Etzioni, O., 1993. Intelligence without robots (a reply to Brooks). *AI Magazine, 14(4)*.

Evans, G., 1978/1996. Can there be vague objects? In Keefe, R. and Smith, P., eds., *Vagueness: A Reader*, p. 317, MIT Press, Cambridge.

Field, H., 1980. *Science without Numbers: A Defence of Nominalism*. Princeton University Press, Princeton.

Fiell, C. and Fiell, P., 1997. *1000 Chairs*. Taschen, Cologne.

Fine, K., 1975/1996. Vagueness, truth and logic. In Keefe, R. and Smith, P., eds., *Vagueness: A Reader*, pp. 119–150, MIT Press, Cambridge.

Fodor, J., 1975. *The Language of Thought*. Thomas Crowell, New York.

Fodor, J., 1987. *Psychosemantics*. MIT Press, Cambridge.

Fodor, J., 1994. Making mind matter more. In *A Theory of Content and Other Essays*, pp. 137–159, MIT Press, Cambridge.

Fodor, J., 2000. Is science biologically possible? Comments on some arguments of Patricia Churchland and of Alvin Plantiga. In *In Critical Condition*, pp. 189–202, MIT Press, Cambridge.

Forbes, G., 1985. *The Metaphysics of Modality*. Clarendon Press, Oxford.

Foucault, M., 1980. Truth and power. In Gordon, C., ed., *Power/Knowledge*, pp. 109–133, Pantheon Books, New York. Trans. C. Gordon, L. Marshall, J. Mepham, and K. Sopher.

Franchi, S., 2005. Chess, games, and flies. *Essays in Philosophy, 6(1)* (www.humboldt. edu/~essays/franchi.html).

Freeman, D., 1999. *The Fateful Hoaxing of Margaret Mead*. Westview Press, Boulder.

Frege, G., 1967. *The Basic Laws of Arithmetic*. University of California Press, Berkeley. Trans. and ed. M. Furth.

Frege, G., 1977. Thoughts. In Geach, P., ed., *Logical Investigations*, pp. 1–30, Yale University Press, New Haven. Trans. P. Geach and R. H. Stoothoff.

Frege, G., 1978. *The Foundations of Arithmetic* (2nd rev. ed.). Basil Blackwell, Oxford. Trans. J. L. Austin.

Friedman, M., 1999. *Reconsidering Logical Positivism*. Cambridge University Press, Cambridge.

Galison, P., 1987. *How Experiments End*. University of Chicago Press, Chicago.

Giere, R., 1990. *Explaining Science*. University of Chicago Press, Chicago.

Giere, R., 1999. *Science without Laws*. University of Chicago Press, Chicago.

Gigerenzer, G., Todd, P., and the ABC Research Group, 1999. *Simple Heuristics that Make Us Smart*. Oxford University Press, Oxford.

Goguen, J. A., 1968–1969. The logic of inexact concepts. *Synthese, 19*, 325–373.

Goldfarb, W., 2001. Frege's conception of logic. In Floyd, J. and Shieh, S., eds., *Future Pasts*, pp. 25–41, Oxford University Press, Oxford.

Gombrowicz, W., 1985. *Cosmos and Pornografia*. Grove Press, New York. Trans. E. Mosbacher and A. Hamilton.

Goodman, N., 1979. *Fact, Fiction and Forecast* (3rd ed.). Hackett, Indianapolis.

Gottwald, S., 2006. Many-valued logic. In Zalta, E. N., ed., *The Stanford Encyclopedia of Philosophy* (http://plato.stanford.edu/archives/win2006/entries/logic-many-valued).

Gould, J. L. and Gould, C. G., 1989. *Sexual Selection*. W. H. Freeman, New York.

Graff, D., 2003. Gap principles, penumbral consequence, and infinitely higher-order vagueness. In Beall, J. C., ed., *Liars and Heaps*, pp. 195–221, Oxford University Press, Oxford.

Graff, D. and Williamson, T., 2002. *Vagueness*. Ashgate, Aldershot.

Gross, S., 2006. Can empirical theories of semantic competence really help limn the structure of reality? *Nous, 40(1)*, 43–81.

Grover, D., 1992. *A Prosentential Theory of Truth*. Princeton University Press, Princeton.

Gupta, A., 1980. *The Logic of Common Nouns*. Yale University Press, New Haven.

Haack, S., 1996. *Deviant Logic, Fuzzy Logic*. Chicago University Press, Chicago.

Hacking, I., 1982. Language, truth and reason. In Hollis, M. and Lukes, S., eds., *Rationality and Relativism*, pp. 48–66, MIT Press, Cambridge.

Hamilton, A. and Haber, M., 2006. Clades are reproducers. *Biological Theory, 1(4)*, 381–391.

Hampshire, S., 1953. Self-knowledge and the will. *Revue Internationale de Philosophie, 7*, 230–245.

Hare, R. M., 1972. 'Nothing matters.' In *Applications of Moral Philosophy*, pp. 32–47, Macmillan, London.

Harman, G., 1986. *Change In View: Principles of Reasoning*. MIT Press, Cambridge.

Hart, W. A., 1979. Speaking the truth. *Haltwhistle Quarterly, 7*, 1–15.

Harte, J., 1985. *Consider a Spherical Cow*. William Kaufmann, Los Altos.

Heine, B., Claudi, U., and Hünnemeyer, F., 1991. *Grammaticalization*. University of Chicago Press, Chicago.

Hempel, C., 1958. The theoretician's dilemma. *Minnesota Studies in the Philosophy of Science, 2*, 37–98.

Hempel, C., 1988. Provisos: A problem concerning the inferential function of scientific theories. *Erkenntnis, 28*, 147–164.

Henrich, D., 1975. Die Deduktion des Sittengesetzes: Über die Gründe der Dunkelheit des letzten Abschnittes von Kants "Grundlegung zur Metaphysik der Sitten." In *Denken im Schatten des Nihilismus*, pp. 55–112, Wissenschaftliche Buchgesellschaft, Darmstadt.

Herman, B., 1993. *The Practice of Moral Judgment*. Harvard University Press, Cambridge.

Hodgkin, H., 1995. *Paintings*. Modern Art Museum of Fort Worth, Fort Worth. Ed. and intro. M. Auping, J. Elderfield, and S. Sontag; with a catalogue raisonné by M. Price.

Holland, J., Holyoak, K., Nisbet, R., and Thagard, P., 1986. *Induction*. MIT Press, Cambridge.

Horgan, T., 1998. The transvaluationist conception of vagueness. *Monist*, *81(2)*, 313–330.

Horwich, P., 1990. *Truth*. Basil Blackwell, Oxford.

Hughes, G. E. and Cresswell, M. J., 1996. *A New Introduction to Modal Logic*. Routledge, New York.

Husserl, E., 2001. *Logical Investigations, vol. I*. Routledge, New York. Trans. J. N. Findlay.

Hutcheson, F., 1726/2004. *An Inquiry into the Original of Our Ideas of Beauty and Virtue in Two Treatises*. Liberty Fund, Indianapolis. Ed. W. Leidhold.

Hyde, D., 2005. Sorites paradox. In Zalta, E. N., ed., *The Stanford Encyclopedia of Philosophy* (http://plato.stanford.edu/archives/fall2005/entries/sorites-paradox).

Jackson, F., 1998. *From Metaphysics to Ethics*. Oxford University Press, Oxford.

Kant, I., 1797/1994. Metaphysical principles of virtue. In *Ethical Philosophy*, pp. 31–161, Hackett, Indianapolis. Trans. J. Ellington.

Kant, I., 1900–. *Kants gesammelte Schriften*. de Gruyter, Berlin. 29 vols., ed. Berlin-Brandenburg Academy of Sciences (formerly the Royal Prussian Academy of Sciences).

Kant, I., 1999. *Correspondence*. Cambridge University Press, Cambridge. Trans. and ed. A. Zweig.

Keefe, R., 2000. *Theories of Vagueness*. Cambridge University Press, Cambridge.

Keefe, R. and Smith, P., 1996. *Vagueness: A Reader*. MIT Press, Cambridge.

Kelly, T., 2003. Epistemic rationality as instrumental rationality: A critique. *Philosophy and Phenomenological Research*, *66(3)*, 612–640.

Kitcher, P., 1990. *Kant's Transcendental Psychology*. Oxford University Press, Oxford.

Kneale, W. and Kneale, M., 1962. *The Development of Logic*. Oxford University Press, Oxford.

Kuhn, T., 1970. *The Structure of Scientific Revolutions*. University of Chicago Press, Chicago.

Kusch, M., 1995. *Psychologism*. Routledge, New York.

Kvanvig, J., 2003. *The Value of Knowledge and the Pursuit of Understanding*. Cambridge University Press, Cambridge.

Lakatos, I., 1976. *Proofs and refutations*. Ed. J. Worrall and E. Zahar. Cambridge University Press, Cambridge.

Lakoff, G., 1973. Hedges: A study in meaning criteria and the logic of fuzzy concepts. *Journal of Philosophical Logic, 2(4)*, 458–508.

Laqueur, T., 1990. *Making Sex*. Harvard University Press, Cambridge.

Latour, B., 1996. *Aramis or The Love of Technology*. Harvard University Press, Cambridge. Trans. C. Porter.

Lewis, D., 1973. *Counterfactuals*. Harvard University Press, Cambridge.

Lewis, D., 1983–1986. *Philosophical Papers*. Oxford University Press, Oxford.

Lewis, D., 1986. *On the Plurality of Worlds*. Blackwell, Oxford.

Lewis, D., 1999. *Papers in Metaphysics and Epistemology*. Cambridge University Press, Cambridge.

Lewis, D., 2000. Causation as influence. *Journal of Philosophy, 97(4)*, 182–197.

Lewis, D., 2004. Void and object. In Collins, J., Hall, N., and Paul, L. A., eds., *Causation and Counterfactuals*, pp. 277–290, MIT Press, Cambridge.

Locke, J., 1690/1924. An essay concerning the true original, extent and end of civil government. In *Two Treatises on Government*, Dutton, New York.

McDowell, J., 1998. *Mind, Value, and Reality*. Harvard University Press, Cambridge.

MacFarlane, J., 2000. What Does it Mean to Say that Logic is Formal? PhD thesis, University of Pittsburgh.

McGinn, C., 2000. Truth. In *Logical Properties*, pp. 87–108, Oxford University Press, Oxford.

MacIntyre, A., 1997. *After Virtue* (2nd ed.). University of Notre Dame Press, Notre Dame.

McMullin, E., 1985. Galilean idealization. *Studies in the History and Philosophy of Science, 16(3)*, 247–273.

McPhail, B. 1996. *Stiffy*. Independent Filmmakers Cooperative of Ottawa.

Maddy, P., 1992. Indispensability and practice. *Journal of Philosophy, 89(6)*, 275–289.

Massey, G., 1992. The indeterminacy of translation: A study in philosophical exegesis. *Philosophical Topics, 20(1)*, 317–345.

Mayr, E., 1984. Species concepts and their application. In Sober, E., ed., *Conceptual Issues in Evolutionary Biology*, pp. 531–540, MIT Press, Cambridge.

Mehlberg, H., 1958/1996. Truth and vagueness. In Keefe, R. and Smith, P., eds., *Vagueness: A Reader*, pp. 85–88, MIT Press, Cambridge.

Melia, J., 2003. *Modality*. McGill-Queen's University Press, Montreal and Kingston.

Menzies, P., 1996. Probabilistic causation and the pre-emption problem. *Mind, 105(417)*, 85–117.

Mill, J., 1869. *Analysis of the Phenomena of the Human Mind*. Longmans, London. "New Ed. with Notes Illustrative and Critical by Alexander Bain, Andrew Findlater, and George Grote, Edited with Additional Notes by John Stuart Mill"; originally published in 1829.

Mill, J. S., 1967–1989. *Collected Works of John Stuart Mill*. University of Toronto Press/Routledge and Kegan Paul, Toronto/London.

Millgram, E., 1991. Harman's hardness arguments. *Pacific Philosophical Quarterly*, *72(3)*, 181–202.

Millgram, E., 1997. *Practical Induction*. Harvard University Press, Cambridge.

Millgram, E., 2005. *Ethics Done Right: Practical Reasoning as a Foundation for Moral Theory*. Cambridge University Press, Cambridge.

Millgram, E. 2008. Lewis's epicycles, possible worlds, and the mysteries of modality. Unpublished manuscript.

Mishler, B., 1999. Getting rid of species? In Wilson, R., ed., *Species: New Interdisciplinary Essays*, pp. 307–315, MIT Press, Cambridge.

Moore, G., 1978. The origins of Zermelo's axiomatization of set theory. *Journal of Philosophical Logic*, *7(3)*, 307–329.

Nasar, S., 1998. *A Beautiful Mind*. Simon & Schuster, New York.

Neta, R., 2003. Skepticism, contextualism, and semantic self-knowledge. *Philosophy and Phenomenological Research*, *67*, 396–411.

Nietzsche, F., 1873/1995. On the truth and lies in a nonmoral sense. In Breazeale, D., ed., *Philosophy and Truth: Selections from Nietzsche's Notebooks of the Early 1870's*, pp. 79–91, Humanity Books, Amherst. Trans. D. Breazeale.

Nietzsche, F., 1989. *On the Genealogy of Morals and Ecce Homo*. Vintage Books, New York. Trans. W. Kaufmann.

Niiniluoto, I., 1998. Verisimilitude: The third period. *British Journal for the Philosophy of Science*, *49*, 1–29.

Nixon, K. and Carpenter, J., 2000. On the other 'phylogenetic systematics.' *Cladistics*, *16*, 298–318.

Nozick, R., 1981. *Philosophical Explanations*. Harvard University Press, Cambridge.

Nozick, R., 1989. *The Examined Life*. Simon & Schuster, New York.

Nozick, R., 2001. *Invariances*. Harvard University Press, Cambridge.

Oddie, G., 1981. Verisimilitude reviewed. *British Journal for the Philosophy of Science*, *32*, 237–265.

Oddie, G. 2001. Truthlikeness. In Zalta, E. N., ed., *The Stanford Encyclopedia of Philosophy* (http://plato.stanford.edu/archives/fall2001/entries/truthlikeness).

O'Leary-Hawthorne, J. and Oppy, G., 1997. Minimalism and truth. *Nous*, *31(2)*, 170–196.

O'Leary-Hawthorne, J. and Price, H., 1996. How to stand up for non-cognitivists. *Australasian Journal of Philosophy*, *74*, 275–292.

Oliver, A., 1996. The metaphysics of properties. *Mind*, *105(417)*, 1–80.

Pennisi, E., 2001. Linnaeus's last stand? *Science (New Series)*, *291(5512)*, 2304–2305, 2307.

Pietroski, P. and Rey, G., 1995. When other things aren't equal: Saving *ceteris paribus* laws from vacuity. *British Journal for the Philosophy of Science*, *46*, 81–110.

Plutynski, A. and Evans, W., 2005. Population genetics. In Sarkar, S. and Pheiffer, J., eds., *Routledge Encyclopedia of Science*, pp. 578–585, Routledge, London.

Pohl, F. and Kornbluth, C., 1958. *The Space Merchants*. St. Martin's Press, New York.

Priest, G., 2001. *An Introduction to Non-Classical Logic*. Cambridge University Press, Cambridge.

Priest, G., 2003. A site for sorites. In Beall, J. C., ed., *Liars and Heaps*, pp. 10–23, Oxford University Press, Oxford.

Psillos, S., 1999. *Scientific Realism*. Routledge, London.

Putnam, H., 1975a. Brains and behavior. In *Mind, Language and Reality*, pp. 325–341, Cambridge University Press, Cambridge.

Putnam, H., 1975b. The mental life of some machines. In *Mind, Language and Reality*, pp. 408–440, Cambridge University Press, Cambridge.

Putnam, H., 1981. *Reason, Truth and History*. Cambridge University Press, Cambridge.

Putnam, H., 1983. Models and reality. In *Realism and Reason*, pp. 1–25, Cambridge University Press, Cambridge.

Putnam, H., 1990. *Realism with a Human Face*. Harvard University Press, Cambridge. Ed. J. Conant.

Putnam, H., 2004. *Ethics without Ontology*. Harvard University Press, Cambridge.

Quine, W. V., 1960. *Word and Object*. MIT Press, Cambridge.

Quine, W. V., 1963. *From a Logical Point of View*. Harper & Row, New York.

Quine, W. V., 1969. *Ontological Relativity and Other Essays*. Columbia University Press, New York.

Quinn, W., 1993. *Morality and Action*. Cambridge University Press, Cambridge.

Raffman, D., 1994. Vagueness without paradox. *Philosophical Review*, *103(1)*, 41–74.

Ramsey, F. P., 1990. Theories. In Mellor, D. H., ed., *Philosophical Papers*, pp. 112–136, Cambridge University Press, Cambridge.

Ramsey, F. P., 1991. The nature of truth. *Episteme*, *16*, 6–16.

Ravetz, J., 1979. *Scientific Knowledge and Its Social Problems*. Oxford University Press, New York.

Ray, G., 2004. Williamson's master argument on vagueness. *Synthese*, *138*, 175–206.

Reissland, J. A., 1973. *The Physics of Phonons*. John Wiley, New York.

Richard, M., 2000. On an argument of Williamson's. *Analysis*, *60(2)*, 213–217.

Ringer, F., 1990. *The Decline of the German Mandarins*. Wesleyan University Press, Hanover.

Rorty, R., 1979. *Philosophy and the Mirror of Nature*. Princeton University Press, Princeton.

Rosen, G., 1990. Modal fictionalism. *Mind*, *99(395)*, 327–354.

Roush, S., 1999. Conditions of Knowledge. PhD thesis, Harvard University.

Roush, S., 2003. Copernicus, Kant, and the anthropic cosmological principles. *Studies in History and Philosophy of Modern Physics*, *34*, 5–35.

Rueger, A. and Sharp, W. D., 1998. Idealization and stability: A perspective from nonlinear dynamics. *Poznán Studies in the Philosophy of the Sciences and the Humanities*, *63*, 201–216.

Ruskin, J., 1906. *Modern Painters*. George Allen, London.

Russell, B., 1905/1973. On denoting. In Lackey, D., ed., *Essays in Analysis*, pp. 103–119, George Braziller, New York.

Schiffer, S., 1991. Ceteris paribus laws. *Mind, 100(1)*, 1–17.

Schlick, M., 1959. The foundation of knowledge. In Ayer, A. J., ed., *Logical Positivism*, pp. 209–227, The Free Press, Glencoe. Trans. D. Rynin.

Schweber, S., 1994. *QED and the Men Who Made It*. Princeton University Press, Princeton.

Searle, J., 1979. *Expression and Meaning*. Cambridge University Press, Cambridge.

Searle, J., 1983. *Intentionality*. Cambridge University Press, Cambridge.

Shapiro, S., 1998. Logical consequence: Models and modality. In Schirn, M., ed., *Philosophy of Mathematics Today*, pp. 131–156, Oxford University Press, Oxford.

Shapiro, S., 2006. *Vagueness in Context*. Clarendon Press, Oxford.

Shope, R., 1983. *The Analysis of Knowing*. Princeton University Press, Princeton.

Simon, H., 1957. *Models of Man*. John Wiley, New York.

Skyrms, B., 1976. Possible worlds, physics and metaphysics. *Philosophical Studies, 30(5)*, 323–332.

Smart, J. J. C., 1987. Philosophical problems of cosmology. *Revue Internationale de Philosophie, 160*, 112–126.

Smith, M., 1987. The Humean theory of motivation. *Mind, 96(381)*, 36–61.

Soames, S., 1999. *Understanding Truth*. Oxford University Press, Oxford.

Sorensen, R., 2001. *Vagueness and Contradiction*. Oxford University Press, Oxford.

Sorensen, R., 2003. Vagueness. In Zalta, E. N., ed., *The Stanford Encyclopedia of Philosophy* (http://plato.stanford.edu/archives/fall2003/entries/vagueness).

Sperber, D., 1985. Anthropology and psychology: Towards an epidemiology of representations. *Man (N.S.), 20*, 73–89.

Stalker, D., 1994. *Grue! The New Riddle of Induction*. Open Court Publishing Company, La Salle.

Stella, F., 1986. *Working Space*. Harvard University Press, Cambridge.

Stevenson, C. L., 1959. The emotive meaning of ethical terms. In Ayer, A. J., ed., *Logical Positivism*, pp. 264–281, The Free Press, Glencoe.

Stewart, I., 1995. The anthropomurphic principle. *Scientific American, 273(6)*, 104–106.

Stich, S., 1983. *From Folk Psychology to Cognitive Science*. MIT Press, Cambridge.

Stich, S., 1990. *The Fragmentation of Reason*. MIT Press, Cambridge.

Suppes, P., 1972. *Axiomatic Set Theory*. Dover, New York.

Tabor, W., 1993. The gradual development of degree modifier *sort of* and *kind of*: A corpus proximity model. In Beals, K., Cooke, G., Kathman, D., Kita, S., McCullough, K.-E., and Testen, D., eds., *Papers from the Twenty-Ninth Regional Meeting of the Chicago Linguistics Society*, pp. 451–465, Chicago Linguistics Society, Chicago.

Tarski, A., 1935/1986. Der Wahrheitsbegriff in den formalisierten Sprachen. In Givant, S. and McKenzie, R., eds., *Alfred Tarski: Collected Papers, vol. 2*, pp. 51–198, Birkhäuser, Basel.

Tarski, A., 1944. The semantic conception of truth. *Philosophy and Phenomenological Research, 4*, 341–376.

Teller, P., 2001. Twilight of the perfect model model. *Erkenntnis, 55*, 393–415.

Teller, P., 2004. The law-idealization. *Philosophy of Science, 71*, 730–741.

Thomason, R., 1982. Identity and vagueness. *Philosophical Studies, 42*, 329–332.

Thompson, M., 2008. *Life and Action*, Harvard University Press, Cambridge.

Travis, C., 2000. *Unshadowed Thought*. Harvard University Press, Cambridge.

Tutte, W. T., 1984. *Graph Theory*. Addison-Wesley, Menlo Park.

Tye, M., 1994/1996. Sorites paradoxes and the semantics of vagueness. In Keefe, R. and Smith, P., eds., *Vagueness: A Reader*, pp. 281–293, MIT Press, Cambridge.

Tye, M., 1995. Vagueness: Welcome to the quicksand. *Southern Journal of Philosophy, 33(Supplement)*, 1–22. Spindel Conference proceedings.

Unger, P., 1979. There are no ordinary things. *Synthese, 41*, 117–154.

van Fraassen, B., 1980. *The Scientific Image*. Clarendon Press, Oxford.

van Fraassen, B., 2002. *The Empirical Stance*. Yale University Press, New Haven.

van Valen, L., 1976. Ecological species, multispecies, and oaks. *Taxon, 25(2/3)*, 233–239.

Velleman, J. D., 2000. *The Possibility of Practical Reason*. Oxford University Press, Oxford.

Vogler, C., 2001. Anscombe on practical inference. In Millgram, E., ed., *Varieties of Practical Reasoning*, pp. 437–464, MIT Press, Cambridge.

Walker, R., 1978. *Kant*. Routledge, London.

Weatherson, B., 2005. The problem of the many. In Zalta, E. N., ed., *The Stanford Encyclopedia of Philosophy* (http://plato.stanford.edu/archives/win2005/entries/problem-of-many).

West-Eberhard, M. J., 2003. *Developmental Plasticity and Evolution*. Oxford University Press, Oxford.

Williams, B., 1973. Deciding to believe. In *Problems of the Self*. Cambridge University Press, Cambridge.

Williams, B., 1978. *Descartes: The Project of Pure Enquiry*. Penguin, Harmondsworth.

Williams, B., 2002. *Truth and Truthfulness*. Princeton University Press, Princeton.

Williams, M., 1996. *Unnatural Doubts*. Princeton University Press, Princeton.

Williamson, T., 1992/1996. Vagueness and ignorance. In Keefe, R. and Smith, P., eds., *Vagueness: A Reader*, pp. 265–280, MIT Press, Cambridge.

Williamson, T., 1994. *Vagueness*. Routledge, New York.

Williamson, T., 1997. Précis of *Vagueness*. *Philosophy and Phenomenological Research, 57(4)*, 921–928.

Wilson, M., 2006. *Wandering Significance*. Oxford University Press, Oxford.

Wilson, W. K., 1990. Some reflections on the prosentential theory of truth. In Dunn, J. M. and Gupta, A., eds., *Truth or Consequences*, pp. 19–32, Kluwer, Dordrecht.

Wimsatt, W., 1987. False models as means to truer theories. In Nitecki, M. and Hoffman, A., eds., *Neutral Models in Biology*, pp. 23–55, Oxford University Press, New York.

Winston, J., 1999. *Describing Species: Practical Taxonomic Procedure for Biologists.* Columbia University Press, New York.

Wittgenstein, L., 1975. *Philosophical Remarks.* University of Chicago Press, Chicago. Ed. R. Rhees and trans. R. Hargreaves and R. White.

Wittgenstein, L., 1998. *Philosophical Investigations* (2nd ed.). Blackwell, Oxford. Trans. G. E. M. Anscombe.

Woodward, J., 2002. There is no such thing as a *ceteris paribus* law. *Erkenntnis, 57*, 303–328.

Wright, C., 1999. Truth: A traditional debate revisited. In Blackburn, S., editor, *Truth*, 203–238, Oxford University Press, Oxford.

Yablo, S., 1987. Identity, essence, and indiscernibility. *Journal of Philosophy, 84(6)*, 293–314.

Yaqub, A., 1993. *The Liar Speaks the Truth.* Oxford University Press, Oxford.

Zadeh, L. A., 1965. Fuzzy sets. *Information and Control, 8*, 338–353.

Index

Index

DATE DUE

3/2/13			